VICTIMS'
RIGHTS

A Reference Handbook

Other Titles in ABC-CLIO's
CONTEMPORARY WORLD ISSUES
Series

Abortion, 2d ed.	Marie Costa
American Homelessness, 2d ed.	Mary Ellen Hombs
Animal Rights	Clifford J. Sherry
Childhood Sexual Abuse	Karen L. Kinnear
Children's Rights	Beverly C. Edmonds and William R. Fernekes
Crime in America	Jennifer L. Durham
Domestic Violence	Margi Laird McCue
Environmental Justice	David E. Newton
Gangs	Karen L. Kinnear
Gay and Lesbian Rights	David E. Newton
Global Development	William Savitt and Paula Bottorf
The New Information Revolution	Martin K. Gay
The Ozone Dilemma	David E. Newton
Rape in America	Rob Hall
The Religious Right	Glenn H. Utter and John W. Storey
Sports Ethics	Lawrence H. Berlow
United States Immigration	E. Willard Miller and Ruby M. Miller
Violence and the Media	David E. Newton
Violent Children	Karen L. Kinnear

Books in the Contemporary World Issues series address vital issues in today's society such as terrorism, sexual harassment, homelessness, AIDS, gambling, animal rights, and air pollution. Written by professional writers, scholars, and nonacademic experts, these books are authoritative, clearly written, up-to-date, and objective. They provide a good starting point for research by high school and college students, scholars, and general readers, as well as by legislators, businesspeople, activists, and others.

Each book, carefully organized and easy to use, contains an overview of the subject; a detailed chronology; biographical sketches; facts and data and/or documents and other primary-source material; a directory of organizations and agencies; annotated lists of print and nonprint resources; a glossary; and an index.

Readers of books in the Contemporary World Issues series will find the information they need in order to better understand the social, political, environmental, and economic issues facing the world today.

VICTIMS'
RIGHTS

A Reference Handbook

Leigh Glenn

**CONTEMPORARY
WORLD ISSUES**

ABC-CLIO

Santa Barbara, California
Denver, Colorado
Oxford, England

Library of Congress Cataloging-in-Publication Data

Glenn, Leigh.
    Victims' rights : a reference handbook / Leigh Glenn.
       p. cm. — (Contemporary world issues)
    Includes bibliographical references and index.
    ISBN 0-87436-870-7
    1. Victims of crimes—Legal status, laws, etc.—United States.
    I. Title. II. Series.
    KF9763.G58 1997
    344.73'03288—dc21   97-41945

02 01 00 99 98   10 9 8 7 6 5 4 3 2   (cloth)

Cover illustration: Standing behind police barricades in a downpour on 26 March 1988, members of the Guardian Angels wait for Robert Chambers to leave his New York City townhouse to begin serving jail time for the murder of Jennifer Levin. Bettmann Archive.

ABC-CLIO, Inc.
130 Cremona Drive, P.O. Box 1911
Santa Barbara, California 93116-1911

This book is printed on acid-free paper ∞ .

For Mom and Dad

Contents

Preface, xiii

1 Introduction, 1
  Defining Crime Victims' Rights, 1
    What Are Crime Victims' Rights?, 2
  Constitutional Amendments and
    Rights of the Accused, 5
      Fourth Amendment, 5
      Fifth Amendment, 7
      Sixth Amendment, 8
      Eighth Amendment, 10
      Fourteenth Amendment, 11
  Politics, Social Activism, and
    Victims' Rights, 12
      Law Enforcement Assistance
        Administration, 13
      Rape Crisis Centers and Early
        Success, 15
  Ronald Reagan and Victims'
    Rights, 17
  Victims' Rights and Other Issues, 18
      State Constitutional
        Amendments, 19
      Victims' Advocates, 19
      Victim Impact Evidence, 20
  The Future of Victims' Rights, 23

2 Chronology, 35

3 Biographical Sketches, 111
Cesare Beccaria, 111
Frank G. Carrington, 112
Ken Eikenberry, 114
Margery Fry, 116
Judge Lois Herrington Haight, 117
Hans von Hentig, 119
Charlotte Hullinger and Robert (Bob) Hullinger, 121
Beniamin Mendelsohn, 122
Bob Preston, 123
Ronald Reagan, 124
Roberta Roper, 126

4 Policy, Legislation, and Court Cases, 131
Policy, 131
Commissions and Task Forces, 131
Speeches, 136
Legislation, 139
Omnibus Crime Control Act of 1970, 139
Parole Reorganization Act of 1976, 139
Penalties for Crimes against Government Officials, 140
Missing Children's Act of 1982, 140
Victim and Witness Protection Act of 1982, 140
Justice Assistance Act of 1984, 141
Victims of Crime Act of 1984, 142
Brady Handgun Violence Prevention Act of 1993, 142
Violent Crime Control and Law Enforcement Act of 1994, 142
Antiterrorism and Effective Death Penalty Act of 1996, 144
Megan's Law (1996), 144
Senate Joint Resolution 6, 145
Court Cases, 146
Cases Concerning the Exclusionary Rule, 147
Fourth Amendment Cases, 154
Fifth Amendment Cases, 155

Sixth Amendment Cases, 161
Eighth Amendment Cases, 166
Fourteenth Amendment Cases, 173
Habeas Corpus Review Cases, 174

5   Directory of Organizations, 183

6   Selected Resources, 195
Print Resources, 195
Indexes, Abstracts, and Annual Reports, 195
Directories, 196
Yearbooks, Dictionaries, and Encyclopedias, 197
Books and Monographs, 198
Articles, 213
Nonprint Resources, 215
CD-ROMs, 215
Videotapes and Audiotapes, 215

Index, 219

Preface

Exactly when the movement to outline and strengthen the rights of crime victims got its start is not known. But sometime during the late 1960s and early 1970s, after a decade in which the U.S. Supreme Court specified, some critics would say created, rights for the criminally accused—rights never detailed in the U.S. Constitution—crime victims and their advocates were not content to watch the scales of justice tip farther toward the accused. Victims' advocates, the media, and politicians began to rally for the rights of crime victims.

The existence of the victims' rights movement has helped to make people aware of the need for protection of victims, to enact victims' rights amendments in various states, and to change the way police and courts treat crime victims. But at the turn of the century, many victims' rights experts and advocates still say more sensitivity toward victims is needed among people employed in law enforcement and the judicial system and that a federal constitutional amendment outlining the rights of crime victims would guarantee rights that are due victims.

If the American criminal justice system is taken to be a set of scales with the accused on one side and the victim on the other, many victims and their advocates say there should be a balance of rights. But ensuring the rights of one without infringing on the rights of the other is the central problem and one many legal rights experts say a victims' rights amendment will not solve. Still, proponents of such an amendment say they don't want to scale back defendants' rights; they simply want victims to have the chance to right the wrongs against them.

How and why did the American criminal justice system grow in such a way that many people believe in the need for victims' rights? As rights for victims expand, what effects are there on the system? What effects will be possible if state constitutions are amended or if the U.S. Constitution is amended to secure rights for victims?

Chapter 1 explores the the answers to some of these questions. It examines the role of the victim in history and how that role has been diminished in the United States as the stature of prosecutors has grown. It looks at the roots of constitutional amendments pertaining to the accused. The chapter also considers how the Supreme Court has interpreted the Constitution in decisions concerning the treatment of the accused. It provides some actual scenarios of cases to show the way in which victims have been treated. Lastly, it outlines the movement's current goals and tries to pinpoint its future course.

For readers who want a brief rundown of the places in society victims' rights traditionally have occupied as well as significant dates of legislation and court rulings that spawned, solidified, and advanced victims' rights, chapter 2 offers a chronology with succinct descriptions of events.

The people who played and play key roles in the movement—those who push for legislation, who argue against setting down rights for victims, who first offered victim services, who made the rules, and who set judicial standards—are identified in chapter 3.

Understanding the motives of the victims' rights movement and the response of courts and policymakers means looking at U.S. Supreme Court decisions delineating the rights of the accused, and later, confirming certain rights of victims, as well as evaluating how presidents and Congress have treated victim issues. Chapter 4 covers policy issues, Supreme Court cases, and congressional legislation.

Chapter 5 lists organizations involved in some aspect of the victims' rights movement or in issues regarding crime.

The last chapter features resources such as books and articles, films, and any other avenues of information that might help students better understand the issues revolving around crime victims.

Introduction

1

Defining Crime Victims' Rights

Bonnie Garland was 20 when her college sweetheart Richard Herrin hammered her head while she slept in her parents' home in Scarsdale, New York, in 1977. They met as students at Yale University and had dated for three years when Bonnie began to distance herself from him and the relationship.[1] After the murder, Herrin drove around trying to find a way to kill himself. But he ended up at a Catholic church in Coxsackie, New York, where he confessed the killing to a priest. They decided to call the police. The Coxsackie police chief asked Herrin whether Garland was dead. "She has to be," he said. The chief asked why. "I hit her with a claw hammer," Herrin said.[2]

The Catholic community at Yale as well as Herrin's friends rallied around him because, as one said in a letter included in Herrin's bail application, "While we are left only to mourn Bonnie's tragic death, it is important, that having lost one life, we do what we can to salvage another."[3] After 35 days of detention, Herrin was released to the Christian Brothers, an order of monks, at LaSalle Academy in Albany. The academy was a temporary home to many young people who had gotten into trouble with the law, and the monks agreed to look after Herrin, although they had never before taken in anyone accused of murder.[4]

The reaction of the community and Herrin's resumption of a fairly normal life at LaSalle Academy incensed Yale alumnus Paul Garland and his wife Joan, who felt everyone had forgotten their daughter. After all, *she* was the victim, not Richard Herrin.[5]

The verdict in the case did not leave the Garlands with any sense of justice: Herrin was convicted, not of murder but of manslaughter, and was sentenced to eight and one-third to twenty-five years in prison.[6]

According to an article in the *New York Post*, after the trial Paul Garland said, "The jury let Bonnie down, let the family down, and the community down. . . . What happened today is another stage in our tragedy. Richard Herrin has successfully got away with murder."[7]

Joan Garland's remarks were similar and biting: "If you have a $30,000 defense fund, a Yale connection, and a clergy connection, you're entitled to one free hammer murder. Because you're a Yale graduate shouldn't let you get away with murder. . . . Because you can buy fancy psychiatric testimony shouldn't let you get away with murder."[8]

When author Willard Gaylin spoke with some Yale faculty about Paul Garland's reaction and ongoing pursuit of justice for his daughter, a few said they could not judge him; they were not sure how they would have reacted in that situation. But the same faculty also said Garland's reaction far outlasted the grieving period and that he was "irrational" about the situation.[9] When this crime occurred, the idea that victims—in this case Bonnie Garland, her parents, and other family members—should be given compassion and help in pursuing justice was relatively new. Specific rights for victims of crime were talked about in a few academic and legal circles, but not in the popular press in the way they would be talked about when Ronald Reagan became president.

What Are Crime Victims' Rights?

Within the last 30 years, the concept of "crime victims' rights" has grown out of the American understanding of the rights of the criminally accused as guaranteed in the U.S. Constitution. Essentially, victims, their families, victims' advocates, and certain policymakers became tired of seeing convicted criminals receive sentences lighter than what they believed served the ideals of punishment and deterrence. They pressed for a balancing of the scales of justice by giving more weight to what they thought should be rights for crime victims.

Consider the following scenario: if someone robs a convenience store, he is entitled to

- Be informed of his right to an attorney
- A speedy trial by a jury of his peers
- Be present throughout the trial against him
- Confront his accusers
- Appeal for a reexamination of his case under the writ of habeas corpus if he believes he has been wrongfully incarcerated

But perhaps the robber beat the store clerk during the robbery. The clerk does *not* have a right to

- A speedy trial
- Be informed of when the trial will take place
- Be present throughout the trial proceedings
- Have the state pay for a lawyer if he cannot afford one
- Make his views known regarding a plea bargain or parole of the prisoner

The U.S. Constitution does not require that crime victims have a trial to address the accused and the crime committed against them. It does not require that they be told what happens—whether an arrest is made, whether a trial is scheduled, or whether the trial is delayed so they can arrange to be at work instead of taking time off for court. If they are not pleased with the way the trial was handled, if they later have evidence of the defendant's wrongdoing, or if they feel a defendant should have been sentenced to more time in prison, they have no mechanism to reexamine a case. If they have the money to hire a good attorney, they can sue the defendant in civil court, but this may not necessarily satisfy their need for justice. Only recently have some states begun to grant crime victims some of these rights.

Crime victims were not always ignored in America. The criminal process in early America adhered to the traditions of British law, giving victims a visible position in the criminal judicial process. In fact, centuries ago, victims and their families arranged for justice, first by blood feuds, and later by compensation (with material compensation set by the victim and his family). But the state gradually began to get involved in victims' affairs.[10] This trend was similar to what happened during the Middle Ages, when rulers saw criminal dispute settlements as potential revenue and began to arbitrate disputes between victims and offenders, taking a portion of the settlement in exchange for their service. This method was abused when kings began selling pardons to criminals despite the seriousness of the crime and the accused person's guilt or innocence. In this way, the state profited from the victim's injuries, and the victim had no recourse through payment or punishment of the criminal.[11]

By the 1700s, Americans still regarded crime as a private matter between the victim and the offender. A colonist who fell victim to crime could hire someone to bring charges against the accused, to collect evidence, and to prosecute the case. The crime victim paid the costs of the case and was reimbursed for court costs only when he was successful.[12] Gradually, this type of system disappeared. Victims' treatment as an invisible party in the criminal justice process was established a few decades before the colonies revolted against Great Britain. The role of crime victims was subordinated to that of the state when, by 1751, they had to consult with a deputy attorney before filing complaints or affidavits in a criminal case.[13]

After the Revolutionary War, the purpose of criminal law shifted from enforcing moral behavior to maintaining social order and promoting the physical security of people. At that time, the scope of the prosecutor expanded. A victim only served in criminal law as the state's witness. Victims who attempted to resolve criminal conflicts privately were punished for "violating the public welfare and usurping the state's authority." Their rights were limited to the civil law system.[14]

As the state began to take on an increasing share of the responsibility in resolving offender-victim conflicts, the idea that humans are endowed with natural rights also began to grip the minds of the day's thinkers and statesmen. The concept of natural rights—that people by their nature have certain basic rights, such as life, liberty, and the pursuit of happiness, that precede the establishment of any government—was incorporated into the Declaration of Independence and the U.S. Constitution. The framers of the Constitution wrote the document with an eye for redressing historical wrongs regarding the criminally accused, who, as citizens, are due certain rights.

Constitutional Amendments and Rights of the Accused

In the first ten amendments to the Constitution—the Bill of Rights—four amendments address rights of the criminally accused. One other, the Fourteenth Amendment, passed after the Civil War, contains the Due Process Clause through which the U.S. Supreme Court in past decades has applied the rights and privileges in the Bill of Rights to the states. Before the Supreme Court began this process of incorporating the first ten amendments and applying them to the states, it adopted the view that the Due Process Clause required only "fundamental fairness"—avoiding cruel or capricious procedures. States could essentially try people fairly and justly without relying on the privileges specified in the Bill of Rights. Those protections, such as the privilege against self-incrimination or protection against illegal searches and seizures, restricted only the federal government's power over the individual, not the states'.[15]

Fourth Amendment

This amendment, unique to American law, grew out of heavy-handed searches by the British in the colonies. At the time, the British were trying to stop smuggling by colonists. They searched colonists' living quarters to turn up smuggled goods to be used as evidence. The Fourth Amendment served to set up a buffer between police and citizens.[16]

It states, "The right of the people to be secure in their persons, houses, papers, and effects against unreasonable searches and seizures, shall not be violated, and no Warrants shall issue, but upon probable cause, supported by Oath or affirmation, and particularly describing the place to be searched, and the persons or things to be seized."

The Supreme Court typically has interpreted the amendment to define a reasonable search as one that takes place under a warrant, while an unconstitutional search is one that does not. At times, the Court has ruled that a search may run aground of civilized standards making it unreasonable even with a warrant. At other times, the Court has held a reasonable search to depend less on a warrant than on the "total atmosphere of the case." The Court used the "total atmosphere" standard extensively in the two decades preceding the 1960s, when a spate of Fourth Amendment cases caused the court to interpret more strictly the searches and seizures clause. This was the standard—albeit not based on the provisions of the Fourth Amendment—the Court adhered to until the 1960s. At any rate, there are exceptions to the warrant requirement including the search of an arrestee and the surrounding area to protect an officer and prevent evidence destruction; the stop and search of a car or truck based on probable cause; the "hot pursuit" of a felon and the area into which he runs; and the "stop and frisk" of suspects who may be dangerous. A law enforcement officer also does not need a warrant when he sees a wrongdoing or an emergency.[17]

In the case of a search, probable cause generally means that a reasonable person would believe evidence relating to a crime is in the area to be searched. In the case of an arrest, it means evidence that the suspect committed a certain offense.[18]

What is not written in the Constitution but has come about through judicial interpretation is the exclusionary rule. This is the principle that evidence procured in violation of a defendant's constitutional right to unreasonable searches and seizures may not be used against him. The case that gave birth to the exclusionary rule was *Weeks v. United States*.[19] In his pretrial petition, Weeks objected to the introduction of lottery tickets sent through the mail as evidence because they were seized in an unconstitutional, warrantless search. In lower courts, Weeks was convicted on charges of using the mail to transport lottery tickets, but the Supreme Court unanimously ruled that allowing the documents to be used as evidence denied the rights of the accused and that the trial court has no authority to admit unconstitutionally seized evidence.[20]

Wolf v. Colorado expanded the Fourth Amendment's search and seizure protections to the states via the Fourteenth Amendment's Equal Protection Clause.[21] But the 6–3 majority did not make the exclusionary rule mandatory for state courts. Only in *Mapp v. Ohio* did the Supreme Court extend the exclusionary rule to the states when it found that no other workable alternative existed to compensate the accused for the violation of the search and seizure protection.[22] Supporters of *Mapp* said it led law enforcement agencies to instill in police a standard for searches. Police administrators and politicians spoke derisively of *Mapp* because they believed it "handcuffed" law enforcement. Other critics said it could not influence police behavior because it did not directly reprimand them for offenses committed during searches. Instead, it put the burden on society when the accused was released. While the number of failed prosecutions due to excluded evidence is small, many cases are not brought to trial because the evidence could be suppressed.[23]

Fifth Amendment

The concept of due process appears in the Fifth Amendment as a restraint on the federal government's powers.[24] "No person shall be held to answer for a capital, or otherwise infamous crime, unless on a presentment or indictment of a Grand Jury, except in cases arising in the land or naval forces, or in the Militia, when in actual service in time of War or public danger; nor shall any person be subject for the same offence to be twice put in jeopardy of his life or limb; nor shall be compelled in any criminal case to be a witness against himself, nor be deprived of life, liberty, or property, without due process of law; nor shall private property be taken for public use, without just compensation."

The idea of due process of law, however, was not new when the framers drafted the U.S. Constitution. It stemmed from the Magna Carta, the charter of liberties drawn up by nobles in 1215 to limit King John's power. Furthermore, the idea that people should not be coerced to testify against themselves appeared initially in the king's courts of the twelfth century. The church courts adhered to an inquisitorial approach. A bishop could require a person to take an oath to tell the truth about all he or she knew. But in the king's courts, the accusatorial approach was taking hold. The prosecutor developed evidence to which the accused had the freedom of choice to respond.[25]

By the 1500s, the idea that no one should be pressed to accuse himself was bounced around a lot but not necessarily put into practice. Judicial bodies such as the Court of Star Chamber or the High Commission made it a standard procedure to force suspects to give evidence against themselves or even used torture to make the accused speak.[26]

By the time the British were settling in North America, however, the privilege not to testify against oneself was part of the British common law. The idea was transported to the colonies where it appeared in the constitutions of many of the original states. The privilege was among the proposals of the First Congress and became part of the Bill of Rights in 1791.[27]

The thrust of due process doctrine is to make sure the government acts fairly when it imposes a burden on someone. It aims to protect citizens from arbitrary government and deprivations that turn out to be mistakes. It also allows people to know about charges against them and gives them the opportunity to respond to such charges. Moreover, the privilege guards against torture and physical and psychological intimidation by police.[28]

In the twentieth century, the 1964 case of *Malloy v. Hogan* was the first in which the Supreme Court applied Fifth Amendment privileges strictly to states. Malloy, who pled guilty to participating in an illegal gambling operation, was sentenced, served some time, and then was placed on probation. During his probation, he was called on to testify in a state inquiry into gambling. He refused, pointing to his Fifth Amendment protection against self-incrimination.[29]

In *Malloy*, the Court diverged from the old, long-held view that states could administer justice fairly. Seven justices believed that the states were bound by the Fifth Amendment's privilege against self-incrimination. The decision overturned two similar cases: *Twining v. New Jersey*,[30] a 1908 case in which the Supreme Court let stand a trial judge's charge to the jury that the defendant's refusal to testify on his own behalf could be taken into account when determining guilt, and *Adamson v. California*,[31] in which the Court decided in 1947 that a prosecutor's action of calling the jury's attention to the defendant's refusal to testify was acceptable because it did not result in an unfair trial.

Sixth Amendment

Among the 15 rights aimed at the criminal process in the first eight amendments, 7 are included in the Sixth Amendment.[32]

The amendment states, "In all criminal prosecutions, the accused shall enjoy the right to a speedy and public trial, by an impartial jury of the State and district wherein the crime shall have been committed, which district shall have been previously ascertained by law, and to be informed of the nature and cause of the accusation; to be confronted with the witnesses against him; to have compulsory process for obtaining witnesses in his favor, and to have the Assistance of Counsel for his defence."

The right to a speedy trial is meant to prevent unnecessary and oppressive incarceration before a trial, to lessen the anxiety and concern that go along with public accusation, and to diminish the possibility that a long wait will hamper the accused in his ability to defend himself. This timeliness is based on arrest or a guilty plea, whichever comes first. Defendants may forfeit this right if they do not invoke it before the trial or before pleading guilty. If this right is violated, the violation may be remedied only by dismissing the charges.[33]

In 1972, the Supreme Court adopted a test in *Barker v. Wingo* to determine whether the right to a speedy trial is denied.[34] After six to eight months, the delay is presumed to be prejudicial to the defense. The Court also considered the reason for the delay—a deliberate attempt to impair the accused's ability to defend himself, negligence or overcrowded courts, or a missing witness. The first weighs heavily against the government. The second weighs less heavily but should still be considered since the government is responsible for such circumstances. The third can justify a delay.

The right to a public trial is to circumvent abuse of judicial power and ensure the validity of testimony. The right is protected as long as there is public access to the trial, but this does not mean that everyone who wants to attend the trial may be allowed to do so. The right also is not absolute; someone who seeks to close a trial must balance his or her interests with the interests of the accused.[35]

A defendant's right to a jury trial acts as a safeguard against the fury of a prosecutor and the whims of a judge and basically prevents governmental oppression. This right is limited to a jury's finding of guilt or innocence and does not apply to sentencing. It is not invoked with petty offenses—those punishable by six months or less time.[36]

While juries traditionally have consisted of 12 people, the Supreme Court has upheld 6-person juries. Juries also must represent cross sections of the population.[37]

The provision that defendants must be notified of the charges against them prevents a defendant from being indicted on one charge and convicted of an entirely different crime. The charge also must be specific, not generic.[38]

Defendants are entitled to be present at their trials, but they may give up this right if they are disruptive. They also are allowed to cross-examine witnesses who are testifying against them. This right may not be observed when there are compelling reasons. Likewise, defendants are protected against hearsay when prosecutors lack a good basis for judging the accuracy of a prior statement.[39]

Included in his right to a "compulsory process for obtaining witnesses in his favor" is the chance for the defendant to testify on his own behalf. A defendant also has the right to subpoena witnesses to testify. This right may not be undermined by the state "as when a trial judge drives a defense witness off the stand by unnecessarily strong warnings against perjury." Part of the right is subordinated to a statutory provision that makes accomplices incompetent to testify on behalf of one another. Another testimonial privilege—the protection against self-incrimination—also may make someone unavailable to testify as a defense witness.[40]

Defendants also are entitled to the assistance of counsel, not just during trials but before they are questioned by police. The right to counsel was expanded through the most famous incorporation case, *Miranda v. Arizona* (1966).[41] Like the exclusionary rule, Miranda rights never were stated explicitly in the U.S. Constitution; in *Miranda*, the Supreme Court decided that prosecutors may not use statements from people held in custody unless, before any questioning takes place, they are informed of their right to "remain silent" and that any statements they make may be used as evidence against them. People in custody also must be told of their right to an attorney, one they themselves hire or one appointed for them by the state. Defendants may forego these rights as long as they do so knowingly and voluntarily. And, under no circumstances may people held in custody be questioned if they indicate "in any manner and at any stage of the process" that they want to consult with an attorney before they say anything.

The Supreme Court also ruled in the 1963 case of *Gideon v. Wainwright* that indigent defendants must be provided counsel by the state.[42] However, poor defendants are not entitled to state-provided counsel in cases in which there is no possibility of imprisonment. Defense counsel must be professionally competent and loyal to the defendant. This right is violated if the defendant shows that there is a conflict of interest that adversely affects his attorney's handling of the case. To prove a constitutional violation, the defendant must illustrate that the defense attorney made professional errors and that, if not for these professional errors, the case would have turned out differently.[43] While the right to defense counsel may be waived, courts are quite strict as to whether a defendant has knowingly and intelligently given up his right to counsel and decided to represent himself.

Eighth Amendment

This amendment, rooted in the British Bill of Rights of 1689, states, "Excessive bail shall not be required, nor excessive fines imposed, nor cruel and unusual punishments inflicted."

While the Supreme Court has not often interpreted the "excessive fines" clause, it has held that bail may not be so steep that a defendant cannot afford to pay. But bail may be high enough to ensure a defendant's trial appearance. The Court also has upheld statutes allowing arrest without bail when the accused is believed to be dangerous to people even though he has not been convicted of a crime.[44]

In the 1960s, two primary groups, concerned that administration of the death penalty weighted unfairly on the shoulders of black men, launched "an all-out legal attack" against it. The American Civil Liberties Union and the National Association for the Advancement of Colored People Legal Defense Fund had evidence that most of the people put to death since 1930 were black.[45]

The Court ended the death penalty in 1972 in *Furman v. Georgia* when the majority in separate opinions argued that it was cruel and unusual and that "a punishment may not be so severe as to be degrading to the dignity of human beings."[46] The majority of justices also noted that death sentences were applied disproportionately and were therefore "not compatible with the idea of equal protection of the laws that is implicit in the ban on 'cruel and unusual' punishments." The ruling invalidated every death penalty statute in the United States, but legislators examined the case to try to develop the type of statute that might be constitutional.[47]

Some states created new death penalty statutes, and it was one of these that came before the court in 1976 in *Gregg v. Georgia*.[48] The majority found that Georgia had sufficiently narrowed the number of crimes for which someone can be sentenced to death and added procedures that required juries to consider the circumstances surrounding the crime and the criminal before recommending a sentence. In again evaluating the constitutionality of death as punishment, the justices ruled that the Georgia statute imposed death in a consistent, nondiscriminatory fashion. When such a statute requires that the death penalty be administered in this manner, it is constitutionally acceptable.

Fourteenth Amendment

The Fourteenth Amendment, drafted after the Civil War, classified all people born in the United States as citizens of the United States and the states where they reside. The first section of the amendment prohibits states from intruding on the privileges and immunities of U.S. citizens and from depriving them of the due process of law and equal protection of the laws.[49]

The first case that raised the issue of Bill of Rights' applicability to the states was *Barron v. Baltimore* in 1833.[50] The Supreme Court decided that the first ten amendments applied only to the federal government; Americans needed to look to their state constitutions to protect civil and political liberties. But the issue of applicability came up again in 1884 in *Hurtado v. California*,[51] in which the California constitution allowed felony prosecutions based on information collected solely by the prosecution and a judge's examination—without a grand jury indictment as required by the Fifth Amendment. On information filed by a district attorney, the defendant was tried for murder and sentenced to die. He argued that his Fifth Amendment rights—part of his due process privileges under the Fourteenth Amendment—had been violated. The Court rejected this argument; in its opinion, the California procedure did not violate the defendant's due process rights.

The decisions of the Supreme Court in *Twining v. New Jersey* (1908)[52] and *Palko v. Connecticut* (1937)[53] clung to the idea that the Fourteenth Amendment only restrained the federal government, not the states. In *Wolf v. Colorado* (1949),[54] however, the Court agreed that the provisions of the Fourth Amendment extended to the states.

It was not until Earl Warren's term as chief justice that the Fourth, Fifth, and Sixth Amendments were fully applied to the states through the Fourteenth Amendment in *Mapp v. Ohio* (1961).[55]

Politics, Social Activism, and Victims' Rights

The so-called liberal Supreme Court decisions made during the 1960s were coupled with an actual increase in crime as baby boomers entered their teens and twenties.[56] The combination thrust crime issues to the front of national consciousness where they remain today.

Based on opinion polls taken in the last two decades, such rulings have led 90 percent of people to believe they would receive a fair trial if they were accused of committing a crime.[57] But those same people also believe courts are not harsh enough with criminals (80 percent) and that most crimes go unpunished today (86 percent). They believe police can do little to combat crime because the courts have restricted them to a great degree (68 percent), and many think judges sympathize more with criminals than with victims (55 percent).[58]

These perceptions helped to fuel the growing prominence of victims' rights beginning in the mid-1970s. The movement burgeoned as politicians at the national level—with their tough law-and-order stances—merged in the public mind with grassroots activists at the state and local levels.[59]

To understand the top-down forces at work is to understand the influence of politics on crime issues and the influence of public perception on politicians. By the mid-1960s, anxiety about crime consumed the public and took on political dimensions. Since Sen. Barry Goldwater employed a law-and-order, crime-in-our-streets theme in his 1964 presidential campaign, almost every candidate for the highest executive office has played up a get-tough stance when it comes to criminals. In 1968, Richard Nixon made crime into a campaign issue. Television spots showed frightened women who claimed the situation would only worsen unless voters launched an offensive against criminals.[60]

Law Enforcement Assistance Administration

The first president to respond to concerns about crime was Lyndon B. Johnson. In 1965, he created the President's Commission on Law Enforcement and the Administration of Justice (commonly known as the Katzenbach Commission). The commission published the results of its examination of crime in *The Challenge of Crime in a Free Society* in 1967. The report revealed widespread apprehension of crime and criminals—an apprehension that forced many Americans to change their lifestyles by self-imposed restrictions on freedom. Rather than put themselves in potentially dangerous confrontations, Americans moved to safer neighborhoods and avoided strangers.[61] In addition to the rise in violence given the antiwar and civil rights movements, the 1960s were marked by rising violence against individuals. In 1968, President Johnson formed the National Commission on the Causes and Prevention of Violence (the Violence Commission), which evaluated the status of the nation in terms of violence.

While both commissions focused national and political interest on the problems of crime, it was the Katzenbach Commission that set up the administrative and political apparatus for the forming of the Law Enforcement Assistance Administration (LEAA)—and for long-term federal involvement in what had always been considered a state and local responsibility.[62]

The LEAA, established by Congress through the Omnibus Crime Control and Safe Streets Act of 1968, almost seemed like a showpiece—a little Potemkin village politicians could point to and say, "Look what we're doing!" The overriding political concern for get-tough standards and crime-free streets "assumed that the police, prosecutors, and courts were ineffective in controlling or reducing crime, and that better planning was necessary to put more criminals in prison." This planning included measuring the success of LEAA programs by "operations research analysts." Success depended on decreasing crime and increasing convictions, but such goals were not to be met. Part of the problem was that LEAA planners did not know very much about real crime or everyday police work.[63]

Initially, the LEAA was modestly funded—$300 million for the first full year of operations in 1970. Theoretically, it should have provided monetary assistance to all sectors of the criminal justice system, but it primarily provided support to police agencies since they were already in a position to receive federal money. The act that created the LEAA stipulated that no more than one-third of the money in any given grant go toward personnel. This locked out programs requiring a lot of manpower, such as community-related crime prevention programs or those based on social work. For the first two years, the majority of federal assistance went to police agencies that could use it on equipment.[64]

The act was amended in 1970 to drop the one-third expenditure requirement for programs besides police. The 1970 changes also specifically recognized corrections and public defender programs to allow them to receive money.[65]

In its attempt to measure the success of its programs, the LEAA developed the first national survey on crime victimization in 1972. Cosponsored annually by the Census Bureau, the survey always showed crime rates higher than what police statistics showed. Politicians needed to be concerned about the LEAA statistics since many of their constituents appeared in them. This, in turn, pumped up support for crime victims.[66]

Conviction rates also served as a success yardstick for the LEAA. While many reasons exist for lack of conviction of a guilty person, one primary reason is that victims—the key witnesses—are not there to testify or do not cooperate with prosecutors. To respond to this problem, the LEAA in 1974 set up the Crime Victim Initiative to act as a grant resource for victim/witness programs in prosecutors' offices. This could be viewed as a success in itself since, by 1980, about 400 victim/witness programs across the country were funded through the initiative. The program also marked the birth of victims' advocates, although they may not have been called that at the time. The success of the victim/witness programs hinged on there being specially trained people who knew how to handle the social and emotional problems of victims and their families. Through LEAA-sponsored training conferences, the National Organization for Victim Assistance was born in 1975. The organization trained victim social service workers and victims' advocates. But at that point in time, such a program was used to increase conviction rates first of all, and to help victims and victims' families later. In evaluating victims' programs, the agency often would look first at whether its services helped increase convictions by promoting victims' pursuit of cases.[67] These evaluation methods led some local victims' grassroots organizations to see the LEAA funding as not necessarily worth fighting for especially when the legal results mattered more than the emotional health of the victim.

Despite the success of getting victims and witnesses more involved in the system and the achievement of creating some programs that given their high price tag would not have been realized except through federal money, crime continued to rise along with the federal deficit. In 1980, the last year of Jimmy Carter's presidency, the $486 million proposed for the LEAA was cut. President Ronald Reagan's advisor Edwin Meese said the LEAA had accomplished "a lot of good," but he also referred to money "wasted" on "so-called crime prevention and treatment programs" through social workers. So, although plenty of groups opposed the termination of the LEAA, it ceased to exist in 1981.[68]

Despite its demise, 70 percent of programs started through the LEAA were taken on by the states, albeit with decreased funding. For the most part, the crowning achievement of the LEAA was to get all sectors of the criminal justice system to coordinate their efforts together instead of dropping their problems on one another.[69]

Rape Crisis Centers and Early Success

Partly because of LEAA programs and partly because of the LEAA's foibles, grassroots groups got involved in helping crime victims and promoting concern for them and their families. This often meant criticizing police and prosecutors who tended to treat victims in such a way that victims felt victimized by the system. Frank J. Weed notes in *Certainty of Justice: Reform in the Crime Victims Movement*:

Many local activists came from the middle class that by-and-large had faith in the legal system until they became part of it. They found that the crime against them did not matter much to insensitive insular bureaucrats. They discovered that the criminal case and the offender had to be processed and "disposed of" in a lengthy procedure to which they were not really an important part. The offender's rights were constitutionally protected, and he or she had a personal advocate in the defense attorney. Yet the prosecutor did not play the same role for the victim; the prosecutor instead is an advocate for the state, and the interests of the state may not correspond with the interests of the victim.[70]

In the beginning of the crime victims' rights movement, there was no general movement. The grassroots victims' groups focused on crimes that did not rate high on police and prosecutors' priority lists: domestic violence, rape, child abuse, and drunk driving. Victims and victims' families networked with other victims and their families when they discovered they had something in common. Typically, there was someone who led a particular group and acted as its public voice.[71]

Many early grassroots responses to victims grew out of the women's movement. For feminist activists, rape was symbolic of men's domination and oppression of women. They established the first rape crisis center in Berkeley, California, in 1972. A rape crisis hotline was set up that same year in Washington, D.C. Other centers opened in Ann Arbor, Boston, Philadelphia, and Hartford. They were staffed by volunteers who viewed the way in which police, prosecutors, and mental health workers treated rape victims as "revictimization."[72]

Rape crisis centers today differ little from those that were first formed. They still want to serve victims, educate the public about rape, and change community attitudes and state laws. The centers still provide 24-hour hotlines, information, referral and escort services, and short-term group and individual counseling.

Little public attention to rape and rape victims existed when the National Organization for Women created a National Rape Task Force in 1974. In the same year, the LEAA concluded in a study that "treatment of rape cases and rape victims was 'poor' and 'haphazard.'" The study also stated that rape convictions could be increased by treating victims in a more dignified manner.[73]

Reforms in laws concerning rape helped to give the victims' rights movement political legitimacy. Before the 1980s, laws presumed that women who said they had been raped were falsely accusing men. New laws have tried to change this attitude by classifying rape as sexual assault, which is a crime of violence against men as well as women. They have included varying degrees of sexual assault so that even the person who commits a rape with less force can still be convicted. And so-called rape shield laws prevent attorneys from using a victim's sexual history to prove that she or he "wanted it."[74]

Ronald Reagan and Victims' Rights

Although the victims' rights movement made small strides before the 1980s, it found a catalyst for greater success in the first presidential term of Ronald Reagan. The United States' fortieth president went beyond other presidents' tough-on-crime stance and shined the spotlight on crime victims. Reagan was the first president to proclaim National Victims' Rights Week (the week of 19 April 1981).

Most significant among Reagan's accomplishments on the victims' rights front was his appointment in 1982 of the President's Task Force on Victims of Crime. Its job was to examine victims' treatment within the system and to recommend ways to fix the imbalance. The task force traveled to six cities throughout the country and listened to more than 1,000 people who shared stories of problems they encountered in the criminal justice system. Lois Herrington Haight, former chairwoman of the task force, said the group concluded the way crime victims in America are treated is "a national disgrace." Many of the people who spoke to the task force said they were ignored, mistreated, and even blamed by the system and that they would never again be involved with the courts. Herrington stated the task force deemed this insensitivity as "unjust" and "unwise." The success of the system at making criminals responsible for their crimes and quashing future crime depends on victims' willingness to report crime and testify.[75]

The task force made 68 recommendations, among them changing bail laws to prevent the release of those dangerous to society, providing restitution for victims in all cases, abolishing parole, accepting hearsay evidence in preliminary hearings so that crime victims do not need to testify, and allowing employers to examine potential employees' sexual assault or child molestation arrest records when those employees will be working with children.[76]

Also in 1982, Congress passed the Justice Assistance Act and the Omnibus Victim and Witness Protection Act, the latter of which included provisions for victim impact statements during sentencing, protection from intimidation, restitution paid to victims of federal crimes, fair treatment guidelines for victims and witnesses in federal criminal trials, and strengthening of bail laws. The Justice Assistance Act permitted Justice Department money to be used for various criminal justice programs, including those supporting victims' services. Little money, however, was allocated to victims' services. That changed a few years later with the passage of the Victims of Crime Act of 1984 (VOCA). Initiated by the Reagan administration, the legislation authorized $75 million to be collected from federal fines and bail forfeitures. The money compensates federal crime victims, assists compensation programs in the states, and helps private and public victims' assistance activities.

When Congress passed VOCA, it established a Crime Victims Fund with an initial allotment of $100 million. In addition to fines and bail forfeitures, it permits the collection of new penalty assessments ($50 per felon, for example) and garnishes payments prisoners receive from anything they publish that involves the crime(s) they committed. The purposes of the fund as Congress passed it were the same as those set forth by the Reagan administration. VOCA money could not be used for lobbying, public awareness, crime prevention programs, or any effort of which crime victims were not the primary or only beneficiaries.

Victims' Rights and Other Issues

Through the first years of Reagan's presidency, the bulk of activity on the victims' rights spectrum concentrated on the federal end via the administrative and legislative branches of government. After the President's Task Force on Victims of Crime presented its first report, in which it proposed an addition to the Sixth Amendment to allow victims to be "present and to be heard at all critical stages of judicial proceedings" in criminal prosecutions, victims' rights organizations and state legislatures took their cue and began to amend their constitutions to reflect crime victims' evolving status. These amendments spawned new ways for dealing with crime victims; new courtroom procedures, including the victim impact statement permitting crime victims or their relatives or friends to share how a crime has affected their lives during the sentencing phase of a trial; and mandatory restitution payments.

State Constitutional Amendments

By November 1996, the citizens of 29 states had amended their constitutions. These amendments typically grant crime victims the following rights:

1. To be informed of their case's outcome
2. To be told when a court proceeding for which they are scheduled to appear has been postponed
3. To be protected from intimidation and to be told how much protection is available
4. To be told of the procedure for receiving witness fees
5. To be allowed to wait, when practical, in a secure area separate from the defendants' waiting area
6. To have law enforcement officials return personal possessions as soon as possible, and when possible to have police agencies photograph possessions and return them within ten days
7. To have someone intercede with an employer so that victims suffer only minimal pay and benefits loss when they go to court.[77]

While state attorneys' offices generally are responsible for notifying victims of court dates, victims' advocates also may oversee notification as well as a variety of other duties, especially when a case is very serious.

Victims' Advocates

Beginning in the early 1980s, even before many states passed victims' bills of rights, some law enforcement agencies developed victims' advocate programs. A victims' advocate handles myriad responsibilities ranging from being at the scene of a crime to comfort a victim and assisting him or her with counseling to helping the victim understand legal proceedings and directing him or her to fill out forms relating to compensation. Advocates, many of whom work directly for a police department or sheriff's office, also may help victims formulate victim impact statements and accompany them to court.

As a victims' advocate for the Pinellas County Sheriff's Office since 1982, Laura Scott fills a niche that the sheriff's deputies do not have the time or frame of mind to fill. Advocates must be well versed in criminal justice and social service, Scott said. "You need to be someone who is an effective listener, who can relate to people, who is able to not be prejudiced."[78] You must always have an open mind and "put yourself in that person's shoes, never think I couldn't have been in that situation to begin with," Scott said. "You have to totally forget that."[79]

Victims' advocates generally become involved in a case after a deputy has passed it on to a detective. But with homicides, suicides, sexual battery, and child abuse cases, advocates may be called immediately to the scene. Upon arrival, they determine what victims need, whether it is food or shelter or intervention with an employer. They also handle death notifications and arrange to have crime scenes cleaned. Later, they help victims with the court process.

In an incest case, for example, Scott explained to the victim what she had to do and prepared her for the trial. She showed her the courthouse to give her an idea of the surroundings in which she would testify. Scott also explained that since the defendant was the father—the family's primary earner—the girl and her mother would have their income reduced by 50 percent. They would qualify for food stamps but would lose their house. In an effort to alleviate some of the pain and humiliation, Scott was trying to work with private individuals to obtain help with extra food.[80]

Victim Impact Evidence

Not all states allow victims to be present throughout the trial involving the crime against them, or to have a say in plea bargaining and parole proceedings. Most, however, now permit victims—or in homicide cases victims' friends or relatives—to tell judges and juries, before sentencing, how a crime has affected them. Known as the victim impact statement, it does not factor in a defendant's criminal culpability, but it may affect the stiffness of a penalty.

The statement dates to 1976 when Fresno County, California, Chief Probation Officer James Rowland created the first victim impact statement to give judges an objective inventory of victims' injuries before sentencing. In 1982, Reagan's President's Task Force on Victims of Crime recommended the enactment of legislation to require victim impact statements at sentencing. By July 1987, 48 states permitted victim impact statements, and two types generally are used: (1) a statement written by a victim or by his or her family or friends, which includes an objective analysis of the crime's effects on the victim and his or her family as well as subjective input pertaining to their feelings and opinions about the crime and the sentence and (2) oral testimony from the victim or his or her family during the sentencing hearing.[81]

The victim impact statement has been a lightning rod for controversy, and three cases have come before the Supreme Court regarding its constitutionality and admissibility. The first case, *Booth v. Maryland,* was decided in 1987.[82] John Booth was convicted of killing Irvin and Rose Bronstein during a robbery in their home. The prosecutor called for the death penalty, and under Maryland law, Booth decided to have the jury rather than the judge determine the sentence. The presentence report contained information about Booth—his employment history, education, and criminal record. It also provided information about who the victims were, their economic loss, the seriousness or permanence of any physical injury, changes in the victims' welfare or family relationships, any requests for psychological services by the victims' family, and any other information about the crime's effects on the victims or victims' family that the court required.[83] Given to the jury, the written statement emphasized the Bronsteins' "outstanding characteristics," their close relationship, their number of friends, and the size of the funeral, as well as the emotional and personal problems family members had suffered since the murders. Many family members believed that Booth could not be rehabilitated or forgiven. Booth's defense counsel rejected the impact statement based on its irrelevance, inflammatory nature, and violation of the Eighth Amendment.[84]

Booth was sentenced to die for Irvin Bronstein's murder and sentenced to life in prison for Rose Bronstein's murder. The state court of appeals upheld the sentence based on the impact statement's factual account of the effects of the murders on the Bronstein family.[85] The Supreme Court, however, reversed the decision based on its violation of the Eighth Amendment. In the Court's 5–4 view, the victim impact statement was not relevant to Booth's culpability and injected arbitrariness into the jurors' decision. The family's opinions only served to inflame the jurors who already knew about the anger and grief a murder victim's family feels.[86]

The dissenters believed defendants could be liable for the harm they cause, including the effects of murder on the victims' family. They also believed that victims should be viewed as individuals whose death is a loss to society and particularly to the victims' family.[87]

The second victim impact decision came in the 1989 case of *South Carolina v. Gathers*, in which a majority of justices again ruled that information about the victim had no connection with the defendant's moral culpability and expanded victim information to include that presented by prosecutors.[88] The prosecutor in the case was allowed to read from religious tracts and prayer cards the victim was carrying at the time of the murder. The prosecutor also inferred that the victim was a registered voter. The dissenting justices again would have admitted victim impact comments.[89]

In the third ruling, in the 1991 case of *Payne v. Tennessee*,[90] the Supreme Court, with a different makeup of justices, allowed *Booth* and *Gathers* to be overturned. In the case, Charisse Christopher, 28, and her two children, Nicholas, 3, and Lacie, 2, were stabbed several times with a butcher knife used by Pervis Tyrone Payne. Payne's girlfriend lived across the hall from the Christophers. Without invitation, Payne came into the Christophers' apartment after he had been drinking for several hours, using cocaine, and reading pornography. Charisse Christopher's refusal of his sexual advances sparked his violent outbreak. The apartment was covered with blood when police arrived. Charisse and Lacie were dead, but Nicholas, whose wounds extended from the front to the back of his body, survived.[91]

Payne was convicted of two counts of first-degree murder and one count of assault with intent to commit murder. During sentencing, four witnesses testified to Payne's good character, lack of criminal history, abstinence from drinking and using drugs, and mental handicap based on a low IQ score.[92] In violation of *Booth* and *Gathers*, Charisse Christopher's mother testified to Nicholas's reaction to the crime. She said Nicholas "missed his mother and sister, worried about them, and did not understand why they did not come home." The prosecutor included this testimony in the closing argument and asked jurors to concentrate on the victims, not the "alleged good reputation of the defendant." The jury sentenced Payne to death.[93]

The Tennessee Supreme Court ruled that although Nicholas's grandmother's testimony regarding her grandson's reaction to the crime was not relevant, it did not make the death penalty in the case unconstitutional. However, the court also ruled that Nicholas's physical and mental condition when he was left to die were relevant to Payne's culpability.[94]

The U.S. Supreme Court upheld the ruling of the Tennessee Supreme Court and cited dissenting opinions from *Booth* and *Gathers*. The ruling opinion quoted Justice Byron White's dissent in *Booth:* "The State has a legitimate interest in counteracting the mitigating evidence which the defendant is entitled to put in, by reminding the sentencer that just as the murderer should be considered as an individual, so too the victim is an individual whose death represents a unique loss to society and in particular to his family."[95]

The Court left it up to state legislatures to decide the bases upon which a death sentence may be imposed and stated that defendants would have recourse through the Fourth Amendment Due Process Clause if highly prejudicial evidence resulted in an unfair trial. A lot of the evidence questioned in *Booth* would already have been heard during the trial's guilt phase. The Court also stated that juries do not have to determine the worth of different victims, that the purpose of victim impact statements is not to promote comparisons between victims' worth.[96]

In his dissent in *Payne,* Justice John Paul Stevens said the Court "ventures into uncharted seas of irrelevance" when it concludes that prosecutors "may introduce evidence that sheds no light on the defendant's guilt or moral culpability, and thus serves no purpose other than to encourage jurors to decide in favor of death rather than life on the basis of their emotions rather than reason."[97]

The Future of Victims' Rights

An often touted fact of the criminal justice system is that of all cases only 10 percent actually go to trial. The other 90 percent are resolved through plea bargaining, a process, which, depending on the laws of the jurisdiction in which plea bargaining is taking place, can exclude many crime victims. In those cases that do make it to trial, Federal Rule of Evidence 615 prohibits witnesses from being present at trials before they testify. Only a few states allow crime victims to be present throughout trial proceedings before they give their testimony.[98]

One of the most controversial recommendations of the 1982 President's Task Force on Victims of Crime called for a federal constitutional amendment stating, "Likewise, the victim, in every criminal prosecution shall have the right to be present and to be heard at all critical stages of judicial proceedings."[99] At the time, even some victims' groups regarded the recommendation as unachievable. They preferred to start small by amending state constitutions to recognize victims.

Although the idea of a federal constitutional amendment faded, it resurfaced at a 1985 conference when Bob Preston, a south Florida businessman whose daughter Wendy was murdered, revived it. He said the state amendments provide no legal redress when someone in an official position does not acknowledge a victim's rights. A federal constitutional amendment would guarantee victims a say in the proceedings that involve the crime against them.[100]

In 1986, during a conference sponsored by the National Organization for Victim Assistance, the Victim Constitutional Amendment Network (VCAN) was born to debate the language of constitutional amendments and to work to pass them in the states where they could test the amendments' effects on victims and the system. Today, members of what is now known as the National Victim Constitutional Amendment Network (National VCAN) attempt to rally support for constitutional amendments on the state and federal levels.[101]

In the 104th Congress, Sens. John Kyl (R-Ariz.) and Dianne Feinstein (D-Calif.) and Rep. Henry Hyde (R-Ill.) introduced a proposal to amend the U.S. Constitution and held preliminary hearings in both judicial committees. Neither acted on it before Congress adjourned. Kyl and Feinstein introduced another draft of the proposal, Senate Joint Resolution 6, again in January 1997. The proposal gives crime victims "the rights to notice of, and not to be excluded from, all public proceedings relating to the crime; to be heard, if present, and to submit a written statement at a public pretrial or trial proceeding to determine a release from custody, an acceptance of a negotiated plea, or a sentence; to the rights described in the preceding portions of this section at a public parole proceeding, or at a non-public parole proceeding to the extent they are afforded to the convicted offender; to notice of a release pursuant to a public or parole proceeding or an escape; to a final disposition of the proceedings relating to the crime free from unreasonable delay; to an order of restitution from the convicted offender; to consideration for the safety of the victim in determining any release from custody; and to notice of the rights established by this article."[102]

Although the proposal makes it constitutional for victims to assert these rights, it does not give them a basis "to challenge a charging decision or a conviction; to obtain a stay of trial; or compel a new trial. . . ." Victims also have no basis to claims "for damages against the United States, a State, a political subdivision, or a public official." The proposal additionally would not "provide grounds for the accused or convicted offender to obtain any form of relief."[103]

Opponents ask why an amendment is needed when, it appears, all states eventually will have altered their constitutions to acknowledge victims. Proponents use the cases of *United States v. McVeigh* and *United States v. Nichols*—the Oklahoma City bombing trial—to promote the argument for a federal constitutional amendment. In these cases, Chief United States District Judge Richard P. Matsch ruled that victims of the bombing or their family may either attend pretrial and trial proceedings or testify during the sentencing phase, but not both. Those petitioning Matsch to reverse his ruling cited the Victims Bill of Rights, which Congress passed in 1990 and the victims allocution law, passed as part of the 1994 crime bill, which gave victims of violent federal offenses the right to speak at sentencing. The Victims Bill of Rights guarantees victims "the right to be present at all public court proceedings related to the offense unless the court determines that testimony by the victim would be materially affected if the victim hears other testimony at trial."[104]

The exclusion of witnesses during trials dates to the 1975 congressional passage of Federal Rule of Evidence 615, which authorizes judges to bar witnesses from a trial so they cannot hear other witnesses' testimony. A witness who, before taking the stand, listens to the testimony of another witness could alter his or her testimony, imposing on the defendant's right to a fair trial.[105]

During pretrial proceedings in the summer of 1996, the court invoked Rule 615 with respect to victim impact witnesses, but attorneys for the United States explained that impact witnesses would share only how the bombing affected their lives. They would not contribute testimony to determine the defendants' guilt or innocence. However, attorneys for McVeigh and Nichols said Rule 615 should apply even to impact witnesses "to avoid the risks" of hearing something that could affect their impact testimony. The court agreed.[106]

U.S. attorneys filed to reconsider, stating that the Victims Bill of Rights superseded Rule 615. McVeigh and Nichols again asked that victims be excluded and cited the opinions of psychologists and a psychiatrist. Dr. Robert Henderson Fairbairn, a clinical psychiatrist who has worked with Vietnam veterans suffering from post traumatic stress disorder,[107] issued a declaration on Nichols's behalf, stating that "a victim who later testifies as to the emotional damage inflicted by the crime will have difficulty distinguishing the emotional trauma inflicted by the event itself, from the emotional trauma caused by witnessing counsel for the alleged perpetrators trying to obtain a not guilty verdict." Again, the court agreed with the defendants. Regarding Rule 615, Matsch said, "Well, you know, Rule 615, the enactment of Federal Rules of Evidence, is not the first time that courts have excluded witnesses under a sequestration order. That clearly predated the Federal Rules of Evidence, and I think has been a part of the common law of evidence. And it goes back through history beyond the history of the republic. . . ."[108] Matsch stuck to his previous ruling, and victims had to decide: either attend the trial or testify during sentencing.

Several of the victims petitioned the U.S. Court of Appeals for the Tenth Circuit for a writ of mandamus to get Matsch to comply with the Victims Bill of Rights in his courtroom or to issue an alternative appellate ruling.

In mid-March 1997, Congress approved the Victim Rights Clarification Act of 1997. It is legislation that would allow victims of the Oklahoma City bombing to attend the trial if they planned to provide only impact testimony. The clarification law applies only to federal cases, and generally only 5 percent of crimes are prosecuted under federal law.[109]

One group that opposes the proposed federal amendment is the National Legal Aid and Defenders Association (NLADA). Scott Wallace, who is special counsel with the NLADA, wrote an op-ed in the *Washington Post* in June 1996 citing reasons for opposition. Although the wording of the proposed amendment has changed some since then, Wallace says several of his points still are pertinent. For example, he wrote that "Prosecutors' offices would be tied in knots. They currently resolve nine out of 10 cases by plea agreement. Letting a victim block a plea agreement means a lengthy trial, and it takes away a prosecutor's best tool for inducing [a low-level offender to testify] against more serious criminals."[110] National Victim Center Assistant Director for Legislative Services Susan Howley, however, says the amendment does not permit victims to block plea bargains. They may only address the court regarding plea bargains. States that currently provide victims such rights have not registered any delays in the system, and according to Howley, prosecutors in those states support the right.[111]

Wallace predicts that the notification requirements of the current version of the amendment will impose overwhelming burdens on authorities to track victims and maintain extensive databases. He bases this prediction on the fact that at any given time, the criminal justice system controls about 5 million people through incarceration, probation, or parole and that their victims would be entitled to notification of every hearing or action in the case.[112] Howley, however, says expanded notification would only affect victims of violent crimes. Corrections departments throughout the country are setting up notification programs, and the American Corrections Association has endorsed the federal amendment. And contrary to what the amendment's opponents say about the impossibility of locating and notifying victims, most victims' rights laws require victims to request notification of proceedings and to keep their address and phone numbers up-to-date. She claims the same would be the case with laws to implement the federal amendment. States such as Kentucky are developing ways to do this cheaply through an automated, computerized system that dials the victim until he or she answers.

Wallace says that despite the amendment's wording preventing victims from suing for damages, they would be able to file other types of suits, such as those for declaratory judgments or injunctions and fines for contempt against public officials who fail, for example, to notify them of a parole hearing or an escape. While victims themselves may not recover damages, "their lawyers would be well compensated under statutes allowing all 'reasonable' attorneys' fees in suits to protect people's constitutional rights." Howley claims relief would be limited to injunctions or writs of mandamus that would require the noncomplying agency to start complying immediately. Other forms of assistance in conjunction with a federal amendment also may be appropriate, including a victims' ombudsman—such as in Minnesota and South Carolina—who investigates and mediates complaints. But opponents say a federal amendment's requirement for "reasonable" efforts on the part of victims and officials could cost states lots of money and lead to many lawsuits. Wallace says that "injunctions are enforced by fines for contempt, which will be paid by government officials. There can be absolutely no doubt that, in a country where someone can collect millions of dollars in damages for spilling coffee in their own lap, either the courts or legislatures will find some way—with some label other than 'damages'—to compensate victims who have been seriously harmed by a clear governmental violation of their constitutional rights." Regardless of the type of legal action—injunction, mandamus, declaratory judgment—victims' attorneys will be able to recover their fees under a section of the U.S. Code.

Proponents of the amendment say they are not out to "trump" defendants' rights but to balance them with victims' rights. One of the main reasons for the amendment is to establish a basic and uniform "floor of rights" such as the one defendants have enjoyed since the Constitution was drafted and passed, according to Howley. Currently, the 29 states that have amended their constitutions to reflect victims' interests have created a "hodgepodge" of victims' rights and protections. Some are stronger, some are weaker. A crime victim in Florida or Maryland may have more rights than a crime victim in another state. Howley maintains, "It shouldn't depend on (which) side of a state line you were standing on when the crime occurred." A federal amendment, according to proponents, would give equal weight to defendants and victims, whereas now defendants' rights automatically supersede any victims' statutory law that conflicts with them.

Conversely, opponents argue that victims' rights have never been "trumped" by defendants' federal constitutional rights because "in two cases where a trial judge made such a ruling, he was promptly overturned on appeal."[113] But proponents disagree, citing enforcement of current victims' rights as a key problem. For example, if a state or jurisdiction is not vigilant about enforcing the victims' laws they have passed, crime victims "often are left with no remedy. If those rights were guaranteed in the U.S. Constitution, victims could seek court orders to enforce their rights," Howley says. An amendment, therefore, also would combat "bureaucratic inertia" and clamp down on traditional disregard for victims and would allow citizens to know what their rights were should they become victims of crime. As Howley states, law schools are single-minded about defendants' rights; after all, they are in the Constitution. That focus on defendants' rights carries over into the real world when law graduates become attorneys and judges.

Just as Americans are familiar with the Fourth, Fifth, Sixth, Eighth, and Fourteenth Amendments and the rights they provide defendants, so should they be familiar with rights for victims instead of having to find an attorney to scan the law books to determine what their rights are. Howley believes that civil servants and officials in states with strong victims' rights laws adapt to the laws so that they are enforced as a matter of routine.

Lastly, for the same reason some people oppose the amendment, others favor it: permanence. What legislators give one day, they can take away the next. Just as the amendment is difficult to enact, it also would be difficult to remove. "These are fundamental rights," Howley says. "They're human rights. People ask, 'Don't victims have this already?' Surely they belong in our fundamental law—the U.S. Constitution."

Notes

1. Willard Gaylin, M.D. 1984. *The Killing of Bonnie Garland.* New York: Simon & Schuster.

2. Ibid., 103, citing Herrin's suppression hearing.

3. Ibid

4. Ibid.

5. Ibid.

6. Ibid.

7. Ibid.

8. Ibid.

9. Ibid.

10. Deborah P. Kelly. 1987. "Victims." *The Wayne Law Review* 34, no. 69: 81.

11. Ibid., 82.

12. Ibid.

13. Ibid., 83.

14. Ibid.

15. Kermit L. Hall et al., eds. 1992. *The Oxford Companion to the Supreme Court of the United States.* New York: Oxford University Press.

16. Ibid.

17. Ibid.

18. Ibid.

19. *Weeks v. United States,* 232 U.S. 383 (1914).

20. Hall.

21. *Wolf v. Colorado,* 338 U.S. 25 (1949).

22. *Mapp v. Ohio,* 367 U.S. 643 (1961).

23. Hall.

24. Ibid.

25. Ibid.

26. Ibid.

27. Ibid.

28. Ibid.

29. *Malloy v. Hogan*, 378 U.S. 1 (1964).

30. *Twining v. New Jersey*, 211 U.S. 78 (1908).

31. *Adamson v. California*, 332 U.S. 46 (1947).

32. Hall.

33. Ibid.

34. *Barker v. Wingo*, 407 U.S. 514 (1972).

35. Hall.

36. Ibid.

37. Ibid.

38. Ibid.

39. Ibid.

40. Ibid.

41. *Miranda v. Arizona*, 384 U.S. 436 (1966).

42. *Gideon v. Wainwright*, 372 U.S. 335 (1963).

43. Hall.

44. Ibid.

45. Robert F. Cushman. 1989. *Cases in Constitutional Law*. Englewood Cliffs, NJ: Prentice-Hall.

46. *Furman v. Georgia*, 92 S. Ct. 2726 (1972).

47. Cushman.

48. *Gregg v. Georgia*, 428 U.S. 153 (1976).

49. Hall.

50. *Barron v. Baltimore*, 32 U.S. 243 (1833).

51. *Hurtado v. California*, 110 U.S. 516 (1884).

52. *Twining v. New Jersey*, 211 U.S. 78 (1908).

53. *Palko v. Connecticut*, 302 U.S. 319 (1937).

54. *Wolf v. Colorado*, 338 U.S. 25 (1949).

55. *Mapp v. Ohio*, 367 U.S. 643 (1961).

56. Frank J. Weed. 1995. *Certainty of Justice: Reform in the Crime Victims Movement*. New York: Aldine de Gruyter.

57. David W. Neubauer. 1992. *America's Courts and the Criminal Justice System*, 4th ed. Belmont, CA: Wadsworth Publishing Company.

58. Ibid.

59. Weed.

60. Ibid.

61. Alan R. Gordon and Norval Morris. 1985. "Presidential Commissions and the Law Enforcement Assistance Administration." In *American Violence & Public Policy: An Update of the National Commission on the Causes and Prevention of Violence*, edited by Lynn A. Curtis. New Haven, CT: Yale University Press.

62. Gordon and Morris.

63. Weed.

64. Ibid.

65. Ibid.

66. Ibid.

67. Ibid.

68. Gordon and Morris.

69. Ibid.

70. Weed.

71. Ibid.

72. Ibid.

73. Ibid.

74. Ibid.

75. President's Task Force on Victims of Crime. 1982. *Final Report.* Washington, DC: Government Printing Office.

76. Ibid.

77. Christopher R. Goddu. 1993. "Victims' 'Rights' or a Fair Trial Wronged?" *Buffalo Law Review* 41: 251.

78. Author's 1996 interview with Laura Scott, victims' advocate, Pinellas County Sheriff's Office, Pinellas County, FL.

79. Ibid.

80. Ibid.

81. Valerie Finn-DeLuca. 1994. "Victim Participation at Sentencing." *The Criminal Law Bulletin* 30, no. 5: 408.

82. *Booth v. Maryland,* 182 U.S. 496 (1987).

83. Finn-DeLuca, 409.

84. Ibid.

85. Ibid., 409–410.

86. Ibid., 411.

87. Ibid.

88. *South Carolina v. Gathers,* 109 S. Ct. 2207 (1989).

89. Finn-DeLuca, "Victim Participation," 412.

90. *Payne v. Tennessee,* 111 S. Ct. 2597 (1991).

91. Finn-DeLuca, 412–413.

92. Ibid., 413.

93. Ibid.

94. Ibid., 414.

95. Ibid.

96. Ibid., 414–415.

97. Ibid., 417.

98. Steven R. Donziger, ed. 1996. *The Real War on Crime: The Report of the National Criminal Justice Commission.* New York: HarperCollins.

99. President's Task Force on Victims of Crime.

100. Author's correspondence with Bob Preston, cochairman, National Victims Constitutional Amendment Network, 1996.

101. Ibid.

102. Senate Joint Resolution 6 (a proposal to amend the U.S. Constitution to protect the rights of crime victims), 1997.

103. Ibid.

104. Draft of a brief filed on behalf of Marsha and Tom Kight and other victims of the Oklahoma City bombing in the Tenth Circuit U.S. Court of Appeals, requesting a writ of mandamus or other relief to allow victims to attend the trials in the cases of *United States v. McVeigh* and *United States v. Nichols* and give victim impact statements at sentencing, 11.

105. Ibid.

106. Ibid.

107. Ibid.

108. Ibid.

109. H.R. 924. Victim Rights Clarification Act of 1997. 105th Congress, 1st Session.

110. Scott Wallace. 1996. "Mangling the Constitution: The Folly of the Victims' Rights Amendment." *The Washington Post* (28 June): A-21.

111. Author's 1997 interview and correspondence with Susan Howley, assistant director for legislative services at the National Victim Center.

112. Author's correspondence with Scott Wallace, special counsel with the National Legal Aid and Defenders Association.

113. Ibid.

Chronology 2

F ew records are available about the way in which prehistoric peoples related to victims and offenders, but researchers in this area offer some speculative examples. For instance, family groups joining to form tribes considered who was most capable among them to look after the tribe's interests. The duty of going to war against a rival tribe may have merged with the duty of enforcing rules within the tribe. It also is likely that the tribal leader delegated police responsibilities to tribe members, with the tribe as a group meting out punishments for violations. Still, such violations could be attributable to the work of evil spirits that needed to be placated. The offender underwent a punishment ritual. Such acts later were deemed voluntary and defined as crimes rather than sins. Tribal blood feuds took offenses out of the realm of evil spirits and led to the development of the *lex talionis*, or "eye for an eye, tooth for a tooth." Based on this way of thinking, offenses could be punished by the entire tribe.

2370 B.C.   Ura-Ka-Gina, a Sumerian king, sets down many key inscriptions regarding his efforts to curb oppression of the poor by some kingdom officials.

2100s Sumerian kings Lipit-Ish-Tar and Eshnunna finally define
B.C. the types of actions considered criminal, and by the eigh-
teenth century B.C., the Babylonian king Hammurabi codifies offenses and their accompanying penalties—ones as
brutal as those defined in the unwritten *lex talionis*. About
a millennium passes before the Mosaic Code, which incorporates the *lex talionis*, is written. Until the mid-1700s,
Western societies continue to use the Code of Hammurabi
as a model for offense-penalty systems of criminal law.

2130 King Nammu issues a code of laws. As later Babylonian
B.C. rulers of the first Amorite dynasty try to practice and add
to these rules, a "common law," similar to the British common law, evolves.

A.D. The British Crown appoints the first attorney general in
1602 Hartford, Connecticut.

1643 In Virginia, an attorney is appointed to represent the interests of the Crown in the colonies. This person acts as
attorney general advising the court.

1655 New Amsterdam is the first Dutch settlement to establish
the office of the schout. The schout has some arrest powers,
notifies the accused of the charges against him, collects
evidence, and acts as a prosecutor in court. Schouts also
are set up in Delaware, New Jersey, and Pennsylvania.

1664– The Dutch and British governments lose and regain con-
1674 trol beginning in 1664. Britain gains permanent control in
1674. Despite the power upheavals, the schout's power is
passed to sheriffs.

1687 The attorney general, at the discretion of the general court,
nominates deputy attorney generals for county courts.

1704 Connecticut becomes the first colony to substitute a public for a private system of prosecution.

1711 Deputy attorney generals are appointed by the governor upon the recommendation of the attorney general.

1751   All accusers and witnesses are required to consult with a deputy attorney general before filing complaints or affidavits in a criminal case. This places the deputy attorney general in the position to review and influence the charging process.

1785   Massachusetts passes legislation to build its first prison on Castle Island in Boston Harbor. People can be sent there when convicted of one or more of 24 crimes, including theft offenses. But whenever the old system of working out payments as compensation for theft can be used, convicted thieves are not supposed to be sent there. Despite the old system's viability, incarceration for convicted thieves becomes more common through court judgments.

1803   Supreme Court Chief Justice John Marshall writes in *Marbury v. Madison* that "the very essence of civil liberty certainly consists in the right of every individual to claim the protection of the laws, whenever he receives an injury. One of the first duties of government is to afford that protection. . . ." The case also sets the stage for the Supreme Court's power of judicial review—its prerogative to examine laws to determine their constitutionality.

1805   A new prison, larger than the one on Castle Island, opens in Charleston, South Carolina. There also is a new penal code with fines, incarceration, or the death penalty as punishment. This eliminates payments by offenders to victims in theft cases.

1833   The Supreme Court decides unanimously in *Barron v. Baltimore* that the first ten amendments offer citizens protection only against the federal government and that they must look to state constitutions to protect their civil and political liberties.

1841   Shoemaker John Augustus visits Boston's criminal court where a judge is about to send a drunk to jail. Augustus intercedes on the man's behalf and suggests that he look after the man. After three weeks, Augustus returns to court with the man, who is sober and remorseful. The court gives

1841   Augustus other cases, and by 1878, Boston has the first
cont.   adult probation system in the country.

1884   In an 8–1 decision in *Hurtado v. California*, the Supreme
Court rules that the Fourteenth Amendment's Due Process Clause does not bind the first ten amendments on the
states and cannot, therefore, make the specific guarantees
in the Bill of Rights applicable to states.

1908   By a vote of 8–1 in *Twining v. New Jersey*, Supreme Court
justices again rule that the Fourteenth Amendment cannot be used to incorporate the Bill of Rights (in this case,
the Fifth Amendment protection against self-incrimination)
and apply it to the states.

1914   In a unanimous decision in *Weeks v. United States*, the Supreme Court gives birth to the exclusionary rule, which
makes illegally seized evidence inadmissible in court. Prior
to this case, courts routinely admitted illegal evidence, as
the defendant's right of possession weighed less than the
needs of justice.

1931   The National Commission on Law Enforcement and Observance (known as the Wickersham Commission) concludes that willing witnesses are necessary for the criminal
justice system to work but that people called to testify encounter unreasonable burdens.

1932   Mississippi is the first state to adopt a constitutional
provision for popular election of local district attorneys.

1937   By an 8–1 decision, the Supreme Court in *Palko v. Connecticut*
rules that the Fifth Amendment's protection against double
jeopardy restrains the federal government but not the
states. The justices also reject the argument that the Fourteenth Amendment's Due Process Clause was violated.

1938   An American Bar Association study concludes that fees
paid to witnesses are too low, courthouse accommodations
are insufficient and uncomfortable, and subpoenaed witnesses are inconvenienced when cases are continued, often arriving at court only to find cases postponed.

1941   Hans Von Hentig writes an article about victim-criminal interaction.

1947   Benjamin Mendelsohn coins the term *victimology* in an article. This gives victims a focal point and creates a new theoretical discipline.

In *Adamson v. California*, the Supreme Court votes 5–4 that a prosecutor who calls jurors' attention to the defendant's refusal to testify does not violate the Fifth Amendment's ban on self-incrimination. The case intensifies the debate on whether the Fourteenth Amendment's Due Process Clause incorporates specific protections in the Bill of Rights to make them apply in state criminal proceedings.

1949   In *Wolf v. Colorado*, the Supreme Court rules 6–3 that the Fourth Amendment's protections against unlawful searches and seizures are applicable to the states through the Fourteenth Amendment's Due Process Clause, but it also rules that illegally seized evidence need not be excluded in state criminal trials.

1951   Margery Fry, an English magistrate, begins to urge sensitivity toward crime victims' issues. She speaks out for reform and victims' compensation.

Early   New Zealand is the first country to have a victims' com-
1960s   pensation program.

1963   The assassination of President John F. Kennedy shocks Americans.

1964   Queens, New York, resident Kitty Genovese is stabbed for more than 30 minutes while 38 witnesses do not call the police. This and Kennedy's death galvanize Americans' awareness of increasing violence.

Republican presidential nominee Sen. Barry Goldwater plays to conservative voters by connecting the violence of the streets to civil rights demonstrators and liberal politicians.

1964
cont.
The Supreme Court rules 5–4 in *Malloy v. Hogan* that states, through the Fourteenth Amendment, are restricted by the Fifth Amendment's protection against self-incrimination.

Sen. Ralph Yarborough of Texas introduces the Criminal Injuries Compensation Act to compensate victims for their injuries. Yarborough says, "Our modern industrial democracy accepts the idea of compensating needy members of a particular class. . . . The failure to recognize the special claims of this group [crime victims] seems to be a gross oversight."

1965
California enacts the first victims' compensation program in the United States after Superior Court Judge Francis McCarty suggests that victims should be compensated by the state. Judge McCarty hears a case involving a middle-aged woman who was robbed and beaten and had to pay more than $1,000 in medical expenses, which she had no way of recouping. McCarty writes a letter to a state legislator requesting legislation to provide assistance to people like the woman whose case he heard.

President Johnson establishes the President's Commission on Law Enforcement and the Administration of Justice, also known as the Katzenbach Commission. The commission is formed to investigate criminals, crime victims, and government agencies and personnel charged with responding to criminals and victims.

1966
Congress mandates the formation of a national commission to examine the overhauling of the federal criminal code. The National Commission of Reform of Federal Criminal Laws is headed by former California Gov. Edmund G. Brown and includes U.S. Appeals Court Judge George G. Edwards, Jr., of Michigan; U.S. District Court judges A. Leon Higginbotham, Jr., of Pennsylvania, and Thomas T. MacBride of California; Senators Sam J. Ervin, Jr. (D-N.C.), Roman L. Hruska (R-Neb.), and John L. McClellan (D-Ark.); Representatives Robert W. Kastenmeier (D-Wis.), Abner J. Mikva (D-Ill.), and Richard H. Poff (R-Va.); and attorneys Donald S. Thomas of Texas and Theodore Voorhees of the District of Columbia.

1967   The Katzenbach Commission releases a landmark report, *The Challenge of Crime in a Free Society*, which states, "The existence of crime, the talk about crime, the reports of crime, and the fear of crime have eroded the basic quality of life of many Americans." The basic quality most eroded is "domestic tranquillity."

1968   President Johnson forms the National Commission on the Causes and Prevention of Violence, also known as the Violence Commission. The commission's task is to qualify and quantify the status of violent crime in the United States.

The Law Enforcement Assistance Administration (LEAA), an independent agency within the U.S. Justice Department, is set up to funnel money to police departments via state block grants. Funding for the LEAA increases from $63 million in 1968 to $800 million by the mid-1970s. During its existence, the agency is a center of controversy. Critics say its funds often go toward pork barrel programs at police departments. Under Nixon, agency administrators try to shift funds into specific program grants to local police and sheriffs' departments.

The Omnibus Crime Control and Safe Streets Act provides for emergency wiretapping and sharpened controls over interstate commerce of firearms and gives hundreds of millions of dollars to localities to upgrade their law enforcement.

1969   The Violence Commission releases findings in which it concludes that the 1960s were much more violent than previous decades and one of the most violent decades in U.S. history. It ranks the United States as the leader among stable democracies in rates of homicide, assault, rape, and robbery. It suggests that the nation's priorities be reorganized to accomplish two purposes set forth in the Constitution: to "establish justice" and to "insure domestic tranquillity."

The state legislature of Nebraska passes a controversial self-defense law over the veto of Gov. Norbert T. Tiemann. The law authorizes people to "use any means necessary" to defend themselves or their property against attack.

1969   After serving since 1966 as an associate justice, Abe Fortas
cont.   resigns due to revelations in *Life* magazine that noted his
        acceptance of a $20,000 honorarium as a consultant to a
        charitable foundation headed by a former client. His fi-
        nancial dealings aside, Fortas's close alliance with Presi-
        dent Lyndon Johnson often drew the ire of opponents, who
        said he violated "separation of powers" principles. Fortas
        is known for his excellent lawyering skills. While on the
        bench, he helped support the Miranda decision and inter-
        preted the Due Process Clause as a wide-ranging guaran-
        tee of fairness.

1970   Attorney General John N. Mitchell announces $236 mil-
        lion in federal grants for 1970 to assist cities and states in
        their fight against crime and in an effort to improve their
        criminal justice systems. The grants, for programs under
        the U.S. Department of Justice Law Enforcement Assistance
        Administration (LEAA), are a "promising beginning for
        the federal-state partnership to defeat crime in the streets,"
        Mitchell says.
            Of the money, $215 million will go toward state and city
        action programs, to be matched partly with money pro-
        vided by the recipients. The action grants are disbursed
        according to population, with California receiving $17.3
        million and New York $16.4 million.
            States also will receive $21 million in 1970 to be used
        for planning. In 1969, the LEAA's first full year of exist-
        ence, most of the $63 million was used for planning projects
        as well as establishing anticrime machinery in every state.

        President Richard Nixon presents his 1971 budget to Con-
        gress. He proposes spending $1.257 billion on anticrime
        and criminal justice programs in 1971. The Department of
        Justice budget would reach $1 billion for the first time. The
        money would go toward hiring more personnel to increase
        strike forces in cities with serious organized crime prob-
        lems and toward hiring more revenue, immigration, and
        narcotics agents as well as postal inspectors to track nar-
        cotics and pornography. The LEAA would get a boost: $480
        million compared to $267 million in 1970 and a first-year
        budget of $63 million in 1969.

Federal Bureau of Investigation Director J. Edgar Hoover reveals that the country's reported crime rate increased almost 11 percent in 1969. All kinds of serious offenses continued to rise, including a 16 percent jump in armed robberies. Hoover says about 61 percent of all robberies in the United States are armed robberies. He also reports that arrests for all crimes, excluding traffic offenses, rose 7 percent in 1969, with arrests of adults up 6 percent and those under 18 up 11 percent.

Nixon nominates Minnesota Judge Harry Andrew Blackmun, 61, to fill the Supreme Court seat vacated by former Justice Abe Fortas in 1969. Blackmun served on the Eighth U.S. Circuit Court of Appeals for 11 years. Blackmun is the president's third choice for the vacant Supreme Court seat, after Judges Clement F. Haynsworth and G. Harrold Carswell. Blackmun is viewed by many as a conservative on crime issues. Less than a month after being nominated, Blackmun is confirmed by the Senate, 94–0, as the ninety-ninth Supreme Court justice.

In three related cases—*McMann v. Richardson, Brady v. United States*, and *Parker v. North Carolina*—Supreme Court justices reject appeals from convicted men who argue that their guilty pleas were in some way coerced. In *McMann*, the justices overturn an appeals court decision that New York prisoners, whose convictions were based on their guilty pleas, were allowed to file habeas corpus petitions in federal court by alleging that their confessions came about through prosecutorial coercion. Justices William J. Brennan, Jr., William O. Douglas, and Thurgood Marshall file dissents.

In *Brady*, Robert M. Brady switched his "not guilty" plea to "guilty" when he learned his codefendant pleaded guilty and would testify against him. In *Parker*, Justices Brennan, Douglas, and Marshall dissent in the case of Charles Lee Parker, a North Carolina resident who pleaded guilty when he was 15 years old to circumvent a stiffer penalty for robbery. The three justices state that the court's action on the appeals would "insulate all guilty pleas from subsequent attack no matter what influences induced them."

1970   In the third case, they all agree that the defendant did
cont.   not prove that his guilty plea stemmed from a fear of being sentenced to death.

In his nationally televised "State of the Judiciary" address
to the opening assembly of the ninety-third annual American Bar Association convention in St. Louis, Chief Justice
Warren E. Burger says the federal judiciary is becoming so
overwhelmed that before approving new reforms, Congress should evaluate the legislation's impact on courts.
He also says federal courts should have more employees
and more funds and should assimilate modern administrative methods.

Congress passes the Omnibus Crime Control Act of 1970,
which authorizes $3.55 billion in federal law enforcement
assistance to states and local communities for the budget
years 1971 through 1973.

1971   President Richard Nixon signs the Omnibus Crime Control Act of 1970.

The Second U.S. Circuit Court of Appeals issues rules to
bring criminal defendants to trial within six months of arrest. Applicable in New York, Connecticut, and Vermont,
the rules take effect in July.
   The court says that if the government is not ready for
trial within that time period "or within the periods extended by the district court for good cause, then upon the
application of the defendant or upon motion by the district court, after opportunity for argument, the charge shall
be dismissed."

The initial report of the first national census of city and
county jails states that many prisoners suffered "less than
human conditions," some in jails built more than 200 years
ago. The Law Enforcement Assistance Administration
(LEAA) authorized the $140,000 study by the Census Bu-
reau. According to the report, as of 15 March 1970, 160,863
people were being held in city and county jails. Among
them, 7,800 were juveniles and 83,000 were awaiting ar-

raignment or trial. State and federal prison populations are not tallied in the report, but they are estimated to total 350,000.

LEAA Associate Administrator Richard W. Velde says that until the study was finished "we didn't even know how many jails there are." He notes that often prisoners, children, habitual offenders, and mentally incompetent people are jailed together "in less than human conditions of overcrowding and filth." He adds that the report will form the basis for additional LEAA assistance for criminal reform programs.

The National Commission on Reform of Federal Criminal Laws, authorized by Congress in 1966 to study the criminal code, urges the abolition of capital punishment for all federal crimes.

The Nebraska Supreme Court declares unconstitutional a self-defense law approved by state legislators in 1969. On behalf of the court, Judge Edward R. Carter writes, "The right to kill another exists only in extremity, where no other practicable means to avoid the threatened harm is apparent. . . . If there is no real or apparent necessity for the killing, the defense fails."

The decision upholds the second-degree murder conviction of Judith W. Goodseal, 26, who argued that the trial judge's instructions declined to inform the jury of the then newly enacted self-defense law.

President Richard Nixon calls for the federal government to spend $500 million to be distributed to states and cities to help them crack down on crime. The $500 million would be distributed by the Department of Justice with recipients permitted to use it as they see fit without having to match it with their own money. The disbursements would be based on population. Nixon also requests $211 million for the LEAA.

The Supreme Court decides in *Durham v. United States* that if someone convicted of a crime dies with his or her appeal pending, the conviction must be reversed and the

1971
cont.

charges dropped. Chief Justice Warren E. Burger and Justices Harry A. Blackmun, Thurgood Marshall, and Potter Stewart file dissenting opinions. In the case, George Washington Durham was convicted of possessing a counterfeit $20 note. He appealed the decision. Several months passed before he wrote to the (Ninth Circuit) Court of Appeals and learned the petition was denied six months earlier. Less than a month later, he petitioned the Supreme Court but died before the justices took any action on his case. While Burger, Marshall, and Stewart agree that Durham's petition to them should be dismissed, it is Blackmun who notes that the indictment should not be dismissed.

Addredding the National Conference on the Judiciary in Williamsburg, Virginia, President Richard Nixon gives a keynote speech calling for "genuine reform" of courts. Nixon says reforms limited to hiring more personnel from judges to police will only create "more backlogs, more delays, more litigation, more jails and more criminals." What is needed is "genuine reform—the kind of change that requires imagination and daring, that demands a focus on ultimate goals."

In its closing session in Williamsburg, Virginia, the National Conference on the Judiciary unanimously approves a proposal to create a national center for state courts and establishes a five-member committee to handle the details.

At a Millburn, New Jersey, dinner in honor of New Jersey State Sen. Harry Sears, U.S. Attorney General John N. Mitchell says the Department of Justice is looking at proposals to restrict defendants' judicial options before trial and after being convicted. He says there should be a "predictable" period after which the opportunities for appeal of a conviction would be depleted.

Mitchell states, "Too often, judicial delays, rehearings, appeals and almost endless collateral attacks after conviction—all these convince the criminal that he will 'beat the rap.' And too often he does." But, he says, due process rights and legitimate appeals must be preserved.

LEAA Associate Administrator Richard W. Velde reports that almost half of the country's serious crimes are committed by juveniles, and the rate of juvenile crime is rising at a rate nearly four times faster than the population of young people. He tells members of the Senate's Juvenile Delinquency Subcommittee that "if a youth is a criminal at 18, the chances are overwhelming that he will be a criminal—a much more adept one—at 24 or 28."

Velde notes that the U.S. procedure regarding youthful offenders is not "fulfilling its mandate, it does not correct . . ., it does not rehabilitate." It does not "even meet ordinary standards of human decency in some cases," he adds.

The Department of Justice submits to Congress proposals to adopt a national pretrial detention procedure and to reverse the presumption of innocence in cases in which convicted felons seek release pending an appeal. A pretrial detention procedure enacted for the District of Columbia would become the standard for all federal courts. The procedure permits federal judges to detain for 60 days defendants charged with "a dangerous or organized crime act" and deemed by judges to threaten community safety. Dangerous acts include loan-sharking, racketeering, selling narcotics, assault related to aircraft hijacking, bombing, kidnapping, and robbery.

The proposal regarding convicted felons who desire to be released before their appeal would put the onus on them to prove they are not likely to flee or endanger other people or their property.

Addressing the National District Attorneys Association, Attorney General John N. Mitchell says the Nixon administration is attempting to bring balance to courtrooms by emphasizing justice for accusers.

"A preoccupation with fairness for the accused has done violence to fairness for the accuser," Mitchell says. Nixon's administration does not have "the slightest intent of taking from the accused any right that constitutionally belongs to him," he says. However, "there is a serious intent to make the courtroom a place where fact is determined and innocence or guilt decided, rather than a place where

1971
cont.   fact is obscured and justice frustrated through the triumph of sophistry over common sense."

The Supreme Court agrees to hear four appeals to decide whether the death penalty is cruel and unusual punishment for people who receive murder or rape convictions. The high court also lifts death sentences, but not convictions, of 39 death-row inmates on the basis of automatic exclusion from the juries of people who oppose capital punishment. Justices linked this decision to the 1968 *Witherspoon v. Illinois* case, in which the high court decided that death sentences are unconstitutional when set by juries from which people who broadly oppose capital punishment are excluded. Among the 39 people whose death sentences are lifted is Richard F. Speck, who received the death penalty for the murder of eight nurses in Chicago in 1966.

The four appeals the Court will hear in the next term are those of John Henry Furman of Savannah, Georgia, for the 1968 burglary-related murder of William J. Micke, Jr.; Earnest James Aikens, Jr., convicted in 1966 in San Francisco for the rape-murders of two women; Lucious Jackson, Jr., of Savannah, Georgia, convicted of rape following his escape from prison; and Elmer Branch, convicted of rape near Vernon, Texas, in 1967.

Speaking before 1,000 delegates at the American Bar Association meeting in London, Attorney General John N. Mitchell criticizes past Supreme Court decisions regarding the rights of criminal suspects and charges the judiciary to "begin to recognize that society, too, has its rights."

The Federal Bureau of Investigation (FBI) releases statistics showing that crime climbed 11 percent in 1970, with the number of serious crimes rising substantially over 1969 figures. The total number of reported crimes is 5,568,200 for 1970, over 4,989,760 for 1969.

FBI Director J. Edgar Hoover suggests people look at the increasing crime rate as a "victim risk rate." He says that "the risk of becoming a victim of crime in this country is increasing and that population growth cannot alone account for the crime increase."

Following the 23 September resignation of Justice John M. Harlan, 72, because of ill health and the resignation and death of Justice Hugo L. Black, 85, President Richard Nixon has a rare opportunity to nominate two justices to fill the vacancies. Meanwhile, the high court postpones key cases, including those involving the constitutionality of the death penalty.

The Judicial Conference of the United States, a 25-member group of ranking federal jurists, asks the Supreme Court to change procedural rules to require all U.S. courts to establish "speedy trial" deadlines for criminal cases. The conference, the administration and policy arm of the U.S. court system, asks the high court to adopt the proposal without waiting for Congress to vote on legislation that would require faster trials. The speedy trial deadlines would be similar to those recently set by the New York State Court of Appeals (90 days) and the Second U.S. Circuit Court of Appeals (six months).

As the Senate Judiciary Committee opens hearings on one of two of President Richard Nixon's Supreme Court nominees, William H. Rehnquist, the American Bar Association's Committee on the Federal Judiciary endorses Rehnquist and Nixon's other nominee, Lewis F. Powell, Jr., for the high court.

1972　　The Law Enforcement Assistance Administration sponsors the first national survey on crime victimization and will continue to sponsor it annually along with the Census Bureau. The survey findings generally show higher crime rates—sometimes twice as high—than the rates police have for violent and property crimes. The survey also indicates that citizens do not trust their police and courts and that they hold little hope for being able to do something about crime.

The first three victims' assistance programs in the United States are created with the establishment of Aid for Victims of Crime in St. Louis, Missouri; Bay Area Women Against Rape in San Francisco, California; and the Rape Crisis Center in Washington, D.C.

1972
cont.
Supreme Court justices decide 5–4 in *Furman v. Georgia* to strike down the death penalty under the cruel and unusual punishment provision of the Eighth Amendment, as the penalty is meted out at random.

1973
The Senate votes to wait until the end of the 1973 legislative session to begin applying new rules of evidence developed by the Supreme Court in November 1972. At a special House judiciary subcommittee hearing, attorney Albert E. Jenner, Jr., of the Judicial Conference's Advisory Committee on Rules of Evidence testifies that the new 40-page code for the first time will give lawyers and judges uniform rules of evidence. Others testify that the Supreme Court is allowed to change the rules if it desires and that the Court's power to develop rules had not been challenged in the last ten years. Others, however, say the new rules break the bounds given the courts regarding rule making on procedural matters, violate the authority given Congress to pass on rules of substance, and are the equivalent of legislation by the judicial branch.

In a radio address, President Richard Nixon charges Congress with restoration of the death penalty and revision of the federal criminal code. "When I say modernize . . . I do not mean to be soft on crime; I mean exactly the opposite," he says. "The time has come for soft-headed judges and probation officers to show as much concern for the rights of the innocent victims of crime as they do for the rights of convicted criminals."

He calls on Congress to create a new death penalty law, toughen narcotics laws, develop laws to limit insanity as a defense in federal criminal cases, reauthorize the Law Enforcement Assistance Administration in the 1974 budget and allocate $891 million to it, and revise the federal criminal code.

President Richard Nixon submits to Congress legislation that contains proposals he recently made regarding criminal justice. The largest component of the proposals is the 680-page Criminal Code Reform Act of 1973, which would eliminate the insanity defense except in the cases of defendants who are so mentally befuddled that they cannot form intent, a principle necessary to convict the accused. The new code would set up nine classes of crimes, with penalties varying from five days to life in prison.

Supreme Court justices rule 7–2 in *Cupp v. Murphy* that police, in certain situations, may obtain "disposable" evidence from criminal suspects without first getting a search warrant.

Since the 1972 Supreme Court *Furman v. Georgia* decision that stated capital punishment was illegal because it was not uniformly applied, 14 states have restored the death penalty and 4 others have passed bills awaiting their governors' signatures.

1974   The Law Enforcement Assistance Administration (LEAA) Crime Victim Initiative provides first-ever grants to prosecutors' offices for victim/witness programs to increase victims' participation in the criminal justice process. Agency funds also are used to train people through conferences on how to handle the social and emotional problems of victims and their families.

The first law enforcement–oriented victims' assistance programs are created in Fort Lauderdale, Florida, and Indianapolis, Indiana.

Congress is interested in spending LEAA money on different social programs. Out of this, LEAA Administrator Donald Santarelli announces funding for a new program named Citizens Initiative 1974, which will be used to involve citizens in the war on crime and to foster more respect for victims, witnesses, and jurors among the key participants in the criminal justice system.

1975   The Senate confirms without debate the nomination of Edward H. Levi as attorney general. The various issues about which senators question Levi include his stance on the death penalty. He says he believes that if it is applied "in a limited area," it deters crime. Its application should be left up to states to decide and must be "acceptable to the community."

1975
cont.

The American Bar Association House of Delegates approves a resolution calling for reform of the country's rape laws at its mid-winter convention in Chicago. Under a new definition included in the resolution, rape would be construed as the penetration against one's will of any area of the body by human or other objects. Current definitions are worded so that only women can be rape victims and only men can be rapists. Additionally, the resolution encourages states to cut down—and in some cases do away with—the need for corroborating evidence, to restrict defense attorneys' sometimes broad cross-examination of victims, and to reexamine the severity of penalties based on the violence of the encounter.

The Supreme Court in *Cox Broadcasting Corporation v. Martin Cohn* overturns a lower court decision confirming the constitutionality of a Georgia law that makes publishing or broadcasting the name of a female rape victim a crime. The justices hold that if such information is available in public law enforcement records, the media cannot be subject to criminal prosecution or civil damage for accurately revealing it. Justice William H. Rehnquist dissents.

The Philadelphia district attorney organizes the first Victims' Rights Week.

President Gerald Ford submits anticrime legislation to Congress shifting priorities from criminals' rights to the rights of "the victims and potential victims." The legislation calls for mandatory jail terms for people who commit crimes using a dangerous weapon; people who commit serious crimes, such as aircraft hijacking, kidnapping, and drug trafficking; and repeat offenders who commit federal crimes with or without a weapon when the crime causes personal injury or has the potential to do so. The proposals grant exceptions to people under 18, those with mental impairments, those who commit crimes under "substantial duress," or those implicated by others and whose participation is "very minor." Ford is "unalterably opposed to federal registration of guns or the licensing of gun owners," but proposes a ban on the manufacture and sale of inexpensive handguns known as "Saturday night specials" and encourages tougher enforcement of current gun laws.

The president also asks Congress to compensate victims of federal crimes for their physical injuries. The compensation money would come from fines and federal prison industry profits. He also requests increases in criminal penalties, from $10,000 to $100,000 for individuals, and from $100,000 to $500,000 for organizations. Ford seeks renewal of the budget for the Law Enforcement Assistance Administration from the current $1.25 billion to $1.3 billion.

Following a 15-month study, the Commission on the Revision of the Federal Appellate Court System says that the Supreme Court is not able to meet the nation's needs for final judicial rulings that affect the entire country and that a new National Court of Appeals is needed. The new court would be set up below the Supreme Court and above the 11 U.S. circuit courts of appeals and the state supreme courts. It would hear cases the high court declined or cases transferred by existing courts of appeals and would be able to provide nationally binding decisions.

Supreme Court justices postpone a review of their 1972 *Furman v. Georgia* decision on the death penalty's constitutionality until the 1975–1976 term.

Grassroots victims' rights activists throughout the country unite to expand victims' services and increase awareness of victims' rights through the creation of the National Organization for Victim Assistance (NOVA).

1976   A government-sponsored study finds that violent crime is worse in eight cities that received federal anticrime money. Street crimes and burglaries were supposed to have dropped by 5 percent within two years in Atlanta, Baltimore, Cleveland, Dallas, Denver, Newark, St. Louis, and Portland, Oregon, all of which received $140 million for 233 anticrime programs through the Law Enforcement Assistance Administration in 1972. Instead, Federal Bureau

1976
cont.
of Investigation statistics for 1968–1974 show "long-term, generally severe crime-rate increases in Atlanta and Portland"; murder rate increases in all the cities except Dallas; and increased rates of robbery and violent crime in all of the cities.

Congress approves and President Gerald Ford signs legislation to reorganize the federal parole system to guarantee prison inmates fair treatment in parole matters.

Ronald Reagan tells a convention of peace officers in Anaheim, California, that "the cards have been stacked long enough against the police and prosecution in favor of the defendant and defense attorneys."

"We do have a problem with lenient judges, but far worse is the problem that laws, precedents, procedures and rules of prosecution are stacked in behalf of the criminal defendant—and hence against the society he threatens." Reagan adds that if federal legislation is needed "to unstack the deck against the prosecution, I am in favor of such legislation."

The National Organization for Women establishes a task force to study battering. The task force members would like the problem of domestic abuse to be researched in depth and are calling for federal money for battered women's shelters.

In a 7–2 decision, the Supreme Court justices affirm the constitutionality of capital punishment in *Gregg v. Georgia*.

Nebraska is the first state to abolish the marital rape exemption.

Supreme Court justices hold 6–3 in *Stone v. Powell* and *Wolff v. Rice* that federal courts may not overturn state convictions based on illegally obtained evidence if defendants had a "full and fair" chance to question the evidence in state courts.

In Fresno County, California, Chief Probation Officer James Rowland creates the first "victim impact statement" to provide the judiciary with an objective inventory of victim injuries prior to sentencing.

Before adjourning, Congress fails to approve several bills, including one proposed by President Ford to ban the manufacture and distribution of certain handguns and another, urged by President Nixon in 1973, revising the federal criminal code.

St. Paul, Minnesota, women's advocates set up the first hotline for battered women, while women's advocates and Haven House (based in Pasadena, California) establish the first shelters for battered women.

In *Moody v. Dagget*, the Supreme Court rules 7–2 that parolees who are convicted for a second crime they commit while on parole do not have a constitutional right to an immediate parole-revocation hearing. Convicts seek immediate hearings so that if the parole board rules they must serve out the time from the first sentence, they can try to have the sentences run concurrently.

1977 In *Brewer v. Williams*, Supreme Court justices rule 5–4 to affirm the overturned conviction of Robert Anthony Williams based on Williams's lack of counsel when he incriminated himself to police.

A report is released by Attorney General Griffin B. Bell in which a special committee of the U.S. Department of Justice urges restructuring of the Law Enforcement Assistance Administration (LEAA). The LEAA has provided state crime-fighting programs with almost $6 billion since 1969, and Bell has often criticized the agency for dumping time and money on bureaucratic red tape.

The special committee recommends that the LEAA emphasize research and send money directly to states. It also encourages the agency to loosen the guidelines regarding detailed spending plans that states must turn in to receive federal money.

One member of the seven-person committee, Paul A. Nejelski, a deputy assistant attorney general, recommends breaking up the LEAA, which would save about $700

1977
cont.
million annually. The money, he suggests, can be better
spent on other programs.

Oregon is the first state to enact laws mandating arrest in
domestic violence cases.

1978
The Supreme Court rules 5–4 in *Bordenkircher v. Hayes* that
prosecutors are allowed to threaten defendants with second, more serious indictments if they refuse to plead guilty
to a lesser charge.

The U.S. House of Representatives approves a resolution
to kill a huge bill the Senate passed earlier in the year. The
resolution quashes the more than 10-year effort to revise
the criminal code. The Senate bill included a measure to
shift sentencing procedures from indeterminate (for example, 5 to 15 years) to fixed, with 10 percent of the sentence shaved for good behavior and parole allowed only
in extraordinary situations. The bill also would have required the creation of a seven-member commission to
recommend fixed sentences for various violations, for example, 4 to 5 years for a first-time bank robber who used
no violence. Another measure would have reduced the
number of various states of mind used to assess
someone's culpability. The current 80 states, including
"wantonly" and "lasciviously," would have been reduced
to 4: "intentional," "knowing," "reckless," and "negligent."
Other provisions would have channeled federal fines into
assisting victims of federal crimes, made spousal rape a
crime, outlawed pyramid sales schemes, and made possession of less than 15 grams of marijuana punishable only
by fines of $100 or less.

Congress enacts the Child Abuse Prevention and Treatment Act, which creates the National Center on Child
Abuse and Neglect. The center acts as an information clear-
inghouse, provides technical assistance and training, and
promotes research and model programs.

The National Coalition Against Sexual Assault (NCASA)
is created to combat sexual violence and to push for services for survivors.

The National Coalition Against Domestic Violence (NCADV) is set up as a national voice for the battered women's movement.

1979 The Supreme Court decides 6–2 in *Dunaway v. New York* that police may not detain criminal suspects for questioning unless they have "probable cause" to justify an arrest.

In *Gannett Co. v. DePasquale*, Supreme Court justices decide 5–4 that the public and press do not have a constitutional right to be present at pretrial criminal hearings, thereby giving judges leeway to close their courtrooms if they believe an accused person's due process rights would be harmed by the publicity.

Congress provides a final $1 billion for the Law Enforcement Assistance Administration through 1981, and federal funding for victims' programs is phased out. Attention swings from the federal government to state legislatures.

1980 A survey is released showing substantial differences among criteria prosecutors use to decide whether to prosecute crimes. Congress ordered the survey due to concern that heavy caseloads were straining federal prosecutors, who, as a result, were not prosecuting cases that could be prosecuted. The U.S. Department of Justice survey, said to be the first to document the lack of national standards under which to prosecute criminal defendants, discovers that 83 of 94 U.S. attorneys had secret guidelines they used to decide not to prosecute certain federal crimes, including narcotics offenses, embezzlement and bank fraud, interstate shipment thefts, illegal aliens, government fraud, U.S. Treasury check forgeries, and 30 other violations.

In embezzlement and fraud cases, for example, attorneys in two federal districts would not prosecute cases involving less than $5,000. Five would consider only cases involving more than $2,500. In another ten districts, attorneys would not prosecute cases of less than $1,000.

The study states that guidelines are not rigid and are not meant to prevent prosecutions of important cases in which there is an unusual circumstance. To develop

1980
cont.

guidelines, federal attorneys consider the availability of state or local authorities to prosecute; the gravity of the offense according to the injury or loss; and the accused person's age and prior criminal record, if there is one.

The Supreme Court rules 6–2 in *United States v. Bailey* that inmates who escape from a federal corrections facility must quickly surrender to authorities if they want to defend their escape by citing bad prison conditions as the reason.

Candy Lightner founds Mothers Against Drunk Driving (MADD) after her 13-year-old daughter Cari is killed by a repeat drunk driving offender. The first two chapters are based in Sacramento, California, and Annapolis, Maryland.

By an 8–1 vote, the Supreme Court reverses an armed robbery conviction, citing that a Louisiana man had incriminated himself by talking to police without knowingly waiving his Miranda rights. The responsibility for proving a voluntary waiver in such a case lies with police, not with defendants, according to the decision in *Tague v. Louisiana,* which the Court sends back to the Louisiana Supreme Court.

Supreme Court Chief Justice Warren E. Burger, in an address to the American Bar Association, calls for a new method for creating federal judgeships "when they are needed, not eight, not nine or 10 years later, depending upon whether the same political party is in control of the White House and the Congress."

Burger says the 152 judgeships Congress created in 1978 would soon be overtaken by the ever-expanding caseload in federal courts. He proposes the creation of judgeships by the Judicial Conference of the United States, not Congress. The conference, comprising 26 federal judges and the chief justice as chairman, is the administrative body of the federal judiciary and conducts most of its work in secret.

The National Coalition Against Domestic Violence (NCADV) establishes the First National Day of Unity to mourn battered women who have died, celebrate those who have survived the violence, and honor everyone who has helped to defeat domestic violence. This day evolves into Domestic Violence Awareness Week and from 1987 on becomes a month of awareness activities held in October.

The NCADV this year also has its first national conference in Washington, D.C. Federal officials, elected representatives, and others begin to recognize the critical issues that battered women face. Several state coalitions are born.

A Council of State Governments survey notes that in 1979, 18 states had passed mandatory sentencing laws and 5 others approved fixed, or determinate, sentencing. Mandatory sentencing requires prison sentences for certain crimes such as murder, rape, drug trafficking, armed robbery, and crimes by repeat offenders. Fixed, or determinate, laws specify a term of imprisonment typically within a narrow range that allows a judge to give additional penalties—restitution of stolen items, for example. Both types of sentencing diminish or even do away with parole boards' authority so that theoretically, a judge's sentence and the time an inmate actually serves are about equal. In many cases, parole boards specify the actual prison sentence under a judge's limits. According to prison and parole officials, conservatives, who want to control crime, and liberals, who want more equitable sentences, combined their efforts to pass laws for mandatory or determinate sentencing.

The same day the survey is released, the *New York Times* reports that in several states such sentencing tactics have increased the prison population and prosecutors' power in the plea-bargaining process.

By a 7–2 margin in *Whalen v. United States*, the Supreme Court decides courts are not allowed to impose consecutive prison sentences for different violations in a single crime unless authorized specifically by law to do so.

In a 7–2 decision in *Carlson v. Green*, the Supreme Court permits prisoners or their survivors to bypass the Federal Tort Claims Act and sue federal prison officials under the Eighth Amendment.

1980 In *United States v. Havens*, the Supreme Court rules 5–4 that
cont. illegally seized evidence may be presented in a criminal
case to void the testimony of a defendant.

In a 7–2 decision in *Jenkins v. Anderson*, the Supreme Court
upholds the murder conviction of Dennis Jenkins, a Michigan resident, when the justices rule that he had to answer
questions in court regarding his failure to talk voluntarily to
police before his arrest. The majority opinion states that a
defendant testifying in his own behalf throws off "the cloak
of silence" and must help to advance "the truth-finding
function of the criminal trial." The majority contrasts this
with the post-Miranda period following arrest when, if a
defendant refuses to answer questions for the police, he is
not allowed to be cross-examined about his refusal.

The Supreme Court rules 6–3 in *United States v. Payner* that
federal judges are not allowed to suppress illegally obtained evidence unless taking such evidence directly violates the defendant's constitutional rights.

In separate decisions in *United States v. Salvucci* and *Kentucky v. Rawlings*, the Supreme Court rules 7–2 that people
charged with illegal possession do not have a right to automatically challenge police searches.

A congressional conference committee quashes a bill authorizing $65 million over three years to help domestic
violence victims. Much of the money would have gone to
emergency shelters for battered wives. The measure was
supported by several women's, civil rights, and social service organizations and was opposed by conservative Christian and "pro-family" groups that lobbied against it.

Ronald Reagan is elected president. He makes victims'
concerns and issues a top priority.

Wisconsin passes the first "Crime Victims' Bill of Rights."

At its adjournment, the Ninety-Sixth Congress fails to revise the federal criminal code through legislation first proposed in 1973.

1981   Supreme Court Chief Justice Warren E. Burger addresses the American Bar Association in Houston, telling members that America's legal system is weighing in too often on the side of criminal defendants. "Our search for justice must not be twisted into an endless quest for technical errors, unrelated to guilt or innocence," he says. He wonders whether society is "redeemed if it provides massive safeguards for accused persons, including pretrial freedom for most crimes, defense lawyers at public expense, trials, retrials and more and more appeals—almost without end—and yet fails to provide elementary protection of its decent law-abiding citizens."

To solve the overall problem, Burger recommends tightening bail standards, shortening waiting periods before criminal trials, limiting the amount and length of criminal appeals, rehabilitating inmates in prisons, and providing new educational and vocational opportunities for prisoners.

President Ronald Reagan proclaims a National Victims' Rights Week in April. He is the first president to do so.

In a unanimous decision in *Hudson v. Louisiana*, the Supreme Court rules that trial judges are permitted to overturn convictions if they determine there was not enough evidence to support the verdict.

Frank G. Carrington, whom many consider to be the "Father of the Victims' Rights Movement," founds the Victims' Assistance Legal Organization, Inc. (VALOR) to push for the rights of crime victims in the civil and criminal justice systems.

Supreme Court Justice William H. Rehnquist berates fellow justices for their refusal to review the appeal of convicted Georgia murderer Wayne Coleman in *Coleman v. Balkcom*. Coleman appealed his death sentence for the 1973 murders of six members of a family, but the high court decided not to hear that appeal in 1977. Rehnquist writes that Coleman likely would continue to file more appeals. He wants the justices to examine Coleman's case and other similar cases to end the appeals process and determine the fate of death-row inmates.

1981
cont.

The Supreme Court decides 5–4 in *Bullington v. Missouri* that constitutional protections against double jeopardy cover death penalty hearings. The ruling means defendants who are granted a retrial in states with bifurcated trial systems—in which juries decide a defendant's guilt or innocence and then decide punishment at a separate hearing—may not face the death penalty a second time.

In *Estelle v. Smith* and *Edwards v. Arizona*, the Supreme Court votes unanimously to expand Fifth Amendment protections against self-incrimination.

Chief Justice Warren E. Burger criticizes Congress for weighing down the caseload of the federal judiciary by enacting poorly written laws. When the high court is forced to decide issues raised by the legislation, it is accused of "legislating," Burger tells a conference of Washington, D.C., federal judges at a meeting in Williamsburg, Virginia.

In an 8–1 decision in *Rhodes v. Chapman*, the Supreme Court rules that prison officials may place more than one inmate in a small cell without violating the constitutional protection against cruel and unusual punishment.

The Attorney General's Task Force on Violent Crime recommends the creation of a separate task force to evaluate victims' issues.

Justice Potter Stewart, who was appointed to the Supreme Court in 1958 by President Dwight D. Eisenhower, resigns.

President Ronald Reagan nominates Judge Sandra Day O'Connor to the Supreme Court. The 51-year-old member of the Arizona Court of Appeals is the first woman to be nominated to the country's highest court. She is characterized as a conservative, but not a hard-liner. As an Arizona senator, she wrote a death penalty bill, and as a trial judge, she sentenced at least one man to death.

1982

In two cases, *United States v. Frady* and *Engle v. Isaac*, the Supreme Court limits convicted criminals' use of habeas corpus petitions.

In *Tibbs v. Florida*, the Supreme Court decides 5–4 that criminal defendants whose convictions are overturned on appeal may be retried when the appeals court bases its decision on the "weight of the evidence."

At an American Bar Association (ABA) convention, Justice John Paul Stevens says the Supreme Court does "a poor job" of selecting the cases it hears. This results in "unnecessary lawmaking" by the court. Given the increasingly heavy caseload, justices are too busy to decide what to do about being too busy, Stevens says. Stevens's law clerks screen petitions that come his way. The high court receives about 4,000 petitions per month. "I do not even look at the papers in over 80 percent of the cases that are filed," he tells ABA members. Stevens recommends that the Supreme Court not hear cases regarding purely statutory— not constitutional-related—conflicts, those involving legal technicalities or judicial errors, those highlighting issues not raised in lower courts, and those affecting only limited geographical areas.

President Ronald Reagan appoints the Task Force on Victims of Crime in a Rose Garden ceremony. The task force holds public hearings in six cities throughout the country, thereby focusing national attention on the problems crime victims suffer. The Task Force *Final Report* puts forth 68 recommendations that become the basis for new programs and policies at the federal, state, and local levels.

The California Supreme Court rules 4–3 that passage of the state's Victims' Bill of Rights does not violate the state constitution. The measure, known as Proposition 8, was approved by 56 percent of voters in a primary election. The court majority holds that "Proposition 8 survives each of the four constitutional challenges raised by petitioners." The main challenge was that the initiative's ten provisions violated state laws restricting citizen initiatives to one subject. The court decides that the one subject was enhancement of crime victims' rights. Proposition 8 calls for the admission of all "relevant evidence" in criminal trials, including evidence obtained illegally, longer sentences for repeat offenders of serious felonies, and abolishment of plea

1982
cont. bargaining in serious felonies and cases of drunken driving. It also permits judges to refuse bail when public safety is at stake. The court's ruling does not involve the initiative's effect on the state penal code and constitution.

President Ronald Reagan sends Congress legislation—the Criminal Justice Reform Act of 1982—that would restrict use of insanity pleas and the exclusionary rule in federal criminal cases. The act also includes a proposal to bar appeals to federal courts on issues not brought out in state courts. Under the act, defendants would have only up to a year after state appeals are exhausted to appeal to federal courts.

Mothers Against Drunk Driving (MADD) sponsors the first Victim Impact Panel in Rutland, Massachusetts, to educate drunk drivers about how their criminal acts devastate innocent victims.

President Ronald Reagan signs legislation under the title Penalties for Crime against Government Officials, making the killing, kidnapping, or assault of certain federal officials, including Supreme Court justices and senior White House and cabinet officials, a federal crime. The legislation stemmed from the 1981 assassination attempt on Reagan.

President Ronald Reagan signs legislation to assist the search for children who are missing. The Missing Children's Act of 1982 expands descriptive information that is included in the Department of Justice's central computer file and allows parents to access the information.

President Ronald Reagan signs the Victim and Witness Protection Act of 1982. It imposes penalties on people who try to intimidate victims and witnesses and requires sentencing reports to contain statements concerning the crimes' impact on victims. It also permits judges to order restitution to victims, and in cases where judges do not order restitution requires them to state their reasoning.

Congress passes a crime bill that includes mandatory 15-year sentences without parole for anyone convicted two or more times of robbery or burglary with a handgun. The legislation also creates a cabinet-level narcotics official; allows prisons to test prisoners for drugs via urine samples; authorizes $170 million for local and state crime projects in 1983–1984; and makes tampering with food, pharmaceutical devices, or cosmetics a felony—a response to the killing of seven people by cyanide-laced Tylenol capsules.

1983   Chief Justice Warren E. Burger urges "a national correctional policy" developed by state, local, and federal officials to deal with prison problems. Nationally, the prison population increased 100 percent from 1972 to almost 400,000 in 1982, Burger notes. He says that mandatory sentencing and additional anticrime legislation likely will "enlarge the prisoner population and lead to more prison explosions."

Saying "the war on crime and drugs does not need more bureaucracy in Washington," President Ronald Reagan vetoes an anticrime bill approved by Congress in 1982 that would have created a cabinet-level narcotics official, established mandatory sentences for repeat offenders who commit crimes with handguns, and permitted local prosecutors to veto federal indictments.

The American Psychiatric Association (APA) defends the insanity plea in a position paper but advises that rules on the plea be tightened. The recommendations state the following:

- Insanity acquittals should be reserved for psychotic defendants as opposed to those with antisocial personality disorders.

- Those with disorders should account for their behavior. This type of defendant understands his actions but is not concerned with their consequences.

- Psychiatric testimony should be restricted to defendants' motives or mental state.

1983
cont.

- State or federal authorities should carefully consider the mental state of defendants who are judged to be "not guilty by reason of insanity" before releasing them. The APA paper states that psychiatrists are not able to size up the "dangerousness" of such people.

The U.S. Department of Justice announces longer minimum sentences for violent criminals and major drug offenders in federal prisons. The guidelines by the U.S. Parole Commission differ from previous ones in that they set up an eighth category, with longer minimum sentences for the most serious federal criminals, including those convicted of murder; forcible felonies such as arson, rape, or robbery that end in death; ransom- or terrorism-related kidnapping; aircraft piracy; and the sale of 6.6 or more pounds of heroin. People unlikely to commit more crime would receive eight years four months (from four years four months) before being considered for parole. Those likely to commit more crime would receive fifteen years minimum (from eight years four months). The commission also increases minimum sentences for crimes involving sawed-off shotguns, machine guns, or silencers. People convicted of selling ten or more tons of marijuana would also face higher minimums.

The Office for Victims of Crime (OVC) is established within the U.S. Department of Justice in the Office of Justice Programs to carry out recommendations from the President's Task Force on Victims of Crime. The OVC sets up a national resource center, trains professionals, and develops model legislation to protect victims' rights.

The U.S. attorney general creates a Task Force on Family Violence, which holds six public hearings throughout the United States.

At its mid-winter convention in New Orleans, the American Bar Association approves a resolution placing limits on the insanity plea. Delegates recommend that defendants who can appreciate the wrongfulness of their actions at the time they commit them may be found guilty of the crime.

A Gallup poll finds that 45 percent of Americans are afraid to go out alone at night within a mile of their residences. Seventy-six percent of women who live in urban areas fear walking alone at night near their homes, and 16 percent of Americans feel unsafe in their homes at night. The margin of error is plus or minus 3 percent.

In *Illinois v. Gates*, the Supreme Court rules 6–3 to allow police to get search warrants based on anonymous tips, but it does not consider whether there is a good faith exception to the exclusionary rule.

The International Association of Chiefs of Police Board of Governors adopts a Crime Victims' Bill of Rights and creates a victims' rights committee to renew emphasis by law enforcement officials across the country on the needs of crime victims.

In *Barefoot v. Estelle*, Supreme Court justices decide 5–4 to allow federal courts to expedite death penalty appeals, thereby making it harder for death-row prisoners to lengthen the appeals process.

Justice John Paul Stevens tells the House of Representatives Judiciary Committee's Subcommittee on Courts, Civil Liberties and Administration of Justice that he opposes the creation of a new federal appeals court to ease the Supreme Court's workload. The subcommittee is debating a bill, sponsored by Rep. Robert W. Kastenmeier (D-Wis.), to set up an intercircuit court of appeals to resolve cases referred to it by the high court. Stevens is the only justice to respond to the subcommittee's invitation to comment. He says the creation of such an appeals court would be a "structural change of perhaps major magnitude" and that Congress is partly to blame for increased caseloads given its passage of expansive laws that encourage litigation. Stevens concludes that the new court would only "increase the burdens of our already overworked courts of appeal."

At a Los Angeles meeting, the American Medical Association (AMA) House of Delegates comes out in favor of abolishing the insanity plea in criminal cases. AMA

1983   President-Elect Joseph F. Boyle says, "If our policy had
cont.   been adopted earlier, it would have prevented Dan White
        from pleading diminished capacity and John Hinckley
        would have been found guilty of having the intent to kill."
            To appease abolition opponents, however, delegates
        pass a second resolution encouraging "collaborative ef-
        forts" with the American Bar Association and the Ameri-
        can Psychiatric Association, two groups that recently urged
        restrictions on—but not abolition of—insanity pleas.

1984   In his address to the National League of Cities convention in
        Washington, D.C., President Ronald Reagan urges Congress'
        passage of a bill to revise provisions of the criminal justice
        code. Reagan says it is "high time" to fix the lopsidedness
        that favors criminals over "law-abiding citizens." "Lenient
        judges are only lenient on crooks," he tells the gathering
        of 3,000 city officials. "They're very hard on society."

        For the first time, the Supreme Court rules on the definition
        of ineffective counsel in *Strickland v. Washington,* when it
        decides 8–1 to reverse a Florida appeals court that over-
        turned the death sentence of a confessed murderer.

        In *Schall v. Martin,* the Supreme Court rules 6–3 that states
        may detain juvenile criminal suspects before trial with-
        out violating the Constitution. Detainment is used to pre-
        vent suspects from committing more crimes while awaiting
        trial.

        The Task Force on Family Violence presents its report to
        the U.S. attorney general, recommending action in areas
        such as the criminal justice system's response to battered
        women, prevention and awareness, education and train-
        ing, and date collection and reporting.

        In *New York v. Quarles,* the Supreme Court rules 5–4 that
        police do not have to issue Miranda warnings to criminal
        suspects if doing so would compromise public safety.

        In *Nix v. Williams,* the Supreme Court unanimously deter-
        mines there is an "inevitable discovery" exception to the
        exclusionary rule.

The National Center for Missing and Exploited Children (NCMEC) is founded as the national resource for missing children.

The Supreme Court rules unanimously in *Tower v. Glover* that criminal defendants may sue a public defender for "intentional misconduct" on an allegation that the defense attorney colluded with the prosecution to secure a conviction.

The National Minimum Drinking Age Act of 1984 is approved. It offers incentives to states without age 21 laws to increase the minimum age for drinking. This saves approximately 5,000 young people every year.

In the 5–4 *Hudson v. Palmer* and 6–3 *Block v. Rutherford* cases, Supreme Court justices rule that prison inmates have no constitutional right to privacy in their cells and that prison officials may limit physical contact between prisoners and visitors. The majority in the first case writes that Fourth Amendment unreasonable searches and seizures protections do not extend to prisoners, and in the second, that jail administrators may consider security as a reason for not allowing inmates contact with family or friends.

In a 6–3 decision in *United States v. Leon* and a 7–2 decision in *Massachusetts v. Sheppard*, Supreme Court justices rule that there is a good faith exception to the exclusionary rule.

President Ronald Reagan signs legislation one congressman describes as "the most important crime package passed by any Congress at any time." The Justice Assistance Act applies only to crimes prosecuted on the federal level, or about 5 percent of all crimes, according to the *New York Times*. The legislation allows judges to deny bail to defendants charged with serious offenses when the judges deem the detention necessary to protect "the safety of any other person and the community." The legislation also directs the president to appoint a seven-member commission to establish standardized sentencing guidelines and restricts use of the insanity defense.

1984
cont.
The Victims of Crime Act (VOCA) creates the Crime Victims Fund, which comprises federal criminal fines, penalties, and bond forfeitures that are used to support state victims' compensation and local victims' service programs.

1985
In *Wainwright v. Witt*, Supreme Court justices vote 7–2 to reverse an appeals court ruling and to approve the exclusion of a potential juror who had doubts about the death penalty in a murder case.

Federal Crime Victims Fund deposits amount to $68 million.

In an 8–1 decision in *Ake v. Oklahoma*, the Supreme Court rules that states must provide free psychiatric care to defendants who invoke the insanity defense in their guilty pleas.

The National Victim Center is established in honor of Sunny von Bulow. It promotes the rights and needs of crime victims and educates Americans about the ways crime devastates society. Mrs. von Bulow had been in a coma since 1980. Her husband, Claus, was acquitted on two charges of attempted murder for allegedly inducing, by way of insulin injections, a first coma in 1979, from which she recovered, and a second in 1980.

In a 6–3 decision in *Oregon v. Elstad*, the Supreme Court rules that courts may admit confessions even when suspects confess before they are read their rights and then voluntarily and knowingly confess a second time after they are given Miranda warnings.

The Bureau of Justice Statistics of the U.S. Department of Justice issues the first nationwide study of repeat offenders, finding that 84 percent of people sentenced to state prisons in 1979 already had been convicted of at least one other crime besides the one for which they were being sentenced to prison. Approximately 61 percent of new 1979 inmates had served time in prisons before, and 42 percent were on probation or parole for crimes they previously committed.

The report states that about half of all inmates who had left prison had been sent to prison again within twenty years. Most who returned committed subsequent crimes within three years after being released.

The report compares younger and older convicts. Fifty percent of ex-convicts 18–24 years old return to prison within seven years, while 12 percent of ex-convicts 45 years or older are sentenced to prison again within that period. The study also discovers that more offenders return to prison for theft than for crimes such as murder or rape.

1986   In *Nix v. Whiteside*, the Supreme Court rules unanimously that an attorney's threat to reveal that his client committed perjury does not infringe on the client's right to effective counsel. The client did not share controversial testimony and was convicted of murder. The high court stated that an attorney does not have to present false evidence or otherwise violate the law to help his or her client. Defendants have no right to help in committing perjury, some of the justices said.

In a recommendation that sparks a debate on individual privacy, the President's Commission on Organized Crime calls to fight drugs by employing large-scale drug testing of federal employees and adopting programs to test most employed Americans.

In a 5–4 decision in *Whitley v. Albers*, the Supreme Court rules that wounding a prisoner during a disturbance does not violate the Eighth Amendment's cruel and unusual punishment prohibition. The majority opinion states, "The infliction of pain in the course of a prison security measure does not amount to cruel and unusual punishment simply because it may appear in retrospect that the degree of force authorized or applied for security purposes was unreasonable."

In a unanimous decision in *Holbrook v. Flynn*, the Supreme Court rules that during a trial, the presence of armed, uniformed guards sitting near defendants does not circumvent defendants' rights to a fair trial by giving the impression to jurors that the defendants are dangerous criminals.

1986
cont.

The Supreme Court rules in a 6–3 decision in *Michigan v. Jackson* that law enforcement authorities are not allowed to question defendants at their arraignments once they have asked for legal representation when their attorney is not present.

By a 7–2 margin in *Delaware v. Van Arsdall*, the Supreme Court rules that denying cross-examination of prosecution witnesses is incorrect but not a basis for an automatic conviction reversal. In the case, defendant Robert E. Van Arsdall was not allowed to question a witness about the deal the witness made with the prosecutor in exchange for testimony. Arsdall was convicted of murder in the 1982 case. The Court sent the case back to the Delaware Supreme Court to determine whether the mistake had any effect on Van Arsdall's conviction.

A crime victims' activist shoots and wounds the man suspected of killing his 18-year-old daughter during the man's murder trial. Daniel David Morgan, the alleged murderer, is in a San Francisco courtroom when he is shot. John D. Spiegelman, the girl's father, is charged with attempted murder, assault with a deadly weapon, and possession of a firearm in a courtroom.

In *Batson v. Kentucky*, the Supreme Court rules 7–2 that prosecutors' exclusion of blacks and other minorities from juries violates the Fourteenth Amendment provision of "equal protection of the laws."

In *Lockhart v. McCree*, the Supreme Court rules 6–3 that strict death penalty opponents may be prohibited from judging capital cases.

Chief Justice Warren E. Burger, 78, retires from the Supreme Court. President Reagan says he will make Associate Justice William H. Rehnquist, 61, chief justice and will nominate federal appeals court Judge Antonin Scalia, 50, to fill in the vacancy. Scalia, currently a judge on the U.S. Circuit Court of Appeals for the District of Columbia, is conservative on judicial, social, and political issues and is not expected to alter the high court's ideological makeup.

By a 5–4 margin, the Supreme Court in *McMillan v. Pennsylvania* upholds a law requiring a five-year minimum sentence for anyone possessing a firearm during the commission of certain crimes. Judges must impose the sentence if they determine the defendant possessed a gun by a "preponderance of evidence." Attorneys for four defendants in Philadelphia challenged the law because it did not subject evidence of gun possession to the reasonable doubt test and to a jury's determination.

The Supreme Court rules 5–4 in *Ford v. Wainwright* that executing an insane criminal violates the Eighth Amendment's ban on cruel and unusual punishment.

In joint television and radio broadcasts, President Ronald Reagan and his wife Nancy announce a national push to stop drug abuse.

President Ronald Reagan signs an executive order mandating drug testing for federal workers in "sensitive" posts. He also reveals a package of proposals for combatting the nation's narcotics problem. Like a bill in the House of Representatives, Reagan's proposals would tighten drug penalties and give more money to law enforcement and antidrug education. The Reagan package would provide an additional $900 million in new money, bringing total narcotics spending to $3.2 billion for 1987. Reagan also proposed, as in the House, letting prosecutors use illegally procured evidence as long as the law enforcement officials who collected it had not known they were violating the law. This would extend to all federal criminal cases, not just those focusing on drug infractions. Another of Reagan's provisions would make use of the death penalty acceptable for certain types of drug-related murders. He also asks for mandatory prison sentences for any dealers who sell narcotics used in fatal overdoses. Reagan does not ask to use the military to curb and curtail smuggling.

The Senate by a 65–33 margin confirms William H. Rehnquist as chief justice of the Supreme Court. The Senate Judiciary Committee discussed Rehnquist and voted 13–5 to recommend him as the chief justice. The number

1986
cont.
of opposition votes was the largest ever against any Supreme Court justice. In fact, when he was confirmed as a justice in 1971, Rehnquist received the greatest number ever of opposition votes—26. Senators who opposed Rehnquist as chief justice cited his ideological fervor as a force that could distort his judgment and objectivity. With little discussion, the Senate also confirms Judge Antonin Scalia's nomination by a 98–0 vote.

William H. Rehnquist becomes the sixteenth Supreme Court chief justice and Antonin Scalia is seated as the 103rd justice on the nation's highest court.

Eight hundred people attend funeral services for Jennifer Levin, a New York City teen last seen with Robert Chambers, another young resident of the city. Known as the Preppy Murder, the case generates a lot of publicity given its sexual aspects. Chambers is indicted on two different counts of murder.

Campaigning for a Republican North Carolina senator, President Ronald Reagan lashes out against "liberal judges," saying they are too easy on criminals. "The proliferation of drugs has been a part of a crime epidemic that can be traced to, among other things, liberal judges who are unwilling to get tough with the criminal element in this society," Reagan says. "We don't need a bunch of sociology majors on the bench. What we need are strong judges who will aggressively use their authority to protect our families, communities and way of life; judges who understand that punishing wrongdoers is our way of protecting the innocent; judges who do not hesitate to put criminals where they belong, behind bars."

1987
An internal Justice Department study, made public through a *New York Times* article, encourages the department to do what it can to overturn the Supreme Court's 1966 *Miranda v. Arizona* case, which requires police to tell criminal suspects about their legal rights before interrogating them. The report states that overturning the decision would help to restore "the power of self-government to the people of the United States in the suppression of crime." Attorney General Edwin Meese III, a veteran critic of Miranda rights,

apparently agrees with the report. He was cited in October 1985 as saying the ruling "only helps guilty defendants."

In *Maryland v. Garrison*, the Supreme Court rules 6–3 that although improper, evidence obtained by law enforcement through an "honest" mistake is admissible in court.

The Supreme Court rules 5–4 in *Pennsylvania v. Ritchie* that defendants accused of child abuse have no right to search through state child protective agency records for information that will assist their defense.

In a 6–3 decision in *Arizona v. Hicks*, the Supreme Court rules that law enforcement officers who move stereo equipment to see the serial numbers are conducting an illegal search even though they are at the scene legitimately to look for weapons.

In a 5–4 ruling in *Illinois v. Krull*, the Supreme Court decides that evidence procured by law enforcement authorities under a law determined to be unconstitutional still is admissible in court as long as the authorities believed the law was constitutional.

The U.S. Sentencing Commission releases new guidelines for federal judges to adhere to when sentencing criminals.

The Supreme Court rules 5–4 in *Tison v. Arizona* that defendants who take part in a crime that ends in murder, even if they are not the murderers, may be sentenced to death when they show a "reckless indifference" to life.

In a 5–4 decision in *McCleskey v. Kemp*, the Supreme Court rejects a general racial challenge to capital punishment as lacking proof that the defendant faced discrimination in the system. Although the defendant cited a statistical study showing death penalty sentencing disparities between blacks and whites, the majority states that the study did not prove a specific sentencing disparity in *McCleskey*.

In a 6–3 decision in *United States v. Salerno*, the Supreme Court rules that "preventive detention" before a trial is

1987
cont.

constitutional when a federal court determines a suspect to be dangerous to the public. The decision affirms the constitutionality of the Bail Reform Act of 1984, which allows the government to press for preventive detention and for a court to have a hearing assessing the accused's potential threat to others or society.

Justice Lewis F. Powell resigns from the Supreme Court.

The Supreme Court rules 5–4 in *Booth v. Maryland* that victim impact statements during the sentencing phase of capital cases violate the Eighth Amendment's protection against cruel and unusual punishment. Victim impact statements describe the effect of a crime on the victim and the victim's family.

Defendants in child molestation cases do not have a constitutional right to be present during pretrial hearings in which the child's competency to testify is determined, the Supreme Court decides 6–3 in *Kentucky v. Stincer*.

The Supreme Court decides 6–3 in *New York v. Burger* that warrantless searches of junkyards under a New York anti–car theft law do not come under Fourth Amendment privacy protections since junkyards are "pervasively regulated businesses."

The Supreme Court rules 6–3 in *Sumner v. Shuman* that mandatory death sentences violate the Eighth and Fourteenth Amendments.

In a 5–4 decision in *Rock v. Arkansas*, the Supreme Court decides that defendants' right to testify on their own behalf supersedes a state's interest in barring potentially unreliable evidence when the defendants' memory is enhanced with hypnosis.

Jury selection begins in the prosecution of Robert Chambers for the murder of Jennifer Levin, the so-called Preppy Murder case. Because of the high degree of pretrial publicity, prospective jurors are questioned one at a time in small jury deliberation quarters.

Due to the "clamor" over his admission of smoking marijuana in the past, U.S. Appeals Court Judge Douglas H. Ginsburg withdraws as President Ronald Reagan's second Supreme Court nominee to fill the seat vacated by Justice Lewis F. Powell. The withdrawal comes 15 days after the Senate Judiciary Committee rejects Reagan's nomination of Judge Robert H. Bork.

President Ronald Reagan nominates Federal Judge Anthony M. Kennedy to the Supreme Court. Appointed to the Ninth Circuit Court of Appeals by President Gerald R. Ford in 1975, Kennedy has taken part in more than 1,400 decisions and penned more than 400 opinions in his 12 years on the court. He wrote a 1983 dissent encouraging an exception to the exclusionary rule—which does not admit illegally obtained evidence in trials—to permit evidence obtained by police acting in good faith. Kennedy also wrote several opinions sustaining tough criminal sentences.

1988 Chief Justice William H. Rehnquist notes that Congress is cutting funding for the federal judiciary, although workloads are increasing and the system is understaffed with judges and other court employees. Rehnquist says there are 48 vacancies among federal judgeships and that an advisory panel he chairs recommended adding 56 new trial judgeships and 13 appellate seats, for a total of 117 judges the federal judiciary lacks. Rehnquist also says that more time is now needed to handle existing criminal cases, which add to the workload, and that compensation for federal judges "may not be high enough to attract the first-rate talent that has always been a hallmark of the federal bench."

As the Preppy Murder trial of Robert Chambers concludes, the defense and prosecution, following nine days of jury deliberation, agree to a plea bargain: first-degree manslaughter with a sentence typical of those for second-degree manslaughter, 5 to 15 years.

Ending months of wrangling over the Supreme Court seat vacated by Justice Lewis F. Powell, Jr., in June 1987, the

1988
cont.

Senate votes 97–0 to confirm Judge Anthony M. Kennedy as an associate justice. The Senate rejected Federal Appeals Court Judge Robert H. Bork, President Reagan's first nominee and a conservative. The sticking point in Bork's nomination was the way he interpreted the Constitution, which divided liberals and conservatives. Federal Appeals Court Judge Douglas H. Ginsburg, Reagan's second nominee, withdrew after he admitted to smoking marijuana while a Harvard Law School faculty member. Judge Kennedy, 51, has "a judicial philosophy that places him within the mainstream of constitutional interpretation," says Sen. Edward M. Kennedy (D-Mass.) in encouraging Kennedy's approval.

President Ronald Reagan requests $5.8 billion for the Justice Department—$643 million more than he asked for fiscal year 1988. The request amounts to more than $76 million in increases for federal antidrug programs, including 655 new jobs. Despite the increase in proposed antidrug money, the Justice Department wants to cut $69.5 million in grants for antidrug programs at the state and local levels. Deputy Attorney General Arnold Burns says assets seized from drug traffickers will compensate for the cuts. The request also includes $420 million for new prisons, expansion of existing corrections facilities, and their maintenance. This would allow 5,400 new prisoners to enter the system. Other proposals enlarge the border patrol and the Federal Bureau of Investigation (FBI). More money at the FBI would go toward bolstering investigations of white-collar crime, terrorism, and espionage. The House and Senate later appropriate $5.4 billion to the Justice Department and $1.4 billion to the judiciary by respective margins of 269–141 and 77–13.

Anthony M. Kennedy takes an oath to become a Supreme Court justice and the 104th member of the country's highest court.

The Supreme Court rules 5–4 in *Wheat v. United States* that trial judges have "broad latitude" in denying criminal defendants their chosen attorney when the attorney's representation may be a conflict of interest.

Supreme Court justices agree to examine the constitutionality of a new federal sentencing code that took effect in November 1987. The new code, developed by a congressional commission composed of federal judges, an executive branch official, and private citizens, is being challenged in *United States v. Mistretta*. The case questions whether the commission's membership violated the Constitution's separation of powers requirement and whether Congress is allowed to delegate its authority over criminal sentences to a commission.

Lower courts have been divided on the new code. In its eight months of existence, it has been struck down as unconstitutional by 59 federal judges and upheld by 44, according to the San Diego Federal Defenders program as reported in the *Wall Street Journal*.

The Supreme Court decides to narrow Fifth Amendment protection against self-incrimination for white-collar crime suspects in two separate cases. In *Braswell v. United States*, the Court decides 5–4 that a corporate records custodian must, if subpoenaed, provide the records even if they reveal incriminating information against him. In an 8–1 decision in *Doe v. United States*, the Court rules a suspect may not invoke the Fifth Amendment to avoid signing a form granting authorities access to bank files that may incriminate him.

In a 375–30 vote, the House approves a $2.1 billion anti-drug bill to provide a core of money for expanded drug treatment and education programs. The bill also imposes a federal death penalty for murders related to drugs and fines up to $10,000 on people with previously clean records when they are caught with small amounts of drugs. A provision in the bill would bar convicted drug users from being able to get several federal financial benefits, including grants, housing, loans, contracts, and some benefits for veterans.

A controversial provision would weaken the exclusionary rule by allowing illegally seized evidence to be admitted in federal criminal trials if law enforcement authorities believed in the constitutionality of the seizures. Although the bill originally contained a provision to require a

1988
cont.
seven-day waiting period to conduct background checks on people who want to buy guns, the measure was dropped by a 228–182 vote. Instead, after being intensely lobbied by the National Rifle Association, the House replaced the provision with a directive to the Justice Department to come up with a system that would detect convicted felons who try to buy guns.

Vice President and Republican presidential candidate George Bush airs an advertisement about Willie Horton, a man convicted of raping a woman while on furlough from a Massachusetts prison. Bush uses the ad to shore up his image as a law-and-order candidate while showing Democratic presidential candidate and Massachusetts Governor Michael Dukakis's lack of concern for justice.

Congress votes to budget $5.4 billion for the Justice Department. Many conservatives oppose the bill's inclusion of money for the Legal Services Corporation, which supports the poor with legal assistance.

By margins of 87–3 and 346–11, the Senate and House respectively pass the antidrug bill. The bill is modified from one the House passed earlier. It allows the death penalty for drug-related killings and calls for fines up to $10,000 for possession of small amounts of illegal substances such as marijuana and cocaine. A provision in the bill expands drug treatment facilities, for the first time, with federal money. The bill appropriates close to half a billion dollars for antidrug programs. It creates a cabinet position to oversee antidrug programs and write budget requests. It takes aim at money laundering by requiring domestic and foreign-based banks to record large cash transactions. Overseas banks also would not be permitted to take part in U.S. dollar-clearing or wire-transfer systems if they refused to open their records to U.S. drug investigators. The bill mandates the chemical industry to periodically file reports about materials they ship that could be used to create illicit substances. Unlike the earlier House version, this bill quashes a weakened exclusionary rule. Lastly, Congress requires warning labels on alcoholic beverages.

In a 6–3 decision, the Supreme Court upholds a conviction on a defendant's appeal that police neglected to preserve evidence that might have proven his innocence. In *Arizona v. Youngblood*, a 10-year-old boy, a sexual assault victim, identified the defendant as his attacker. This was the basis for conviction. Although police found semen on the boy's clothing, they did not conduct any identity tests or preserve the clothing so that the defense could perform identity tests.

In *Penson v. Ohio*, the Supreme Court by an 8–1 margin upholds the right of poor defendants to have attorneys represent them when they appeal their convictions.

1989   In a yearly report on the federal judiciary, Chief Justice William H. Rehnquist asks Congress to make 73 new positions for federal judges and raise federal judges' salaries. Federal courts are strapped with an influx of cases. Judges earn less as judges than what they could earn as attorneys in private practice, so the profession does not necessarily attract people with "the talent, experience and temperament" to "protect imperiled rights and to render a fair decision," Rehnquist says.

In a newly released study, the Justice Department's Bureau of Justice Statistics states that more than 60 percent of all released state prisoners are arrested for a serious crime within three years after their release.
   The Bureau examined 16,000 inmates' records (of 109,000 total) for 1983 releases from corrections facilities in California, Florida, Illinois, Michigan, Minnesota, New Jersey, New York, North Carolina, Ohio, Oregon, and Texas. By 1986, about 62.5 percent of them had been arrested either on felony or serious misdemeanor charges, 47 percent were convicted, and 41 percent were returned to prison. According to the study, young prisoners and those with long criminal histories are most likely to commit more crimes.

A Portland, Maine, judge decides that a prisoner convicted of stabbing a man has no right to sue to thwart shutting off the victim's life-support system. Noel Pagan, the convicted

1989 felon, has served three years for stabbing Mark Weaver in
cont. Lewiston, Maine, in 1985. After the attack, Weaver slipped
into a coma and has been kept alive via life-support equipment. Pagan said he should be permitted to stop Weaver's
family from taking out his feeding tube. If the tube is re-
moved and Weaver dies, Pagan could be charged with
murder. But according to Judge Dana Childs, Pagan's interest "has nothing to do with this proceeding." Although
the Constitution guards against double jeopardy, Pagan's
conviction was based on an assault charge, not murder.
Therefore, he could be tried for murder.

President George Bush proposes a $1.2 billion anticrime
package. Its measures include a ban on the import, production, and sale of semiautomatic weapon cartridges with
more than 15 rounds; a permanent ban on the import of
some semiautomatic weapons that Bush originally announced as a temporary ban; 825 new agents for the Bureau of Alcohol, Tobacco and Firearms, the U.S. Marshals
Service, and the Federal Bureau of Investigation; 1,600 new
positions in U.S. attorneys' offices throughout the country; 168 new positions in the Justice Department's criminal
division; $1 billion for new federal prisons; and stronger
penalties for various federal crimes.

The Supreme Court in *Graham v. Connor* unanimously
rules that challenges to use of force by police must be based
on "objective reasonableness" and not on the intent—good
faith or maliciousness—of the officers.

In *South Carolina v. Gathers*, the Supreme Court rules 5–4
to uphold its stance on the inadmissibility of victim impact remarks.

In a 5–4 decision in *Murray v. Giarratano*, the Supreme Court
decides that poor death-row prisoners do not have a constitutional right to an attorney to help them with a second
round of state court appeals.

The Eighth Amendment's protection against cruel and
unusual punishment does not stop execution of mentally
retarded murderers or murderers who were minors when

they committed murder, the Supreme Court rules in three separate 5–4 decisions in *Penry v. Lynaugh*, *Stanford v. Kentucky*, and *Wilkins v. Missouri*.

In *Duckworth v. Eagan*, the Supreme Court rules 5–4 that it is acceptable for police to tell a suspect they cannot provide him an attorney and that if he cannot afford one, one will be appointed "if and when you go to court."

1990   The Supreme Court by a 5–4 vote reaffirms the exclusionary rule in the case of *James v. Illinois*. Allowing an exception to the exclusionary rule in this case would pave the way for overriding citizens' constitutional rights and also would "significantly weaken the exclusionary rule's deterrent effect on police misconduct," Justice William J. Brennan, writing for the majority, states.

The Supreme Court rules 7–2 in *Baltimore v. Bouknight* that Jacqueline Bouknight may not use her Fifth Amendment right against self-incrimination to resist telling authorities the location of her son, who was abused and believed to be dead.

In *Butler v. McKellar* and *Saffle v. Parks*, the Supreme Court rules 5–4 that death-row inmates whose convictions were based on laws in effect at the time of their trials cannot take advantage of any new precedent that came about after their convictions.

The Supreme Court rules 6–3 in *McKoy v. North Carolina* to overturn a state law requiring juries deciding on the death penalty to consider "aggravating" and "mitigating" evidence for and against a convicted defendant. Under the North Carolina law, jury members could take into account only evidence they unanimously agree is proven. The court strikes down the unanimity requirement as it relates to mitigating factors.

By a 5–4 vote in *Michigan v. Harvey*, the Supreme Court rules that evidence that violates the Sixth Amendment's right to counsel provision may be used to "impeach" a defendant's "false or inconsistent testimony."

1990
cont.

In a 5–4 split, the Supreme Court decides that a state appeals court was permitted to judge the elements of a crime and rule whether to sentence the defendant to death if the jury had considered elements that were not proper. The jury in *Clemons v. Mississippi* had called a murder "heinous," a designation the state allowed but one that the high court in a later Oklahoma case had deemed unconstitutional because of its vagueness. The justices state that the Mississippi court had not specified why it upheld the death sentence, and they return the case to the state court for a new hearing.

The Federal Courts Study Committee warns that already overburdened U.S. courts are being slammed with prosecutions under antidrug and anticrime laws Congress passed in the 1980s.

In a speech to the American Law Institute, Chief Justice William H. Rehnquist asks to restrict death penalty appeals to federal courts. In the typical death penalty case, a hiatus of seven or eight years between sentencing and execution is a "serious malfunction in our legal system," he says. Death-row inmates may file any number of habeas corpus petitions, and in recent years, more than half of all death sentences imposed by state courts have been overturned in federal courts during inmates' appeals.

Under the Victim and Witness Protection Act, defendants may be required to pay restitution only for crimes of which they are convicted, according to a unanimous decision by the Supreme Court in *Hughey v. United States*. The defendant in the case was charged with dozens of credit card thefts but pleaded guilty to and was convicted of taking only one card.

The legality of a 1984 law requiring a $25 fine for people convicted of federal misdemeanors is challenged in *United States v. Muñoz-Flores*. The money charged on every count goes into a Crime Victims Fund to compensate crime victims. The Supreme Court unanimously rules to uphold the law, which the justices consider a special program, not a means of raising revenue—something that can originate only in the House of Representatives.

By a 5–4 split in *Grady v. Corbin*, the Supreme Court decides a drunk driver who pleaded guilty to two misdemeanors in a fatal traffic accident may not be prosecuted for homicide. Such a prosecution would violate the Fifth Amendment's safeguard against double jeopardy.

An undercover law enforcement officer posing as an inmate does not need to give a jailed suspect Miranda warnings about his protections against self-incrimination, the Supreme Court decides 8–1 in *Illinois v. Perkins*.

After adding a provision to strengthen the government's power to examine and prosecute fraud in the savings and loan business, the Senate, by a 96–4 margin, passes the Omnibus Crime Bill. It raises the number of federal death penalty crimes from 23 to 34, allows death-row prisoners only one federal appeal, and authorizes money for 2,500 new federal police positions and $900 million for state and local law enforcement agencies. The anticrime legislation is pending in the House of Representatives.

Appointed by President Eisenhower in 1956, Justice William J. Brennan resigns from the Supreme Court. He is remembered for his coalition-building talents in many of the Warren Court's landmark decisions in the 1950s and 1960s and is known in the 1980s and 1990s as a liberal voice on the Court's conservative bench.

President Bush names David H. Souter, 50, a New Hampshire judge, to fill the Supreme Court vacancy left by Justice William J. Brennan. After confirmation hearings in September, the Senate votes 90–9 to confirm Souter as a Supreme Court justice.

In a 368–55 vote, the House of Representatives passes an anticrime bill already approved by the Senate. It includes the Racial Justice Act amendment, which passes 218–186. The amendment requires inmates who want to overturn their death sentences to prove that "at the time the death sentence was imposed, race was a statistically significant factor in decisions to see or impose the sentence of death in the jurisdiction in question." The measure also increases

1990
cont.
the amount of crimes justifying the federal death penalty, limits death-row prisoners' constitutional appeals, and allows the ongoing production of semiautomatic weapons that are made with parts manufactured in the United States.

Members of Congress approve the Omnibus Crime Bill. The bill came up for a vote after many of its sticking points were eliminated in a joint conference. The provisions cut from the bill include expansion of the amount of crimes warranting the federal death penalty, restrictions on death-row prisoners' appeals, and the banning of some types of semiautomatic weapons. The conference committee also stripped from the bill the Racial Justice Act amendment. The bill increases money for local and federal law enforcement and establishes stiffer penalties for drug offenses, financial fraud, and child pornography.

In a 6–2 vote in *Minnick v. Mississippi*, the Supreme Court rules that once criminal suspects request consultation with an attorney, police may not question them unless the attorney is present.

1991
The Justice Department's Bureau of Justice Statistics (BJS) reports a 20 percent decrease in violent crimes against men between 1973 and 1987. The number of violent crimes against women held steady, the report states. The BJS survey reports that 25 percent of violent crimes against women were committed by family members or men the women dated compared to 4 percent of crimes committed against men by family members or female acquaintances.

The Supreme Court dismisses a victim impact case, *Ohio v. Huertas*, stating that it should not have been accepted in the first place. The Court ruled in 1987 that testimony during sentencing by a murder victim's family and friends was too inflammatory for jurors to hear. President Bush and victims' rights organizations have pushed the justices to overturn the 1987 ruling.

President George Bush submits to Congress an anticrime bill similar to ones he proposed in 1989 and 1990. Those proposals did not pass muster with members of Congress. Bush's new proposals include increasing the scope of the federal death penalty to 30 new crimes such as espionage, treason, serious drug offenses, and crimes committed with "weapons of mass destruction," such as bombs; admitting in court evidence police illegally seize as long as they are believed to have seized it in good faith; limiting convicted federal prison inmates' number of appeals; and mandating a five-year minimum prison term for anyone caught with a firearm when the person has been convicted of a violent or drug-related crime (federal law at this time requires a fifteen-year minimum sentence for felons who have three previous convictions and are caught with a firearm).

Senate Judiciary Committee Chairman Joseph R. Biden (D-Del.) says House Democrats are ready to pass many of Bush's provisions, but the president must accept more controls on semiautomatic weapons and raise federal revenue for state and local law enforcement. In 1989 and 1990, Bush rejected those additions.

The Supreme Court in *Arizona v. Fulminante* rules 5–4 that using a coerced confession in a criminal case does not automatically suspend a conviction.

In *McCleskey v. Zant*, the Supreme Court rules 6–3 that second-round habeas corpus petitions can be considered only when inmates show the constitutional violation being appealed actually harmed their cases and when they show how "some external impediment" prevented earlier discussion of the relevant issue. Also, an inmate who provides evidence that demonstrates his or her probable innocence may file a second petition.

Evidence dropped by a fleeing suspect does not fall within the realm of the Fourth Amendment's protections against illegal searches and seizures, the Supreme Court rules 7–2 in *California v. Hodari D.*

In a 6–3 decision in *Demos v. Storrie*, the Supreme Court bars a Washington State inmate from filing certain types of petitions without paying a $300 filing fee to the Court. In the situation that spurred the Court to act, inmate John

1991
cont.

Robert Demos, Jr., had filed 32 petitions during the Court's previous three terms. The Court rules not to let Demos petition for "extraordinary" relief without paying the $300 fee. The justices also dismiss Demos's three pending petitions and decides not to label "indigent" cases it deems "frivolous or malicious."

Supreme Court justices decide whether prosecutors need to show that an alleged juvenile sexual abuse victim is not able to testify in court before statements taken outside the courtroom may be admitted as evidence. The case, *White v. Illinois*, involves Randall D. White, who was convicted of abusing a four-year-old girl named in the case as S. G. The girl was present during the trial but did not testify. Adults, such as her mother and doctor, however, gave testimony about what she had said regarding the alleged abuse. White argued that the adults' testimony was hearsay and violated his right to question those who were witnesses against him. The Supreme Court rules unanimously that prosecutors were not required to have the victim testify, nor were they required to show that she could not testify before statements taken outside the court could be admitted.

In a 5–4 decision, the Supreme Court rules that suspects under warrantless arrests may be detained for a maximum of 48 hours to wait for a judge to decide the arrest's legality. In *County of Riverside, Calif. v. McLaughlin*, Riverside County prisoners filed a class action suit against the county for its policy of routinely detaining suspects one to two days—or three to four if they were arrested before a weekend or holiday—before a judge determined whether there was probable cause to warrant the arrest.

In *Michigan v. Lucas*, the Supreme Court rules 7–2 that states are allowed at certain times to restrict an accused rapist's ability to provide evidence about his previous sexual relationship with the alleged victim.

The Supreme Court holds 6–3 in *Hernandez v. New York* that prosecutors do not necessarily violate the Constitution when they remove potential jurors who speak and understand Spanish in a case with a Hispanic defendant.

Prosecutors not only must consider language ability but must take into account whether potential bilingual jurors will use the court's official English translation transcript and not base judgments on their ability to comprehend Spanish.

The Supreme Court holds 5–4 in *Mu'Min v. Virginia* that a judge in a high-profile criminal case need not ask jurors specifically about their knowledge of the crime based on print or broadcast reports.

In *California v. Acevedo*, the Supreme Court rules 6–3 to permit police without warrants to search bags, suitcases, or other containers in the trunk of a car. They need to have probable cause, however, to justify such searches. The decision overturns the 1979 precedent set forth in *Arkansas v. Sanders,* which made warrantless luggage searches unconstitutional.

The *Miami Herald* reports that federal judges increasingly object to narrow federal sentencing guidelines for drug offenders as established by the Anti-Drug Abuse Act of 1986. The judges say the guidelines provide no leeway for a defendant's criminal background or degree of guilt and force "the courts in many instances to impose sentences which are manifestly unjust and harsh."

The Supreme Court decides 6–3 in *McNeil v. Wisconsin* that with given cases, criminal suspects represented by an attorney in one case are allowed to be questioned by police about a different, unrelated case without an attorney. The ruling restricts *Miranda v. Arizona*, a landmark 1966 case in which the justices decided that police always must tell suspects that they have the right to an attorney under the Fifth Amendment's privilege against self-incrimination.

In the case of *Burns v. United States*, the Supreme Court rules 5–4 that federal judges must notify both parties before meting out a sentence stricter than one specified in the federal sentencing guidelines. The author of the majority opinion, Justice Thurgood Marshall, states that advance notices are required according to the Federal

1991
cont.

Sentencing Reform Act of 1984, the legislation that established the guidelines. The decision reverses that of the U.S. Circuit Court of Appeals for the District of Columbia. A federal judge sentenced William J. Burns, a former employee of the U.S. Agency for International Development who was convicted of stealing money from the government, to five years instead of the 30 to 37 months set up by the guidelines.

In a 5–4 decision in *Wilson v. Seiter*, the Supreme Court rules that to invoke the Eighth Amendment protections against cruel and unusual punishment regarding prison conditions, an inmate must prove such conditions exist because of prison officials' "deliberate indifference."

The Supreme Court decides 6–3 in *Florida v. Bostick* that police may board buses and, with passengers' permission, search luggage for drugs without violating Fourth Amendment protections against illegal searches and seizures.

In *Schad v. Arizona*, the Supreme Court decides 5–4 that jurors need not have a unanimous theory on how a crime was committed to convict the accused on first-degree murder charges.

Failure to follow a state's requirements for filing writs of habeas corpus may cause prisoners to lose their rights to file such appeals in federal court, according to a 6–3 Supreme Court decision in *Coleman v. Thompson*. The decision overturns *Fay v. Noia*, a 1963 landmark case in which state inmates almost always were guaranteed the right to challenge their convictions in federal courts.

Justice Thurgood Marshall, the first African American to sit on the country's highest court, announces his retirement. In the realm of criminal justice, Marshall is known for his belief that the death penalty constitutes cruel and unusual punishment.

In a 6–3 decision in *Payne v. Tennessee*, the Supreme Court rules that victims or their families may make victim impact statements during the sentencing phases of capital cases.

Ruling 5–4 in *Harmelin v. Michigan*, the Supreme Court decides that a Michigan law mandating life imprisonment with no chance of parole for possession of 650 grams of cocaine does not violate the Eighth Amendment's guarantee against cruel and unusual punishment.

President George Bush nominates Judge Clarence Thomas, 43, of the U.S. Court of Appeals for the District of Columbia to fill Thurgood Marshall's seat.

The U.S. Senate passes 71–26 an anticrime bill that sets up a five-day waiting period for handgun purchases; bans for three years the production, sale, and possession of nine kinds of semiautomatic weapons; expands the federal death penalty to an additional 51 crimes; cuts down the amount of appeals death-row prisoners may file; and codifies the exclusionary rule to permit evidence that police obtained acting in good faith or believing that a warrant was legal.

House Democrats introduce an anticrime measure that includes many provisions similar to those in the bill the Senate recently passed. One provision would route approximately $750 million to state and local governments for crime prevention programs such as prison-based drug treatment, community policing, and programs to keep young offenders from committing more crime. Unlike the Senate bill, the House measure does not attempt to codify the exclusionary rule.

In a 305–118 vote, the House of Representatives approves an anticrime bill that expands the scope of the federal death penalty from 2 crimes (airline hijacking resulting in death and some drug-related murders) to more than 50, requires a maximum of one year in which death-row prisoners may file habeas corpus petitions for federal case reviews, and permits warrantless evidence in court as long as a judge finds that police were acting in good faith.

Massachusetts Governor William F. Weld (R) introduces legislation to restore the state's death penalty. Massachusetts' last execution was in 1947 and there has not

1991
cont.

been a death penalty law in place for ten years. Under the proposal, lethal injection could be used for specific categories of first-degree murderers older than 18.

William P. Barr is confirmed as U.S. attorney general to replace Dick Thornburgh, who resigned to run for the Pennsylvania Senate. Barr, 41, says he favors federal funding for juvenile justice programs, supports mandatory minimum sentences for some drug and gun crimes, and backs the Bush administration's stance on restricting prisoners' rights to appeal court decisions.

An anticrime bill dies in the Senate when Democratic leaders do not have enough votes to stem a Republican filibuster. The $3 billion bill passed the House 205–203 the same day. The House and Senate versions of the bill were sent to a conference committee, which achieved a partisan compromise.

In *Simon & Schuster v. New York Crime Victims Board*, the Supreme Court by an 8–0 margin deems unconstitutional a New York law that restricts criminals' ability to sell their stories for books or movies. Justice Clarence Thomas does not participate in the decision. Striking at the 1977 "Son of Sam" law after the "Son of Sam" murders committed by David Berkowitz in New York City, the ruling is expected to affect the 41 other states that have such laws and the federal law that went on the books in 1984.

1992

Fourteen death-row prisoners in California file a lawsuit to have their sperm preserved for artificial insemination. The prisoners ask that they be permitted to donate sperm "for future procreation with a willing woman." They contend that prohibiting them to save their sperm is cruel and unusual punishment because "not only are their lives taken, but the possibility of any future generations of their family are also executed."

In *United States v. Jakobetz*, the U.S. Second Circuit Court of Appeals issues a unanimous ruling making it easier for prosecutors to introduce DNA "fingerprint" evidence in criminal cases. While the court is based in New York City and covers New York, Connecticut, and Vermont, the ruling, applicable only in federal courts, is expected to greatly influence court proceedings in other states.

President George Bush proposes raising law enforcement spending from $14.1 billion—what was budgeted for federal law enforcement activities in fiscal year 1992—to $15.4 billion, an increase that is less than Bush has previously requested. The Justice Department would see more money than in 1992, $10.4 billion, or an increase of 11 percent. But the Federal Bureau of Investigation, the Drug Enforcement Administration, and other federal anticrime task forces would receive less money—$2.93 billion from $2.95 billion in 1992.

As part of the budget proposal, Bush also outlines a plan to make federal prison inmates pay for their first year in prison as long as they have the money to do so. The administration estimates that approximately one-fifth of federal prisoners can afford to pay the $18,000 bill, amounting to about $48 million overall in a given year.

Democratic Party officials sue to make the Federal Election Commission (FEC) reinvestigate links between George Bush's 1988 presidential campaign and the National Security Political Action Committee (PAC). The independent PAC developed the "Willie Horton" advertisement, one of the factors contributing to the defeat of Democratic Party candidate Michael S. Dukakis, who at the time was governor of Massachusetts. The ad showed how Horton, a black felon, was convicted of raping a white woman while on furlough from a Massachusetts prison. It tied the crime to Dukakis's "weak" approach to crime and criminals. Many people said the ad was racist, and Bush campaign officials denied involvement in the making and airing of it.

An FEC investigation publicized in the *Washington Times* stated that Roger Ailes, Bush's campaign media advisor in 1988, had spoken with the Horton ad producer several times throughout the campaign. Also, a former Ailes employee, Jesse Raiford, assisted with the ad's production while working for the Bush campaign. In 1991, the FEC, split along party lines, voted to close the investigation.

1992
cont.

The Supreme Court rules 7–2 in *Hudson v. McMillian* that excessive force by corrections officers against prisoners violates the Eighth Amendment's ban on cruel and unusual punishment even if the force does not seriously injure the prisoner.

The Supreme Court unanimously rules in *United States v. Felix* that first prosecuting an individual for committing a crime and then prosecuting him or her for conspiracy to commit the same crime does not violate constitutional protections against double jeopardy—even if the prosecutions are based on the same incidents.

A three-member California parole board votes unanimously to deny parole to Charles Manson, who supervised the 1969 killings of actress Sharon Tate and eight others. Manson, 57, is serving a life sentence. He is allowed to seek parole every three years. The parole board has denied him parole eight times.

In a 5–4 vote, the Supreme Court overturns a 1963 precedent establishing state inmates' access to federal courts. In the case of *Keeney v. Tamayo-Reyes*, the Court decides that federal courts do not have to grant a federal court hearing to a state prisoner who challenges his convictions even if he can demonstrate that his lawyer in the state appeals process did not properly present important facts of the case.

In a 5–4 decision in *Foucha v. Louisiana*, the Supreme Court rules unconstitutional a Louisiana law that in some cases permits criminal defendants' indefinite detention in mental hospitals. The Louisiana law allowed continued confinement of a criminal defendant—who initially was found not guilty because of insanity and later was determined to have regained sanity—if state officials believed he would endanger society upon his release.

In *Riggins v. Nevada*, the Supreme Court rules 7–2 that states may not force a mentally ill defendant to take antipsychotic drugs during a trial unless they can demonstrate that forcing medication on a defendant is medically acceptable and "essential" to the defendant's or others' safety.

By a 6–3 margin in *Morgan v. Illinois*, the Supreme Court rules that defense attorneys in capital cases may dismiss potential jurors who say they will automatically vote to sentence the defendant to death if he or she is found guilty.

The Supreme Court decides 7–2 that criminal defendants may not exclude potential jurors only on the basis of race. The ruling, in *Georgia v. McCollum*, ends the Court's recent revision of rules concerning the peremptory jury challenge, which allowed defense and prosecuting attorneys to disqualify a specified number of prospective jurors without explaining why.

The Supreme Court by a 7–2 vote in *Medina v. California* holds constitutional a California law requiring criminal defendants to prove themselves mentally unfit, and therefore unable, to stand trial.

The U.S. Senate fails to approve a conference committee version of a major anticrime bill for the second year in a row. Led by Sen. Joseph R. Biden, Jr. (D-Del.), the upper house's Democrats in a repeat of a 1991 vote fail to come up with enough votes to thwart a threatened Republican filibuster. Senate Democrats and Republicans have been at loggerheads on the bill since November 1991. The vote is 55–43, 5 short of votes needed to stop debate on the bill. As presented by the conference committee, the bill includes limits on death-row prisoners' ability to counter their sentences via habeas corpus petitions, extension of the death penalty to more than 50 crimes, and new penalties for gun-related crimes. There also is a provision including the Brady bill, which would mandate a five-day wait for handgun purchases. Republicans oppose the handgun controls, and Democrats do not favor limits on prisoners' ability to challenge their sentences. President George Bush is not against the waiting period as long as it goes into a crime bill with the habeas corpus limits.

Residents of Colorado, Illinois, Kansas, Missouri, and New Mexico by large margins pass crime victims' bills of rights amendments to their state constitutions. This brings the total number of states with such amendments to 13.

1993   In *Herrera v. Collins*, the Supreme Court decides 6–3 that under most circumstances, new federal court trials are not allowed for prisoners sentenced to death by state courts even if the prisoners later produce evidence of their innocence.

President Bill Clinton nominates Miami, Florida, State Attorney Janet Reno to head the Justice Department as attorney general.

In a unanimous vote, the Senate approves the nomination, and she is sworn in on 12 March.

The Supreme Court rules 7–2 in *Arave v. Creech* that an Idaho law that allows capital punishment in cases in which the defendant shows "utter disregard for human life" is not unconstitutionally vague.

In a unanimous decision in *Sullivan v. Louisiana*, the Supreme Court rules that a criminal conviction should be set aside based on a judge's failure to instruct the jury that a defendant's guilt must be proven beyond a "reasonable doubt."

President Bill Clinton nominates Ruth Bader Ginsburg, a District of Columbia U.S. Court of Appeals judge, to replace Justice Byron R. White, who is retiring after serving 31 years on the high court.

In a two-pronged decision, the Supreme Court rules unanimously that prosecutors may be liable for what they say to the media. The justices also decide 5–4 to permit suits against prosecutors for overzealous actions in trying to get a conviction. Both decisions come about through the case of *Buckley v. Fitzsimmons*.

In *Johnson v. Texas*, the Supreme Court rules 5–4 that a Texas law permitting juries to sentence teenagers convicted of murder to death is constitutionally sound.

President Bill Clinton announces anticrime legislation including provisions to tighten federal gun control and add 50,000 new police officers. Several of the provisions were part of an anticrime bill that died in Congress in 1992 when

Senate Democrats did not have enough votes to quash a Republican filibuster.

Measures in the legislative package include:

- The Brady bill. Named after James Brady, who was wounded in the 1981 assassination attempt on President Ronald Reagan, the bill requires a five-day waiting period for handgun purchases.

- A one-time limit on death-row prisoner sentence challenges via a habeas corpus writ. Inmates would have to file such petitions no later than six months after a state court rejects the claim.

- Expansion of the federal death penalty to 50 crimes.

The House of Representatives approves four parts of the anticrime legislation, including the allocation of $3.45 billion over five years to hire more police, $300 million to treat federal and state prison inmates' drug problems, and $200 million to combat gang violence.

The House, 238–189, passes its version of the Brady bill, which calls for a five-day waiting period on handgun purchases. The waiting period provision would be in effect for five years.

Wisconsin voters approve a constitutional amendment for victims' rights bringing the number of states with such an amendment to 14.

The Senate approves 94–4 an anticrime bill authorizing $22.3 billion over five years to hire more police, build new corrections facilities, and establish crime prevention programs. Included in the legislation are $8.9 billion to hire 100,000 more police throughout the country, $3 billion for new regional prisons, $3.5 billion for new jails, $1.8 billion to fight violence against women, and $1.2 billion for drug treatment and antidrug programs. The Senate bill also bans 19 types of semiautomatic assault weapons, allows young people accused of violent crimes to be tried as adults, expands the federal death penalty to 52 crimes, and mandates life imprisonment for anyone convicted of 3 violent crimes.

1993   The House passes a conference committee version of the
cont.   Brady bill.

Senate Republicans accept a Senate-House conference committee version of the Brady bill entitled the Brady Handgun Violence Prevention Act, which President Bill Clinton says he plans to sign.

1994   The Supreme Court chooses not to review *Callins v. Collins*, a Texas death penalty case. While the case is rather ordinary—Bruce Edward Callins, 34, was convicted of murder and robbery after he committed murder while robbing a Fort Worth, Texas, bar in 1980—Justice Harry A. Blackmun's lone, long dissent adds a twist. Blackmun, 85, has supported the death penalty throughout his 23-year career on the Court. In his dissent, however, he argues the death penalty's unconstitutionality given the judicial system's inability to fairly mete out justice. He began voicing such doubts in a 1993 death penalty case. At the time, he gave an interview on ABC's *Nightline*, in which he said he was thinking of changing his capital punishment views.

Writing the majority opinion, Justice Antonin Scalia criticizes Blackmun's dissent. He agrees with Blackmun's statements that established precedents regulating a jury's right to recommend the death penalty are contradictory, but he writes that Blackmun based his dissent on his personal views rather than on the Fifth Amendment provisions allowing states to impose capital punishment.

The Supreme Court lets stand a lower court ruling affirming Montana's ban on the insanity defense. Montana abolished the insanity defense in 1979. In *Cowan v. Montana*, a defendant accused of severely beating a woman claimed insanity at the time of the crime. The Supreme Court decision applies only to this case.

Speaking before the House Appropriations Committee on the Supreme Court's budget, Justice Anthony Kennedy criticizes Congress for imposing mandatory minimum sentences for some federal crimes. Congress in recent years set minimum prison sentences to be given by judges to those convicted of drug- or gun-related crimes. Several federal judges do not like minimum sentences because they are too rigid and do not allow judges the leeway to tailor a sentence to a defendant's particular circumstances.

At the hearing, Justice Kennedy says laws imposing mandatory minimums are "an imprudent, unwise and often unjust mechanism for sentencing." He points out the varying sentence lengths for crack and powder cocaine as an example of the unfairness of such laws. While crack possession will garner a minimum sentence of five or ten years, the minimum for powder cocaine is lower despite its significantly higher price tag.

The Supreme Court upholds murder convictions in two separate cases in which judges told jurors to rely on their "moral certitude" to decide the defendants' guilt beyond a reasonable doubt. The justices rule unanimously in *Sandoval v. California* and by a 7–2 decision in *Victor v. Nebraska*. They make it known, however, that references to jurors' morality in judges' instructions are outdated and may confuse jurors.

The Supreme Court rules 6–3 that attorneys may not use a potential juror's gender to disqualify him or her from participating on the jury. In deciding *J.E.B. v. T.B.*, the high court broadens an established precedent that bans attorneys from using race as a peremptory challenge to disqualify a potential juror.

Rodney G. King is awarded more than $3.8 million by a U.S. district court jury in Los Angeles as compensation in a civil lawsuit against the city that stemmed from King's March 1991 videotaped beating by Los Angeles police officers.

By a 285–141 margin, the U.S. House of Representatives approves an anticrime bill authorizing $27.9 billion to be spent over six years. The House bill authorizes $13.5 billion to construct state prisons, $600 million over three years for state boot camps and alternative corrections programs for young offenders, $6.7 billion for community crime prevention programs, and $2.45 billion for rehabilitation

1994
cont.
programs. The bill also expands the federal death penalty to more than 60 crimes and allows death-row prisoners to employ racial disparity statistics in capital punishment cases to challenge their sentences. The bill allows $3.45 billion to hire 50,000 new police officers over the next six years, prohibits sale or transfer of guns to minors, and mandates life imprisonment for anyone convicted of a third violent felony. While the first two felonies could be either state or federal violent crimes or a significant drug offense, the third must be a violent felony or significant drug offense.

The Supreme Court decides 6–3 in *Custis v. United States* that repeat offenders who are being sentenced under the strict federal laws for so-called career criminals may not have their earlier convictions reviewed. The high court restricts such review requests to cases in which defendants' right to counsel was violated.

The Supreme Court decides 7–2 that juries in death penalty cases need to be told whether defendants will be eligible for parole if the juries give them life imprisonment sentences instead of death. The outcome of *Simmons v. South Carolina* voids a South Carolina law banning trial judges from telling a jury whether parole will be added as an option if the jurors decide on life imprisonment.

The Supreme Court rules 5–4 that police do not have to stop questioning a suspect if he or she makes an ambiguous request for an attorney. In *Davis v. United States*, the case at issue was *Miranda v. Arizona*, the 1966 landmark case that requires police to stop interrogating suspects when they invoke their constitutional right to counsel.

The Supreme Court rules 7–2 that the judge in *Shannon v. United States* did not have to tell the jury that the defendant—who sought acquittal through the insanity defense—would be placed in a mental hospital if judged insane. The main point of controversy in the case revolved around the Insanity Defense Reform Act of 1984, which set up guidelines for insanity pleas.

In a 5–4 ruling in *McFarland v. Scott*, the Supreme Court decides that federal judges are allowed to postpone the executions of death-row prisoners who do not have legal counsel and who want to file habeas corpus writs to request federal reviews of their convictions.

A House-Senate conference committee approves an anticrime bill to allocate $33.5 billion for prevention programs, punishment, and prisons over a six-year period. The bill would establish a $30.2 billion trust fund for the programs, with the money coming from anticipated cuts of more than 250,000 federal jobs over the six years. Congress would appropriate the other $3.3 billion in various programs.

Six states amend their constitutions to provide rights for crime victims. The passage of such amendments in Alabama, Alaska, Idaho, Maryland, Ohio, and Utah brings the total number of states with such amendments to 20.

The House of Representatives votes 225–210 to block a $33.5 billion anticrime bill, recently passed by a conference committee. Of the 58 Democrats who vote against the bill, most do not favor the inclusion of a weapons ban. Of 38 Congressional Black Caucus members, 10 vote against the bill because some oppose expanding the federal death penalty while others do not support the conference committee's exclusion of a provision allowing death-row inmates to use racial disparity statistics in capital punishment cases to challenge sentences they deem discriminatory. Of the 167 Republicans who vote against the bill, many favor neither the weapons ban nor prevention programs—including one that would set up midnight basketball leagues for young people in high-crime areas—which they see as trivial. Republicans also label as a "pork barrel" project a $10 million grant for a criminal justice program at Lamar University in Beaumont, Texas, which lies in the home district of Rep. Jack Brooks (D-Tex.), House Judiciary Committee chairman.

The U.S. Senate by a margin of 61–38 passes the Violent Crime Control and Law Enforcement Act, which allocates $30.2 billion to law enforcement, prisons, and crime

1994
cont.

prevention; bans certain types of assault weapons; mandates life imprisonment for anyone with two prior state or federal felony convictions who is convicted of a federal crime; requires notifying communities of the whereabouts of convicted sex offenders who move there; and expands the federal death penalty to more than 50 crimes. Congress passes the final legislation in August, and President Bill Clinton signs it.

In referenda around the country, voters make their opinions about criminals and crime victims known at the polls. Georgia residents vote by a margin of 81–19 percent to sanction a life imprisonment sentence without parole for second-time violent offenders. California voters approve 72–28 percent a "three strikes" law that imposes life sentences on convicted felons who commit and are convicted of a third serious crime. Utah residents vote 69–31 percent to allow crime victims to be excused from testifying at pretrial hearings.

1995

In a 430–0 vote, the House of Representatives approves a measure requiring people convicted of federal crimes to pay restitution to crime victims who suffered physical, emotional, or financial harm from the crimes. The 1994 anticrime law, the Violent Crime Control and Law Enforcement Act, mandated restitution only for sexual abuse victims and victims of federal child pornography crimes.

By a 289–142 vote, the House of Representatives passes legislation that would allow, in federal trials, evidence obtained without a search warrant as long as it appeared authorities were complying with the Fourth Amendment protections against unreasonable searches and seizures. The House also approves 297–132 legislation curbing death-row inmates' opportunities to file habeas corpus writs to request federal reviews of their convictions. State inmates would be given a year to file such writs, while federal inmates would have up to two years. Both state and federal death-row inmates would be limited to one habeas corpus petition.

By a vote of 265–156, representatives pass a bill to allocate $10.5 billion to prison construction over a five-year period, compared with $7.9 billion in 1994. Of the $10.5 billion, half would go to states that make inmates serve at least 85 percent of their sentences. The other half would not carry such strict requirements.

The House of Representatives by a vote of 238–192 approves anticrime legislation authorizing $10.5 billion in block grants for local governments and eliminating federal funding to add 100,000 officers to police forces across the country, a measure that was passed in a 1994 anticrime law. Over a five-year period, the $10.5 billion would provide local officials with grants to use as they see fit. It would replace $8.8 billion authorized in the 1994 anticrime bill to add police and $4 billion for crime prevention programs. President Bill Clinton vows to veto the measure if the Senate also approves it.

The Supreme Court rules 6–3 in *O'Neal v. McAninch* that judges unable to determine whether an inmate's constitutional rights were violated during a state trial should suppose that they had been and order a new trial.

The Supreme Court decides 8–1 in *Harris v. Alabama* that an Alabama law permitting judges to override juries' sentencing recommendations in death penalty cases is constitutional.

In what is an exception to the exclusionary rule, the Supreme Court rules 7–2 in *Arizona v. Evans* that evidence obtained by police officers acting on an invalid arrest warrant may be permitted in a trial.

New York becomes the thirty-eighth state to have capital punishment when New York Governor George E. Pataki (R) signs a capital punishment measure into law. Since 1977, when the New York Court of Appeals ruled the law unconstitutional, the state legislature passed bills to reinstate the death penalty. Despite their passage, Governors Mario Cuomo and Hugh Carey, both Democrats, vetoed the bills.

The law makes punishable by lethal injection ten categories of murder, including serial and contract murders; the killing of judges, on-duty police officers, and prison guards; and intentional killings that take place in conjunction with

<table>
<tr><td>1995
cont.</td><td>

other violent crimes. Pregnant women and mentally incompetent or mentally handicapped people are exempted, but if mentally handicapped people kill someone while in prison, they could be executed. The law also requires the state from time to time to examine the fairness of the death penalty's application. It sets up a statewide office to help train, choose, and oversee court-appointed attorneys for poor people accused of crimes punishable by death. Under the law, defense attorneys may privately interview potential jurors about race issues to avoid racial partiality.

In *California Department of Corrections v. Morales*, the Supreme Court upholds 7–2 a change in California's parole procedures that decreases the number of parole hearings for some prisoners. Adopted in 1981, the change ended the standard of giving prisoners automatic annual parole hearings. The statute allows parole boards to delay hearings up to three years for prisoners who were convicted of more than one murder.

The Milwaukee, Wisconsin, Common Council approves an $850,000 payment to the family of Konerak Sinthasomphone to settle the family's lawsuit alleging police errors that led to the murder of Sinthasomphone, a victim of Jeffrey Dahmer. In May 1991, police allowed Dahmer to take back the 14-year-old after they found him naked and bleeding outside Dahmer's apartment. In January 1992, Dahmer pleaded guilty but insane in Milwaukee County Circuit Court to charges that he murdered 15 young men and boys, most of them at his Milwaukee apartment. Given his guilty but insane plea, the jury focused only on Dahmer's sanity. Only two members of the jury argued that Dahmer was insane, and in Wisconsin, a minimum of ten jury members must agree on sanity or insanity, so the jury's verdict was that Dahmer was sane at the time of the murders. Dahmer received 16 consecutive life terms but was killed by another prisoner in November 1994.

As part of an effort by Republican Governor Forrest (Fob) James, Jr., to make prison tougher, the state of Alabama brings back chain gangs, in which groups of convicts are chained together and work outdoors. Chain gangs had

</td></tr>
</table>

been common in the South until the late 1960s when Georgia outlawed them. More than 300 Alabama inmates are chained together with leg irons in groups of five and clear ditches, cut weeds, and collect litter along state highways. Arizona and Florida later follow Alabama's lead.

The Supreme Court rules 7–2 that prosecutors must only give a nondiscriminatory reason for their peremptory challenges and that the reason does not have to be "persuasive, or even plausible" to defense attorneys. In the case, *Purkett v. Elem*, a lower court in Missouri decided that a prosecutor motivated by racial partiality had wrongly excluded a black man from a jury.

The Supreme Court rules 7–2 in *Garlotte v. Fordice* to permit prisoners serving time for a crime to file habeas corpus writs to challenge convictions for other crimes for which they already have served time. In the case, the ruling would allow a convicted murderer serving two life sentences in Mississippi to challenge a three-year drug-trafficking sentence he had already served. An overturned drug-trafficking conviction would speed up the parole date for his life sentence.

The New Jersey Supreme Court rules 6–1 to uphold the constitutionality of a law requiring community officials to notify residents of the whereabouts of a convicted sex offender. Named for Megan Kanka, a 7-year-old New Jersey girl who allegedly was killed by a sex offender in her neighborhood, the notification provisions of the 1994 "Megan's Law" were the equivalent of illegal extra punishment, according to a decision by U.S. District Judge Nicholas Politan.

More than $500,000 is given to the Justice Department's Crime Victims Fund. The money comes from assets confiscated in February 1994 when Aldrich and Rosario Ames were arrested and later convicted of spying for the former Soviet Union and Russia.

The House of Representatives and Senate vote 256–166 and 50–48 for $27.3 billion in funding for the Commerce,

1995
cont.

Justice, and State Departments. The bill includes a provision to replace a program authorizing $8.8 billion to hire 100,000 police over six years with state block grants. President Bill Clinton vetoes the bill on the grounds that he objects to the bill's change of a police-hiring program. Clinton requested $1.9 billion for hiring police in 1996, but Republicans wanted to replace the hiring program with block grants that would allow states to support their own crime prevention and crime fighting methods. The bill also would give more prison construction money to states making inmates serve all or much of their sentences.

1996

In his State of the Union address, President Bill Clinton stresses the need for continuing the provision set out in the 1994 anticrime bill for hiring 100,000 new police officers. The president estimates that the passage of the so-called Brady bill in 1993, which requires gun buyers to undergo criminal background checks, prevented 44,000 crimes. Clinton also directs the Federal Bureau of Investigation to target gangs that involve juveniles in violent crime and urges housing authorities and tenant associations to evict tenants after first drug-selling offenses.

The House of Representatives passes an antiterrorism bill, which includes the following provisions: federal death-row prisoners have one year from their conviction dates to file habeas corpus writs, and only one such appeal is allowed with exceptions for new evidence; killing a former or current federal employee because of that person's job is a capital offense punishable by death; convicts must pay restitution to victims; U.S. citizens may bring civil suits against foreign nations for terrorist acts; and tracing materials must be required in plastic explosives.

President Bill Clinton announces an initiative to link federal aid for local public housing to public housing authorities' efforts to evict tenants convicted of crimes. The policy would allow authorities to end leases and evict tenants if they, any member of their household, or any visitor to their home engages in drug dealing or other crimes.

President Bill Clinton signs the Antiterrorism and Effective Death Penalty Act of 1996.

President Bill Clinton signs a bill requiring all states to notify communities of the whereabouts of convicted sex offenders. The bill, known as "Megan's Law," is based on a New Jersey law enacted weeks after Megan Kanka, a seven-year-old resident of Hamilton Township, New Jersey, allegedly was killed by a convicted sex offender who had recently moved into her neighborhood.

The Supreme Court rules 8–1 in *Ornelas v. United States* that defendants challenging convictions on grounds that they were victims of improper police searches are entitled to new reviews of their cases by appellate court judges. In doing so, the justices order a new hearing for two California men, Saul Ornelas and Ismael Ornelas-Ledesma, who were convicted of drug possession in 1993.

The California Supreme Court unanimously rules that judges who consider too severe the prison sentences mandated by the state's "three strikes and you're out" law can mete out lighter sentences. In a nonbinding November 1994 referendum, 72 percent of Californians endorsed the three-strikes law, which went into effect in March 1994 in response to the public outcry over the 1993 kidnapping and murder of 12-year-old Polly Klaas. Klaas, a Petaluma, California, resident, was abducted and killed by paroled ex-convict Richard Allen Davis. The law requires judges to impose a sentence of 25 years to life for a felony by a defendant who has had two "strikes"—two convictions for violent or serious felonies. The law mandates at least twice the usual prison sentence for a second strike. About 20 states and the federal government have versions of the three-strikes law.

In a Rose Garden ceremony surrounded by parents of murder victims and crime victims, President Bill Clinton says he supports and would help to write a measure guaranteeing victims such things as court proceeding notifications, the ability to witness trials, and permission to address the court prior to sentencing or the acceptance of a plea bargain. Of a constitutional amendment guaranteeing such rights, the president says, "This is not an attempt to put legislative responsibilities in the Constitution or to guarantee a right that is already guaranteed. Amending the

1996
cont.

Constitution here is simply the only way to guarantee the victims' rights are weighted equally with defendants' rights in every courtroom in America."

Anticipating that some would see his support of an amendment as election-year stumping, Clinton says, "This is a cause for all Americans. When people are victimized, the criminal almost never asks before you're robbed or beaten or raped or murdered: Are you a Republican or a Democrat?"

The Supreme Court rules unanimously in *Felker v. Turpin* to uphold portions of federal legislation that curb the rights of death-row inmates in state prisons to seek federal reviews of their convictions passed as part of the Antiterrorism and Effective Death Penalty Act of 1996 signed by President Clinton in April.

Santa Clara County Superior Court Judge Thomas C. Hastings sentences Richard Allen Davis, 42, to death for the 1993 kidnapping and murder of 12-year-old Polly Klaas. Under California law, Davis's sentence is subject to automatic appeal and also can be appealed to federal courts. The appeals process could take as long as 15 years.

Senators Dianne Feinstein (D-Calif.) and John Kyl (R-Ariz.) and Rep. Henry Hyde (R-Ill.) introduce a proposal to amend the U.S. Constitution to provide basic rights for victims of crime. Although the proposed amendment is not acted on in committee, Feinstein and Kyl introduce a revision of it based on consultations with the U.S. Department of Justice, members of the White House staff, legal scholars, and victims' advocates and organizations.

A National Institute of Justice–sponsored survey reveals that crime costs Americans $450 billion a year. It accounts for costs ranging from pain, suffering, and diminished quality of life to police work, legal fees, and lost work time in crimes such as child abuse, domestic violence, murder, and rape.

Voters in Connecticut, Indiana, Nevada, North Carolina, Oklahoma, Oregon, South Carolina, and Virginia amend their constitutions to provide rights for crime victims. This brings the total number of states with such amendments to 29.

1997   Senators Dianne Feinstein (D-Calif.) and John Kyl (R-Ariz.) introduce another version of the proposed U.S. constitutional amendment for victims of crime. To become a law, the House of Representatives and the Senate would have to approve it by a two-thirds majority. The amendment then would have to pass muster with three-quarters of state legislatures within seven years of its passage in Congress.

The Supreme Court holds unconstitutional the Brady Handgun Violence Prevention Act in *Printz v. United States.* The five-member majority deems unconstitutional the provision that required state and local authorities to perform criminal background checks on people who wanted to purchase firearms. It bases this judgment on the long-held idea that the federal government may not compel state governments to enact or administer federal regulatory programs. The Brady bill, passed by congress in 1993, had prevented several thousands of convicted felons from buying firearms. The suit was brought by Jay Printz and Richard Mack, chief law enforcement officers for Ravalli county, Montana, and Graham County, Arizona, respectively. Justices John Paul Stevens, David H. Souter, Ruth Bader Ginsburg, and Stephen G. Breyer dissent from the majority opinion.

Jesse Timmendequas, 36, is convicted of the rape and murder of Megan Kanka, whose death sparked passage of state and federal convicted sex offender community notification laws, known throughout the country as Megan's Law. Timmendequas was a twice-convicted sex offender when he moved into Megan's Hamilton township, New Jersey, neighborhood. During the penalty phase, Timmedequas's attorneys cited his tortured childhood, including a career criminal father who beat and raped his children and a promiscuous, alcoholic mother. The attorneys cite their client's low I.Q. as well. Timmendequas himself asks that he be spared the death penalty, so that ". . . someday . . . I can understand why something like this could happen."

1997
cont.

The jury, however, sentences him to death. Although Hunterdon County, New Jersey Superior Court Judge Andrew J. Smithson sets an execution date of 1 August of the same year, Timmendequas's sentence is subject to automatice review by the New Jersey Supreme Court. Following the sentencing announcement, Maureen Kanka, mother of Megan, says "It will not bring our little girl back. . . . It's sad that in today's society, we have people who do not put value on human life like they should. Megan was worth a life."

Biographical Sketches 3

As much as the crime victims' rights movement has blossomed in the last 15 years, there are many people on all levels who work on behalf of victims. The people included in this chapter have played various roles on behalf of victim and criminal justice. These entries are meant to illustrate their roles as well as expand readers' general understanding of the victims' rights movement.

Cesare Beccaria (1738–1794)

Although Cesare Beccaria received a degree in law, his life's work focused on economics and criminal justice. He aligned himself with the Enlightenment, and at the suggestion of Count Pietro Verri, he undertook a critical study of criminal law. While he lacked experience in the administration of criminal justice, he published *Crimes and Punishment* in 1764. Beccaria's work is the first to state the principles controlling criminal punishment. It is based in the philosophy of utilitarianism, the idea that actions should obtain the greatest good for the greatest number of people, including the actions of governments.

Beccaria opposed the capriciousness of officials and torture as punishment. Instead, he stated, punishment should be only severe enough to achieve security and order—hence, proportionate to the corresponding offense. He also came out against capital punishment and recommended its abolition. According to Beccaria, the worst crimes were committed in societies that imposed the worst punishments. Instead of severe punishments, he argued that certainty of punishment is more important, for with little chance of being punished, crime is "rationally and economically justifiable."

Instead of likening the purpose of criminal justice to an aid for victims to obtain redress from offenders, Beccaria argued that the basis for criminal justice was the social contract (a means of keeping society together). Therefore, punishment serves the interests of society—deterrence of criminals, payment of their debts to society, and deterrence of others who would commit similar acts.

Beccaria's ideas reverberated throughout Europe, through utilitarian philosopher Jeremy Bentham and his disciples, and to postrevolutionary America. As the ideals of the Enlightenment, including the philosophy of utilitarianism, took hold in the United States, public prosecutions replaced private ones, and the status of crime victims was reduced to that of witness.[1]

Frank G. Carrington (1936–1992)

President George Bush dubbed Frank Carrington the "father" of the victims' rights movement when he honored him in a Rose Garden ceremony in the spring of 1991.

Indeed, by that time Carrington had been working on behalf of crime victims for more than 20 years. With a law degree from the University of Michigan Law School in 1960 and a criminal law degree from Northwestern University in 1970, Carrington acted as a legal advisor to the Denver Police Department, a narcotics/vice advisor to the Chicago Police Department, and served as an intelligence agent to the Internal Revenue Service. He went on to become the executive director for the Chicago-based Americans for Effective Law Enforcement from 1970 to 1979. And it was during those years that Carrington picked up the pace in his life's work on behalf of crime victims. In *Victims* in 1975, he outlined wide-ranging abuses against victims, from their treatment by police and attorneys to the ways in which judges' interpretation of laws gave defendants the weightier side on the scales of justice. His importance in the field of victims' rights earned him a place on President Ronald Reagan's Task Force on Victims of Crime in 1982.

Above all, Carrington is remembered for several of his innovations in the area of victims' rights and services. He founded VALOR—the Victims' Assistance Legal Organization—in 1979. A nonprofit organization, VALOR receives charitable contributions and government grants to develop programs, national in scope, to address issues that concern crime victims. Like other later organizations, VALOR responds to calls from crime victims who need information and help. To assist them, VALOR directs them to experts who can tell them their rights in the jurisdiction from which they are calling. In addition to working on the expansion and improvement of victims' rights and services, VALOR serves to make adult and juvenile criminals accountable by compiling information that is submitted to policymakers.

Beginning in the mid-1980s, Carrington became involved in efforts to support federal and state legislation to boost security on college and university campuses. He began working with Howard and Connie Clery in 1987 after their daughter Jeanne was raped, sodomized, beaten, and murdered in her dormitory room at Lehigh University. Along with the Clerys, who founded Security on Campus, Carrington and many others were able to pursuade Congress to pass the Campus Security Act in 1990. The act requires colleges and universities receiving federal money to release their security policies and the three most recent years of campus crime statistics for murder, sex offenses, robbery, aggravated assault, burglary, and motor vehicle theft. Schools also must make available statistics for liquor, drug, and weapons violations.

In a broad sense, Carrington's success stemmed from his ability to draw attention to the ways crime victims were treated. In a specific—and likely what will be an enduring—sense, much of his success came through helping victims to pursue civil litigation against perpetrators and others who contributed to their injuries. In writing about crime victims' civil litigation, Carrington noted that beginning in the late 1970s, civil courts started awarding damages to crime victims based on the negligence of third parties, such as corrections officials, probation and parole officers, and landlords. In such cases, victims overcame the doctrine of sovereign immunity by proving gross negligence on the part of officials who released or failed to supervise prisoners with histories of violent behavior or on the part of landlords on whose premises security was lacking. Carrington argued that this trend benefited society at large since the very possibility of tort liability makes government officials more careful and landlords more responsible—both of which can protect people against future crimes.

Carrington designed a database in which he organized and annotated appellate court decisions involving crime victims, with a particular emphasis on civil litigation of campus crimes. The National Victim Center, in a formal agreement with VALOR in 1993, renamed its civil litigation program after Carrington. The Carrington Victims' Litigation Project maintains a database of current cases, offers legal referrals to crime victims and their attorneys, and conducts specialized legal research.

Carrington died in a fire at his house in Virginia Beach, Virginia, in 1992. In a eulogy to Carrington, Dr. Jane Nady Burnley, executive director of VALOR and a close friend of his, said "Frank had the unusual ability to respond to individual victims with a balance of compassion and insight and advice that would enable victims to take action that would aid in their recovery . . . Frank's development of civil remedies for victims has already dramatically affected the lives of thousands of victims and would-be victims. The full effects of his pioneering work will be seen in decades to come. He has created a force, a tool for victims which has enormous strength and will endure as his legacy."

Ken Eikenberry (b. 1932)

Ken Eikenberry's public service dates to the early 1960s with his years as Federal Bureau of Investigation (FBI) special agent (1960–1962) and encompasses his terms as a member of the Washington State House of Representatives (1972–1976), a prosecutor, a municipal judge (1979–1980), and chairman of the Washington State Republican Party (1977–1980). While attorney general for Washington (1981–1992), he was chosen to serve on the President's Task Force on Victims of Crime.

Eikenberry recalled being aware of crime victims' problems in law school and later in the FBI. "I remember a strong resentment against the 'exclusionary rule' as implemented by our courts," he said. "This is not to disagree with constitutional protections which we all cherish, but it is to say that the courts have looked like a collection of fools in those cases where the evidence was clearly reliable and convincing, but nevertheless excluded so that the defendant walked free while the surviving family members looked on. . . . "

What Eikenberry saw made him cognizant "of how the American 'Criminal Justice System' was inherently *unjust* to crime victims, and later experiences gave added reason for wanting a system that would treat me, as a typical citizen, fairly."

In fact, about 15 years before President Ronald Reagan turned the executive branch's spotlight on victims of crime, a cousin of Eikenberry was a typical citizen. As she and her husband were driving back to Seattle from a visit with her parents, she was killed and he was severely injured when a drunk driver hit them head on. Although the Washington State Patrol trooper testified that he pulled the other driver from his wrecked car and that the man was unconscious and reeked of alcohol, that was the only evidence he could present. He was not able, under the law as it was then, to sample—with a breathalyzer, for example—the driver's blood-alcohol level. That the man was unconscious and smelled of alcohol was not enough. The case was dismissed "for lack of prima facie evidence." This incident was the second in which the man escaped charges of negligent homicide for driving under the influence. Eikenberry worked through the legislature to get the law changed to allow law enforcement to obtain specimens that would prove a person's impairment due to alcohol or drugs.

Eikenberry was chosen by Sen. John Ashcroft (R-Mo.), then Missouri attorney general and National Association of Attorneys General president, to be on President Reagan's Task Force on Victims of Crime. Before he was appointed to the task force, Eikenberry said he had thought that "a constitutional reordering of rights had to be declared, *together with statutory adjustments to the process.*" Otherwise, crime victims and others would respect neither the courts nor the law and that possibly could lead to vigilantism.

The need for a constitutional amendment became clear to Eikenberry as a task force member when he questioned everyone with "training or experience which would support an opinion on the subject. . . . " In its recommendation, the task force stated it did not want "to vitiate the safeguards that shelter anyone accused of crime." However, the members also believed, based on what they had heard from crime victims, that as a group, victims were "oppressively burdened by a system designed to protect them."

In addition to maintaining the accused's rights—including a speedy and public trial, an impartial jury, knowledge of the nature and cause of the accusation, favorable witnesses and counsel—the task force suggested the following addition to the Sixth Amendment: "Likewise, the victim, in every criminal prosecution shall have the right to be present and to be heard at all critical stages of judicial proceedings."

The members said they did not recommend the addition in haste. But given what they learned, they decided that the "fundamental rights of innocent citizens cannot adequately be preserved by any less decisive action."

Although he is not currently involved in the victims' rights movement, Eikenberry said that a constitutional amendment guaranteeing the rights of crime victims "is feasible, or it would not have already been adopted in numerous states. . . . "

"It does seem to me that, from a political point of view, there has never been a better time to pursue an amendment to our U.S. Constitution, and (politically) I can see no reason to wait for future developments."

Margery Fry (1874–1958)

An English magistrate, Margery Fry is credited with starting the modern crime victims' movement. Fry's initial interest lay in penal reform and was sparked by her contact with Quaker groups. An interest in social anthropology led her to observe the practice, popular among many tribal groups, of demanding restitution: an offender's family and kin had to pay compensation for harm done to a victim's family and kin. In the case of murder, an offender would have to support the victim's widow and children. As she mentioned in her 1951 book, *Arms of the Law,*

> Have we not neglected overmuch the customs of our earlier ancestors in the matter of restitution? . . . We have seen that in primitive socities this idea of "making up" for a wrong done has wide currency. Let us once more look into the ways of earlier men, which may still hold some wisdom for us.[2]

About the early systems of restitution and the subsequent development of criminal law, Fry said, "It is noteworthy that the aim was to compensate the party aggrieved; the idea of punishment for a public crime came later. It is perhaps unfortunate that we have got so far away as we have from these primitive usages. . . . The tendency of English criminal law in the past has been to 'take it out of the offender' rather than to do justice to the offended."[3]

Fry believed victims' compensation offset society's need for vengeance, but in modern criminal law, the state shoulders the repression of crime while victims are excluded and forgotten. Nevertheless, she viewed crime victims as lacking special rights and not differing from people who encounter "accidents and mischances of life" that qualify them for help from the government.[4]

Fry wanted to model victims' compensation on industrial injuries benefits or workers' compensation. For example, a victim blinded as a result of a violent assault and awarded damages by a court to be paid by the offender at a rate of five shillings per week would continue to suffer since it would take more than 400 years to pay the victim. Instead, it is the government's responsibility to help the victim so that he or she will be compensated more quickly.[5] However, Fry wanted to limit the growth of welfare by supporting the *social welfare* theory of victims' compensation. It limits compensation to those who need it most, those who meet the requirements for government assistance.[6]

Through her various positions as a reformer, writer, and magistrate, Fry was able to advance these ideas among policymakers. At the same time her ideas were circulating—the years between 1948 and the 1960s—the establishment of criminal rehabilitation and the abolishment of capital punishment combined to inspire criticism and fear among Britons. These attitudes set the stage for the passage of victims' compensation laws. New Zealand officials relied on a 1962 British report containing Fry's ideas and incorporated them into the Criminal Injuries Compensation Act, which they passed in 1963. The Conservative Party in Britain followed their lead and, in 1964, set up a Criminal Injuries Compensation Board to review victims' claims.[7]

Judge Lois Herrington Haight (b. 1939)

Judge Lois Haight saw how the criminal justice system operated as a prosecutor in Alameda County, California, in the 1970s. Once when she escorted a rape victim to the sentencing proceeding, the judge in the case told Haight and the victim to leave. She said she was outraged, as the victim had the right to be there.

Her sixth year in that post coincided with the election of Ronald Reagan to the presidency of the United States. A few months after her husband moved to Washington, D.C., to be assistant secretary of the Navy, she also moved to the capital. There she met people who were serving on Attorney General William French Smith's Task Force on Violent Crime. She helped them to understand the issues surrounding crime victims. That task force recommended in 1982 the creation of the President's Task Force on Victims of Crime, which Haight was asked to join. After an interview with President Reagan, she was selected to chair the task force. Haight said she believed the prominence of the "president(ial)" task force demonstrated the importance of the issues the task force would explore.

After holding public hearings in cities throughout the country and listening to the problems victims faced, the task force recommended several ways to improve the justice system for victims. Haight said the issues still are meaningful, and even though many changes have occurred, especially changes in the law, it is a matter of "law versus practice. It takes a long time to change attitudes and practices," she said.

After her tenure on the task force, Haight was appointed assistant U.S. attorney general in 1983, a position she held for five years before chairing a conference for Drug Free America. After Reagan left office, she returned to California and again worked as a prosecutor. She has been a judge in Contra Costa County, California, since 1993.

In addition to her work as a judge, Haight teaches courses on victims of crime. One is a continuing education course for lawyers. Many of the students say, "'I simply never thought of what happens to victims of crime,'" she said. They have not considered the victims' right to speak at sentencing, plea bargaining, or bail hearings. Many of them are rooted in civil law and have not had much experience with criminal law. "Class action suits are different from criminal cases," Haight said. "It's a whole different way of thinking."

While many judges and attorneys who have never thought about victims' rights worry that it will denigrate defendants' rights, Haight said it is a matter of exposure to the problems victims encounter. Such exposure can make those in positions of power take courses of action to safeguard fair treatment of victims.

As Haight said of her own courtroom, it is up to judges to "ensure that the process is fair, fair for the defendant and fair for the victim." That does not mean they have to be partial to one side to be fair.

Some of the task force recommendations still are relevant today as more states join those that already have amended their constitutions to reflect victims' rights. Haight said that states are enacting amendments at a good rate. "The question is are they really putting into practice what they put into law?"

While she opposed the task force's recommendation to amend the U.S. Constitution—it was considered a last resort and the members wanted to give states time to change their constitutions, as the bulk of criminal law is the purview of state and local jurisdictions—she said she is no longer opposed. But she believes that neglect of crime victims is not so much bad intentions as it is oversight.

California's Proposition 8 and a later victims' rights referendum, although they are weak in some ways, have guided attention to victims, down to where victims should sit while they wait before or during trials. When continuing a case, it is easy for a judge to forget to ask a crime victim, "How's that date for you?" That is what is really needed, according to Haight: simple consideration.

Hans von Hentig (1887–1974)

The so-called Golden Age of the victim—that period in which the victim-offender scenario centered squarely on the victim and offenders were required to compensate victims for their losses—had long faded before Hans von Hentig and, a little later, Beniamin Mendelsohn (see separate entry in this chapter) appeared earlier this century.

Pioneers in the field of victim studies, they concentrated on the victim's role in crime and the importance of decreasing victimization as a way of moving humanity forward. Of course, they were not the first to evaluate victim-offender relationships. Cesare Lombroso believed there were "passionate criminals who acted under the pressure of victim-provoked emotions." Raffaele Garofalo theorized that certain victim behaviors pushed offenders to criminal action. In *Penal Philosophy*, Gabriel Tarde criticized the "legislative mistake" of not considering the motives that arise when victims and offenders share significant relations and ignoring the possibility that the responsibility for a crime rests on "some act of the victim's." Jules Simon and Jean Hemard examined criminal-victim relationships from the standpoint of the victim's consent. Kahlil Gibran talked about victim-precipitated crimes when he said "the guilty is oftentimes the victim of the injured." There were others, too, who scrutinized various aspects of victim-offender relations. But Hentig and Mendelsohn were the first to do so in great depth.[8]

Hentig distinguished himself as a professor of criminal law in prewar Germany. When Hitler asked him to join the government,

Professor Hentig—in person—refused.[9] Instead, he came to the United States where he taught at several universities. He was a professor at Yale when he blazed the trail of victimology in *The Criminal and His Victim* in 1948.

This landmark work contains a chapter entitled, "The Contribution of the Victim to the Genesis of Crime." In it, Hentig asserts "that many criminal deeds are more indicative of a subject-object relation than of the perpetrator alone. There is a definite mutuality of some sort. The mechanical outcome may be profit to one party, harm to another, yet the psychological interaction, carefully observed, will not submit to this kindergarten label."[10]

Hentig stated the victim-criminal relationship is not unlike the prey-predator relationship among animals. They complement each other and just as it would be impossible for zoologists to understand the behavior of a hawk without looking at what it feeds upon, so, too, is it impossible for social scientists to understand criminals without looking at victims. But by excluding the role of the victim, that's what criminology has tried to do.

Hentig delineated general classes of victims, including the young, female, old, mentally defective or deranged, immigrants, minorities, and "dull normals." He also carved out psychological niches into which victims fall. There are the depressed whose attitudes may include apathy and lethargy; submissiveness and passivity; cooperation; and provocation, instigation, and solicitation. Depressed victims share a loss of the instinct for self-preservation—a loss that leaves them vulnerable and open to victimization. There are the acquisitive, who given their greed, make excellent victims. Hentig cited those who want to get—and believe in the possibility of getting—something for nothing. These types may be victims of investment schemes or white slavery. Other psychological categories include the wanton (those who desire to seduce others); the lonesome and heartbroken; the tormentor ("The alcoholic or psychotic father tortures wife and children for years; finally the son, grown up, maybe under grave provocation by the old man, kills him," Hentig writes); and the blocked, exempted, and fighting (Businesspeople typically leave themselve open for blackmail when they risk a losing moneymaking scheme. The rich make good victims because they don't pay their employees very much, so it's okay to rob them. And "a half-hearted attempt at fight which does not disarm and overwhelm the aggressor . . . is likely to increase crime statistics by a homicide instead of by an aggravated robbery," he writes).[11]

In arguing for an integrated approach to examining the problems of crime and victimization, Hentig had in mind long-term solutions to the problems of crime. "In most crimes the perpetrator is hidden, the victim—dead or alive—available," he writes in *The Criminal and His Victim.* "With a thorough knowledge of the interrelations between doer and sufferer, new approaches to the detection of crime will be opened. The potentialities of crime prevention will experience a vast expansion. Crime will become a problem of dynamics, and we will build our systems of treatment and prevention around the most seizable and workable of the causative forces."[12]

Charlotte Hullinger and Robert (Bob) Hullinger

Charlotte and Bob Hullinger founded Parents of Murdered Children (POMC) in 1978 in Cincinnati, Ohio, after their 19-year-old daughter Lisa was murdered by an ex-boyfriend while she was studying in Germany. Charlotte Hullinger, a legal secretary and business college teacher, and the Rev. Robert Hullinger, a Lutheran minister, were assisted by Father Ken Czillinger, a Roman Catholic priest who led support groups for the bereaved. He led them to two other couples whose children had been murdered.

Victims themselves, the Hullingers have helped people and the media to understand better the shock and anger that accompanies the violent death of a loved one and to accept that such feelings are natural. As Charlotte Hullinger said in an interview with Bill Robinson of *People* in the 16 March 1981 issue, many friends and neighbors came forth and showed that they cared about the Hullingers, but after a time that outpouring leveled off. "People have their own lives to live, and they went back to them. But a very vital part of my family was gone. My world would never be the same. And it amazed me that the rest of the world went on as usual. How could I do things like shop for groceries or clean the house when Lisa was dead? I couldn't think of anything else. I had a tremendous need to talk about what had happened, but I found few people were able to listen."

Although POMC began as a local support group, it now has chapters throughout the United States. In addition to serving as an emotional outlet for victims and their families, the organization runs the Parole Block Program, in which the POMC on behalf of survivors circulates petitions to protest early release or parole of convicted murderers. POMC also coordinates other programs that raise awareness about the amount of violence prevalent on television and in games and toys and that pool experts together to work on unsolved or complex cases.

Beniamin Mendelsohn

Like Hans von Hentig (see separate entry in this chapter), Beniamin Mendelsohn was a pioneer in the victims' studies field who is credited with coining the term "victimology" and promoting it as a discipline entirely different from criminology. Admitted to the bar in Bucharest in 1934, Mendelsohn's early studies were based on 300-question forms, which, as a practicing attorney, he gave his clients. He also concentrated on the extent of resistance by rape victims.

Mendelsohn formed a new vocabulary for victimology. In his lexicon, he uses "victimal" as the opposite of "criminal," "victimity" as the opposite of "criminality," and takes the "potential of victimal receptivity" to mean one's unconscious aptitude for being victimized.[13] Unlike Hans von Hentig, who based his victim classifications on psychological, social, and biological factors, Mendelsohn grouped victims according to their degree of culpability in a crime. For example, a "completely innocent victim" would include children and those who suffer a crime while unconscious. There also are the "victim with minor guilt" and the "victim due to his ignorance" as well as the "victim as guilty as the offender" in the cases of suicide, euthanasia, and couple suicide. The "most guilty victim" is aggressive, such as an attacker who is killed by another in self-defense. The "victim more guilty than the offender" includes the "provoker victim" who provokes someone to a crime and the "imprudent victim" who causes someone to commit a crime. The "simulating victim" and the "imaginary victim" are people who mislead those who administer justice to obtain punishment against the accused.[14]

Since the creation of victimology, pioneers such as Hentig and Mendelsohn have been criticized for their lack of empirical evidence. But as the field has grown, others have studied victim statistics. The ideas of Hentig and Mendelsohn also would seem to counter the current thinking of not blaming crime victims and act as lightning rods for criticism. But Mendelsohn, like Hentig, believed in the long-term validity of victimology.

As he wrote in *Victimology*'s inaugural issue in 1976, "The essential goal of victimology is fewer victims in all sectors of society to the extent that society is concerned with the problem. Given that man is that part of nature which is integrated into the constitution of society, fewer victims mean fewer losses and more vital energy to ensure man's existence. Given that man is the creative force in society, fewer victims contribute to his progress."[15]

Bob Preston (b. 1927)

As a successful south Florida businessman, Bob Preston never anticipated having to face a great tragedy, but in 1977, his 22-year-old daughter Wendy was murdered. The defendant, "a Quaalude freak, confessed, tried to kill himself, pleaded not guilty by reason of insanity and was committed" to a psychiatric hospital. Preston and his wife Pat attended a bereavement support meeting sponsored by the Fort Lauderdale Police Department in 1979. There they met Greg Novak, whose 20-year-old sister Beverly had been murdered.[16]

Preston and Novak discovered they shared similar goals: to do something to right the wrongs crime victims encounter in the criminal justice system. Along with eight other victims, in 1979 they formed Justice for Surviving Victims, Inc., to create awareness about the plight of victims and to push for legislative changes to restore balance to the system.

The organization's lobbying efforts among Florida legislators led to the passage of the 1984 Florida Victim/Witness Protection Act. It required that crime victims be informed about the arrest, trial, and sentencing of the accused; that courts hear a victim impact statement before sentencing; and that upon victims' requests, officials notify them about parole hearings and allow them to attend. The act also created a crime compensation statute and set up a process for convicted offenders to pay restitution to victims.

Although he did not serve on President Reagan's 1982 Task Force on Victims of Crime, Preston was asked to testify before task force members in Boston in 1982. One of the task force recommendations called for a change in the Sixth Amendment, which outlines the rights of the accused with respect to criminal trials. The change required rights for crime victims to be present and heard "at all critical stages of judicial proceedings." This idea of amending the Bill of Rights came out of the task force as a recommendation by then Washington State Attorney General Ken Eikenberry.

At the time, even victims' rights groups viewed the recommendation as too controversial and the proposal was shelved. But Preston revived it at a 1985 conference. Statutes, Preston reasoned, were not a panacea for the problems crime victims face in the legal system because they provide no legal redress when someone in an official position fails to acknowledge their rights. Endowing victims with constitutional status would guarantee them a voice in the proceedings involving the crime against them.

In the meantime Preston and others, including members of Mothers Against Drunk Driving, Parents of Murdered Children, Justice for Children, People Against Violent Encounters, People Against Crime Together, and the Domestic Violence Coalition, banded together to pursue their mutual goals, namely legislation and a constitutional amendment securing rights for crime victims in Florida. Everyone gathered petition signatures to get the amendment before voters. By the time they collected 170,000, the Florida legislature voluntarily put the amendment on the ballot. It passed in 1988 with 90 percent of the vote.

The Victims Constitutional Amendment Network (VCAN) officially came into being in February 1987 during a conference sponsored by the Sunny von Bulow Victim Advocacy Center (now the National Victim Center) to debate the pros and cons of a constitutional amendment. VCAN members, including Preston, concentrated their efforts on the states where such amendments could test the human and legal limits. In 1995, VCAN members surveyed weak state laws that purported to serve crime victims but in some cases hindered the progress victims had made in states with stronger laws.

Since 1992, Preston has lived in Denver, Colorado, and served as a cochairman of the now named National Victims Constitutional Amendment Network, which promotes the federal constitutional amendment guaranteeing victims' rights following the commission of crimes. In April 1996, Preston testified before the U.S. Senate Judiciary Committee in support of a national constitutional amendment that had been introduced in the 104th Congress.

Ronald Reagan (b. 1911)

While other presidential candidates and presidents campaigned on or sought to encourage tough, law-and-order stances in the realm of criminal justice, Ronald Reagan was the first to have a substantial impact on the victims' rights movement.

As early as 1966 when he was campaigning against incumbent California Gov. Edmund G. Brown (D), Reagan took a conservative tack on lawlessness, sharing his disdain for campus radicals and welfare cheaters. After serving two terms as governor of California, Reagan campaigned unsuccessfully against Gerald Ford for the Republican nomination. But he was successful in 1980, beating Jimmy Carter in his bid for the highest office and ushering in a new era for victim justice.

In his first 100 days, Reagan proclaimed the week of 19 April 1981 as "National Victims' Rights Week." (The week has been observed ever since.) As Frank Carrington and George Nicholson state in "The Victims' Movement: An Idea Whose Time Has Come," "These Presidential Proclamations were of great importance because they placed the imprimatur of the highest office in the land on the cause of victims and their rights."[17] In September of 1981, Reagan, in a speech to the International Association of Chiefs of Police, announced that his administration was going to wage a war on crime. He promised to try to "redress the imbalance between the rights of the accused and the rights of the innocent."[18]

His first step in keeping his promise was appointing the President's Task Force on Victims of Crime in 1982. The task force traveled to six cities around the country, listened to more than 1,000 people, and concluded that crime victims' treatment was appalling. Based on testimony from various people and their encounters with the criminal justice system during the trial phase, the task force stated, "Your character is an open subject of discussion and innuendo. The defense is allowed to question you on incidents going back to your childhood. The jury is never told that the defendant has two prior convictions for the same offense and has been to prison three times for other crimes. . . . Even at the point of conviction of the defendant, the system can place new burdens on the victim; if the defendant wins an appeal, the victim may have to go through the trial process all over again. There might have been more than one defendant, or one might have been a juvenile. This would have meant two or three trials, two or three times as many court appearances and hours of cross-examination, double or triple the harassment. . . . The defendant's every right has been protected, and now he serves his time in a public facility, receiving education at public expense. In a few months, his sentence will have run. Victims receive sentences, too; their sentences may be life long."[19]

The year 1982 also saw the passage of the Omnibus Victim and Witness Protection Act, which provided for victim impact statements during sentencing, protection of federal victims and witnesses from intimidation, restitution from offenders to victims of federal crimes, fair treatment guidelines for victims and witnesses in federal criminal cases, and a general stiffening of bail laws. While the act applied only to federal crimes, it promoted sensitivity toward victims and witnesses at the state and local levels and acted as a model statute for state and local governments.

One of the suggestions coming out of the task force was the creation of a federal crime victims' fund. Although Congress had approved the Justice Assistance Act in 1982, which gave money to the Justice Department to use for criminal justice activities, including victim services, no money was set aside specifically for victim programs. So when the Reagan administration sent a crime victims' compensation bill to Congress on 13 March 1984, the suggestion became a reality. Congress passed the Victims of Crime Act, which provided for $75 million to be raised from federal fines and bail forfeitures. The money would be used to compensate victims of federal crimes, assist state crime victim compensation programs, and pay for public and private victim assistance efforts.

Until Reagan became president, the bulk of progress on the victims' rights front came from below. The activist approach toward crime victims that he took during his first term shifted the progress to the federal level but also ignited growth in victim services and programs at the state and local levels. It is fair to say that the impact of Reagan's first term, as far as the victims' rights movement is concerned, still is being felt.

Roberta Roper (b. 1937)

In April 1982, Roberta Roper's eldest daughter, Stephanie, one month short of graduating with honors from Frostburg State College in Frostburg, Maryland, was kidnapped, raped, and murdered by two men after her car veered off a rural road at night while she was driving home. Like many people who became local activists for crime victims' rights early in the movement, Roberta Roper was spurred by her personal loss to do something about the lack of consideration of victims' needs and services in Maryland.

Roper's is a classic example of double victimization prevalent in what she calls the "dark ages" of victims' rights and services. Given the pretrial media attention, trials for the two defendants in the case were moved from the county in which Stephanie Roper was killed—the county in which she and her family lived—to two different counties, both at least an hour's drive from the Roper residence. That did not stop Roper, who drove to all the proceedings, many times only to learn there had been a continuance. As witnesses, Roper and her husband were not allowed to watch the trial proceedings. And just when she believed she had an opportunity to make a difference in one of the trials with victim impact testimony at the sentencing phase, defense attorneys objected, saying Roper's testimony would only stir up the jurors' emotions and bias them against the defendant. The trial judge agreed. He told Roper to step down and ruled that the impact of Stephanie's death on the Roper family was "irrelevant."[20]

Before Stephanie was killed, Roper had never seen courtroom walls. After her death, a neighbor of the Ropers, Victor Pietkiewicz, gathered friends and other neighbors together to help the Ropers through the funeral and the trials. The nucleus of the group formed the Stephanie Roper Family Assistance Committee. It included relatives, friends, and supporters who were bent on attending court proceedings and in need of educating themselves about the workings of the criminal justice system. When the group met with a state attorney, Roper glimpsed how she would proceed through the judicial process, not as the mother of a young woman whose death reverberated beyond her family but as someone officials swept to the sidelines. That treatment included exclusion from the proceedings—even though the Ropers testified first for the prosecution—until the closing statements; seeing jurors experience her daughter as an abstraction, as someone who never really was alive while the defendants were able to recount all the specifics of their lives; and experiencing the impact of devastation that the lack of fairness had on Stephanie's four siblings. Both defendants received life for murder, life for rape, and 20 years for kidnapping—all with the possibility of parole—to be served concurrently.

In October 1982, the committee became the Stephanie Roper Committee and Foundation (SRC/F) and incorporated. Under Roper's tutelage, the SRC/F has scored a lot of legislation for crime victims, including mandatory victim impact statements, restitution, proceedings attendance rights for victims and survivors, life imprisonment without parole for those convicted of first-degree murder, a state constitutional amendment for victims' rights, and a Maryland crime victims' fund with money from criminal fines. The fund pays for more than 40 programs for victims and does not cost taxpayers any money, Roper said. In addition, the foundation provides victims' services such as court accompaniment; help with impact statements, restitution requests, and correspondence with agencies like the parole commission; and free support groups.

Today, Roper continues to head up the committee and foundation named for her daughter, but her role has expanded to the national scene. She cochairs the National Victims Constitutional Amendment Network and testified before the House Judiciary Committee in July 1996 and January 1997 as to the importance and necessity of the amendment.

Notes

1. Valiant R. W. Poliny. 1994. *A Public Policy Analysis of the Emerging Victims' Rights Movement*. Bethesda, MD: Austin & Winfield.

2. Frank J. Weed. 1995. *Certainty of Justice: Reform in the Crime Victims Movement*. New York: Aldine de Gruyter.

3. Ibid.

4. Ibid.

5. Ibid.

6. Poliny.

7. Weed.

8. Stephen Schafer. 1977. *Victimology: The Criminal and His Victim*. Reston, VA: Reston Publishing.

9. Marvin E. Wolfgang. 1979. Preface to *The Criminal and His Victim,* by Hans von Hentig. New York: Schocken Books.

10. Hans von Hentig. 1979. *The Criminal and His Victim*. New York: Schocken Books.

11. Ibid.

12. Ibid.

13. Schafer.

14. Ibid.

15. Beniamin Mendelsohn. 1976. *Victimology: An International Journal* 1, no. 1 (Spring): 8–28.

16. Charles Whited. 1982. "They're after Justice in World of Insanity." *The Miami Herald* (14 March): Area News, Section B.

17. Frank Carrington and George Nicholson. 1984. "The Victims' Movement: An Idea Whose Time Has Come." *Pepperdine Law Review* 11, no. 1: 7.

18. Poliny.

19. President's Task Force on Victims of Crime. 1982. *Final Report*. Washington, DC: Government Printing Office.

20. Paul Duggan. 1993. "A Giant Hole in Your Life." *The Washington Post Magazine* (29 August).

Policy, Legislation, and Court Cases

4

T his chapter will give readers an idea of how the crime victims' rights movement has played out in public policy and the courts. It examines the ways in which constitutional amendments concerning the accused—the Fourth, Fifth, Sixth, Eighth, and Fourteenth—were interpreted and expanded upon by the Supreme Court. It also gives an overview of some of the actions various commissions have recommended and laws Congress passed regarding the administration of justice. The speeches are included to give readers an understanding of the prevailing attitudes toward crime and criminal justice.

Policy

Commissions and Task Forces

When the government desires a deeper understanding of the extent of a problem or how a solution to a problem might play out, it appoints a commission. Commissions have a set amount of time to examine a problem, often getting input from the public or from experts who work in the field.

The National Commission on Reform of Federal Criminal Laws (1971)

In 1966, Congress authorized a national commission to study overhauling the criminal code. In its 366-page draft, released in 1971, the 12-member National Commission on Reform of Federal Criminal Laws stated that it supported the following:

- Abolishing capital punishment for all federal crimes.
- A drug law that limits penalties for marijuana possession to $1,000 fines and decreases penalties for use of dangerous drugs such as heroin. Penalties for selling dangerous drugs would remain severe.
- Broadening federal jurisdiction to include, in specific situations, crimes that typically had come under state jurisdiction, such as murder, burglary, and sex offenses.
- Outlawing all handguns except those carried by military or police officials and requiring registration of all firearms. Another proposal makes it illegal to stockpile weapons or train "paramilitary" groups for political reasons.
- Simplifying the present penalty system to define maximum penalties for three categories of felonies and two categories of misdemeanors.

Attorney General's Task Force on Violent Crime (1981)

The Attorney General's Task Force on Violent Crime was formed "to recommend specific ways in which the federal government can do more to assist in controlling violent crime without limiting its efforts against organized crime and white-collar crime." The task force concluded that the wave of violent crime the country was experiencing was the result of a breakdown of social order. As such, it stated that there was little the government could do as a whole to change the social order. It directed its suggestions to the Justice Department. Task force members recommended the following:

- The attorney general should take the lead to ensure that crime victims are accorded proper status by the criminal justice system.
- The attorney general should require "as a matter of sentencing advocacy, that federal prosecutors assure that all relevant information about the crime, the defendant, and where appropriate, the victim is brought to the court's

attention before sentencing. This will help ensure that judges have a complete picture of the defendant's past conduct before imposing sentence."

- Legislation should be enacted to permit courts to deny bail to people who "are found by clear and convincing evidence to present a danger to particular persons or the community."
- Evidence should not be excluded from criminal proceedings "if it has been obtained by an officer acting in the reasonable, good faith belief that it was in conformity to the Fourth Amendment to the Constitution."
- The attorney general should establish, either within the Department of Justice or through legislation, federal standards for the Fair Treatment of Victims of Serious Crime.
- The attorney general should "study the principle that would allow for suits against appropriate federal governmental agencies for gross negligence involved in allowing early release or failure to supervise obviously dangerous persons or for failure to warn expected victims of such dangerous persons."
- The attorney general should conduct an inexpensive study of the various crime victims' compensation programs and their results.

President's Task Force on Victims of Crime (1982)

After two months of public hearings involving victims of crime and professionals responsible for serving victims, the President's Task Force on Victims of Crime outlined the problems of victims and came up with several recommendations to help. Lois Herrington Haight, who chaired the task force, wrote that

Something insidious has happened in America—crime has made victims of us all. Awareness of its danger affects the way we think, where we live, where we go, what we buy, how we raise our children, and the quality of our lives as we age. The specter of violent crime and the knowledge that, without warning, any person can be attacked or crippled, robbed, or killed, lurks at the fringes of consciousness. Every citizen of this country is more impoverished, less free, more fearful, and less safe, because of the ever-present threat of the criminal. Rather than alter a system that has proven itself incapable of dealing with crime, society has altered itself. . . .

Victims who do survive their attack, and are brave enough to come forward turn to their government expecting it to do what a good government should—protect the innocent. The American criminal justice system is absolutely dependent on these victims to cooperate. Without the cooperation of victims and witnesses in reporting and testifying about crime, it is impossible in a free society to hold criminals accountable. When victims come forward to perform this vital service, however, they find little protection. They discover instead that they will be treated as appendages of a system appallingly out of balance. They learn that somewhere along the way, the system began to serve lawyers and judges and defendants, treating the victim with institutionalized disinterest.

Based on its interviews, the task force made the following recommendations:

- Police should be sensitive to the needs of victims. Law enforcement officers generally are the first at the scene of a crime. Their treatment of victims affects victims' immediate and long-term ability to handle the crime as well as their willingness to help prosecute it.
- Police departments should set procedures for promptly returning victims' property.
- Prosecutors should assume the "ultimate responsibility" for informing victims as to how their case is proceeding from the initial charge to parole hearings.
- Prosecutors should make the views of crime victims known on matters of bail, continuances, plea bargains, dismissals, sentencing, and restitution, and they should strongly discourage continuances in cases. When continuances are inevitable, however, they should make sure future dates are acceptable to victims and witnesses.
- Trial and appellate judges should take part in training programs that address the needs and legal interests of crime victims.
- Judges or court administrators should set up separate waiting rooms for prosecution and defense witnesses.

- When ruling on continuance requests, judges should weigh equally the interests of victims, witnesses, and defendants. Judges should explain their reasons for such ruling on the record.
- Judges should permit and weigh appropriately sentencing input from victims of violent crime.
- In cases in which victims suffered financial loss, judges should order restitution unless they enter compelling reasons to the contrary into the record.
- Judges should permit the victim and a member of the victim's family to attend the trial, even if they are identified as witnesses, unless there is a compelling need to the contrary.

The U.S. Parole Commission (1983)

The U.S. Parole Commission's 1983 guidelines required longer minimum sentences for violent criminals and major drug offenders in federal prisons. They did this by adding an eighth category of criminals and crime to the previously existing seven categories, with longer minimum sentences for the most serious federal criminals, including those convicted of murder; forcible felonies, such as arson, rape, or robbery, that end in death; ransom- or terrorism-related kidnapping; aircraft piracy; and the sale of 6.6 or more pounds of heroin.

Under the new rules, people unlikely to commit more crime would receive 8 years 4 months (from 4 years 4 months) before being considered for parole. Those likely to commit more crime would receive 15 years minimum (from 8 years 4 months).

The commission also increased minimum sentences for crimes involving sawed-off shotguns, machines guns, or silencers. People convicted of selling ten or more tons of marijuana also faced higher minimums.

President's Commission on Organized Crime (1986)

The President's Commission on Organized Crime ignited a nationwide controversy on individual privacy when it recommended combatting drugs by instituting large-scale drug testing of federal employees and adopting programs to test most Americans in the workplace.

The commission's report cited drug trafficking as "the most serious problem presented by organized crime in this country" and

stated that drug deals made up 40 percent of organized crime activity in the United States, generating $110 billion in illegal profits
every year. The commission also recommended the following:

- Prosecution for possession of even tiny amounts of drugs
- More police and prisons to deal with drug offenders
- More money for drug prevention programs
- Eased restrictions on amounts of seized drug-trafficking
  assets police agencies may keep to help pay for the recommendations
- Use of military personnel to help stem smuggling and a
  "specific formula" determined by the State Department
  as to when to cut off foreign assistance to countries that
  do not decrease their drug crops

The U.S. Sentencing Commission (1987)

The U.S. Sentencing Commission created a new system of sentencing that had 43 levels—as little as no imprisonment, as much as a
life term. Every crime was designated a level. For example, a first-
time offender convicted of fraud was considered a level 6 and received up to 6 months' prison time. If the fraud amounted to
$50,000 to $100,000, the sentence level went to 11, or 8 to 14 months'
prison time. If the same defendant defrauded more than one person, the level went to 13, or 12 to 18 months' prison time. Repeat
offenders were subjected to higher sentencing levels and lengthier
prison terms.

The new guidelines prohibited early release through parole
but allowed probation for some portion of a prison term. Judges
had to follow the code as much as possible. If a situation differed
from a scenario presented in the code, judges were permitted to
depart from the guidelines but had to give their reason in writing.
Such departures were open to appeal.

Speeches

All the players in criminal justice have their ideas of what it takes
to improve the application of justice. A justice's perspective differs
from a president's in that a president's constituents—the entire citi-
zenry—is made up of victims and criminals and those in between,
while a justice's responsibility is to those who come before him
and those who follow. The speeches surveyed below show some
variation between these responsibilities and also give readers a

sense of the status of criminal justice at the times the speeches were made.

Chief Justice Warren E. Burger (10 August 1970)

In a television address broadcast nationally, Chief Justice Warren E. Burger said the federal judiciary is becoming so overwhelmed that before approving new reforms, Congress should evaluate the legislation's impact on courts. In the "State of the Judiciary" speech to the opening assembly of the ninety-third annual American Bar Association convention in St. Louis, Burger also said federal courts should have more employees and more funds and should assimilate modern administrative methods.

Burger ascribed the backlog to an increase in criminal cases and in the length of those cases. He cited "the closer scrutiny we now demand as to such things as confessions, identification witnesses and evidence seized by the police" as procedures that "represent a deliberate commitment . . . to values higher than pure efficiency when we are dealing with human liberty." He suggested considering ways to "screen out frivolous appeals." Burger also said that if federal courts were given the staff and the means to try criminal defendants within 60 days of indictments, the crime rate would go down "sharply" and that by solving the problem of delays, "the heated debates over preventive detention would probably disappear and subside."

Burger compared spending on the federal judiciary in 1969 ($128 million) with "the $200 million cost of a C-5A" military plane and the $58 million budget for legal services of the Office of Economic Opportunity.

President Richard Nixon (11 March 1971)

At the National Conference on the Judiciary in Williamsburg, Virginia, President Richard Nixon opened the keynote speech calling for "genuine reform" of courts. Nixon said reforms limited to hiring more personnel from judges to police will only create "more backlogs, more delays, more litigation, more jails and more criminals." What is needed is "genuine reform—the kind of change that requires imagination and daring, that demands a focus on ultimate goals."

The period between arrest and trial in the United States is "far too long" and "in case after case, the appeal process is misused—to obstruct rather than advance the cause of justice," Nixon said. "A system of criminal justice that can guarantee neither a speedy trial nor a safe community cannot excuse its failure by pointing to an elaborate system of safeguards for the accused. Justice dictates not only that the innocent man go free, but that the guilty be punished for his crimes."

Nixon also stressed the bad effects of the "exploitation of the courts by publicity seekers" as well as the need for judges to maintain order in their courtrooms. The president said that relieving courts of the "endless stream of 'victimless crimes,'" including traffic violations and drunkenness, and adding paraprofessionals such as magistrates to the system would speed up the judicial process.

In addition, Nixon proposed creating a national center for state courts with financial support from the Law Enforcement Assistance Administration to study problems of procedure, administration, and training.

Attorney General John N. Mitchell (16 July 1971)

At a meeting before 1,000 delegates to the American Bar Association meeting in London, Attorney General John N. Mitchell criticized past Supreme Court decisions regarding the rights of criminal suspects and charged the judiciary to "begin to recognize that society, too, has its rights."

"We face in the United States a situation where the discovery of guilt or innocence is in danger of drowning in a sea of legalisms," he said, not referring specifically to former Chief Justice Earl Warren but directing his criticisms at criminal law rulings made while Warren headed up the Supreme Court. Mitchell cited pretrial hearings ("designed mainly to deprive the jury of material and relevant evidence"), in which defense attorneys may move to suppress evidence because of improper police procedures.

The attorney general also urged restrictions on prisoners' rights to repeatedly challenge convictions through habeas corpus petitions. Mitchell said that the American judiciary may have been "too preoccupied in the exhilarating adventure of making new law and new public policy from the bench and that this function of the courts has outdistanced the more sober task of judging guilt and innocence."

President Bill Clinton (25 June 1996)

In a Rose Garden ceremony surrounded by parents of murder victims and crime victims, President Bill Clinton said he supports and would help to write a measure guaranteeing victims such things as court proceeding notifications, the ability to witness trials, and permission to address the court prior to sentencing or the acceptance of a plea bargain. Of a constitutional amendment guaranteeing such rights, the president said, "This is not an attempt to put legislative responsibilities in the Constitution or to guarantee a right that is already guaranteed. Amending the Constitution here is simply the only way to guarantee the victims' rights are weighted equally with defendants' rights in every courtroom in America."

Anticipating that some would see his support of an amendment as election-year stumping, Clinton said, "This is a cause for all Americans. When people are victimized, the criminal almost never asks before you're robbed or beaten or raped or murdered: Are you a Republican or a Democrat?"

Legislation

Omnibus Crime Control Act of 1970

President Richard Nixon signed the Omnibus Crime Control Act of 1970 in 1971. The legislation authorized $3.55 billion in federal law enforcement assistance to states and communities from 1971 to 1973. On 17 December 1970, Congress had approved the legislation, which redirected the focus of aid on urban crime centers. The act retained the bipartisan, three-man leadership of the Law Enforcement Assistance Administration (LEAA). It also made kidnapping, assault, or murder—or the attempt or conspiracy to commit such actions—of a member or member-elect of Congress a federal crime. It prohibited entry without permission into a building or grounds where the president was staying. Other measures set tougher sentences for people who carry firearms while they commit a federal crime, permitted the federal government to appeal rulings ending criminal cases, and authorized a study on wiretapping abuses.

Parole Reorganization Act of 1976

In 1976, Congress approved legislation that President Gerald Ford later signed to reorganize the federal parole system to guarantee prison inmates fair treatment in parole matters. The legislation included the following provisions:

- Entitling prisoners to parole when they obey prison rules.
- Crediting prisoners with time spent out of prison on parole as law-abiding citizens if their parole is cancelled due to technical violations or misdemeanors. If prisoners committed a felony, parole credit would be optional.
- Guaranteeing prisoners adequate notice, an advocate, information access, and a finding with reasons and appeal in parole determination hearings. These were construed as prisoners' rights.
- Making parole available to prisoners serving sentences longer than 1 year after they have served one-third of their sentence, or after 10 years if they receive sentences of 30 years or longer or life.
- Providing a written statement of reasons to inmates denied parole.
- Changing the U.S. Board of Parole to the Parole Commission with nine appointed commissioners—with no more than two six-year terms. Commissioners would be appointed by the president pending Senate confirmation.

Penalties for Crimes against Government Officials

In 1982, President Ronald Reagan signed legislation making the killing, kidnapping, or assault of certain federal officials, including Supreme Court justices and senior White House and cabinet officials, a federal crime. The legislation stemmed from the 1981 assassination attempt on Reagan.

Missing Children's Act of 1982

President Ronald Reagan signed legislation to assist the search for children who are missing. The bill expanded descriptive information that is included in the Department of Justice's central computer file and allowed parents to access the information.

Victim and Witness Protection Act of 1982

President Ronald Reagan signed the federal Victim and Witness Protection Act in 1982. It imposed penalties on people who try to intimidate victims and witnesses and required sentencing reports to contain statements concerning the crimes' impact on victims. It also permitted judges to order restitution to victims and, in cases where judges do not order restitution, required them to state their reasoning.

Justice Assistance Act of 1984

In 1984, President Ronald Reagan signed legislation one congressman described as "the most important crime package passed by any Congress at any time." The bill applied only to crimes prosecuted on the federal level, or about 5 percent of all crimes, according to the *New York Times*.

The legislation included the following provisions:

- Judges who believed that a defendant charged with a serious crime would undermine the safety of any person and the community were allowed to deny bail to the defendant. This was the first time in the nation's history, other than in times of war, that pretrial detention was allowed in cases other than those involving capital crimes. For example, a defendant who faced a serious drug charge should be presumed dangerous and detained until trial. He or she could challenge the ruling.
- The president had to appoint a seven-member commission to set narrow windows for sentencings for myriad federal crimes. The commission, including three federal judges, had to complete the assignment in 18 months. Once the sentencing guidelines were in place, judges who meted out sentences other than those specified had to write their reasons for differing from them. Prosecutors and defense attorneys had the right to appeal sentences that did not adhere to the guidelines. This provision also phased out the granting of federal parole within five years. Sentences, however, still could be reduced by 15 percent for good behavior.
- The burden of proving that defendants who use the insanity defense were insane when they committed a crime shifted from prosecutors to defense attorneys. Also, insanity could be used only if defense attorneys proved defendants were unable to comprehend the wrongfulness of their actions. In the past, defense attorneys had been allowed to argue that insanity made defendants simply lose control of their actions.
- People convicted of the most serious federal drug crimes could be fined up to $250,000, a tenfold increase.

Additionally, government officials had more power to confiscate assets related to drug dealing and other criminal activities.
- A National Drug Enforcement Policy, led by the attorney general, would be formed to coordinate national attempts to reduce the flow of drugs into and throughout the country.
- A fund, created from and maintained with court fines, penalties, and forfeitures and worth up to $100 million per year, would be spread among state victims' compensation programs.
- Career criminals convicted of three serious state-level crimes would face stiff federal penalties.

The legislation also gave federal officials broader jurisdiction over credit card and computer-related crimes, initiated an anticrime grant program for states, and strengthened a program to assist parents who were searching for missing children.

Victims of Crime Act of 1984

In 1984, President Ronald Reagan signed the Victims of Crime Act (VOCA) to establish the Crime Victims Fund, into which federal criminal fines, penalties, and bond forfeitures would go to support state victims' compensation programs and local victims' services.

Brady Handgun Violence Prevention Act of 1993

In 1993, Congress passed and President Bill Clinton signed the Brady Handgun Violence Prevention Act. Named after James Brady, who was shot during the attempted assassination of former President Ronald Reagan in 1981, the act requires that anyone purchasing a firearm wait five days to allow dealers and law enforcement to conduct a criminal history check. Anyone with *any* kind of record would not be allowed to complete the transaction.

Violent Crime Control and Law Enforcement Act of 1994

In 1994, President Bill Clinton signed the Violent Crime Control and Law Enforcement Act. "Let us roll up our sleeves to roll back this awful tide of violence and reduce crime in this country," he said at a White House signing ceremony. "Today the bickering stops, the era of excuses is over, the law-abiding citizens of the country have made their voices heard," said Clinton, referring to the partisan politics that almost defeated the bill.

The legislation authorized spending more than $30 billion on crime with $13.5 billion on law enforcement, including $8.8 billion to hire 100,000 officers over the next six years; $7.9 billion for new state prisons; $1.8 billion to reimburse states for jailing illegal aliens who committed crimes; and $150 million for alternative programs for young offenders. Various crime prevention programs were allotted $6.9 billion, including $1.6 billion for the Violence Against Women Act, a provision to fight violence against women through grant programs and new federal penalties. A program to place nonviolent offenders with substance abuse problems in treatment was funded with $1 billion, and another $567 million was authorized for after-school, weekend, and summer children's programs.

The act also

- Outlawed the manufacture, sale, and possession of 19 types of assault weapons and similar versions of them for ten years and banned guns with two or more features associated with assault weapons and gun clips holding more than ten rounds. About 650 types of semiautomatic weapons were exempted and gun owners legally could keep guns they owned at the time of the act's passage.
- Required life in prison for anyone who had two previous convictions for serious federal or state felonies and was then convicted of a federal crime; provided early release for some first-time, nonviolent drug offenders who were serving mandatory minimum sentences; and permitted federal court trials for juveniles 13 and older who committed certain violent crimes.
- Required notification for communities to which convicted sex offenders move. The offenders would have to continue reporting their addresses to authorities for anywhere from ten years to life. Additionally, accusations of past sexual offenses would be admissible as evidence against a defendant in federal criminal trials, even if the defendant had not been charged in the previous cases.
- Expanded the federal death penalty for more than 50 crimes.

Antiterrorism and Effective Death Penalty Act of 1996

In 1996, President Bill Clinton signed legislation that gave state and federal death-row inmates six months from the date of their final court proceedings to file habeas corpus appeals and limited the number of successive appeals they could file. Other inmates had one year to file their appeals. Although Congress debated expanding federal power to wiretap suspected terrorists, in the end, it did not vote to do so. Instead, it created an Alien Terrorist Removal Court comprising five sitting U.S. district judges chosen by the chief justice. The antiterrorism act also required mandatory victim restitution without regard to defendants' ability to pay. This has been criticized as too inflexible and expensive a replacement of the old way of implementing restitution, which was based on common sense and judicial discretion.

Another provision orders closed-circuit televising of proceedings in federal criminal trials in which the venue is changed from the state in which the trial was originally brought and more than 350 miles from where the proceedings originally would have taken place.

Megan's Law (1996)

In 1996, President Bill Clinton signed a bill requiring states to notify communities of the whereabouts of convicted sex offenders. The legislation, passed by voice vote in the Senate and 418–0 in the House, was presented as an amendment to the 1994 federal Violent Crime Control and Law Enforcement Act.

The bill, known as "Megan's Law," was based on a New Jersey law enacted weeks after Megan Kanka, a seven-year-old resident of Hamilton Township, New Jersey, allegedly was killed by a twice-convicted sex offender who had recently moved into her neighborhood. The new neighbor, Jesse Timmendequas, was arrested and charged in the crime against Megan but did not go to trial until early 1997. Richard and Maureen Kanka, Megan's parents, had not known about Timmendequas's criminal record.

Although almost all states had laws to register and track paroled sex offenders—based on the 1994 anticrime act—only 15 mandated community notification of such offenders. The 1994 law allowed but did not require notification. Megan's Law required states to provide information about people convicted of sexually violent crimes when they are placed on parole or released from prison. The offender's expected address was to be included in the information. States that did not create a system of notification by September 1997 could lose federal anticrime funds.

Senate Joint Resolution 6

Senate Joint Resolution 6 (SJR 6) proposes an amendment to the Constitution of the United States to protect the rights of crime victims. Sens. Dianne Feinstein (D-Calif.) and John Kyl (R-Ariz.) and Rep. Henry Hyde (R-Ill.) introduced the proposal for the first time in 1996, and they reintroduced it in the Senate Judiciary Committee in January 1997.

The proposal reads:

Resolved by the Senate and House of Representatives of the United States of America in Congress assembled (two-thirds of each House concurring therein), That the following article is proposed as an amendment to the Constitution of the United States, which shall be valid for all intents and purposes as part of the Constitution when ratified by the legislatures of three-fourths of the several States within seven years from the date of its submission by the Congress:

Section 1. Each victim of a crime of violence, and other crimes that Congress may define by law, shall have the rights to notice of, and not to be excluded from, all public proceedings relating to the crime;

To be heard, if present, and to submit a written statement at a public pretrial or trial proceeding to determine a release from custody, an acceptance of a negotiated plea, or a sentence;

To the rights described in the proceeding portions of this section at a public parole proceeding, or at a nonpublic parole proceeding to the extent they are afforded to the convicted offender;

To notice of a release pursuant to a public or parole proceeding or an escape;

To a final disposition of the proceedings relating to the crime free from unreasonable delay;

To an order of restitution from the convicted offender;

To consideration for the safety of the victim in determining any release from custody;—And

To notice of the rights established by this article; however, the rights to notice under this section are not violated if the proper authorities make a reasonable effort, but are unable to provide the notice, or if the failure of the victim to make a reasonable effort to make those authorities aware of the victim's whereabouts prevents that notice.

Section 2. The victim shall have standing to assert the rights established by this article. However, nothing in this article shall provide grounds for the victim to challenge a charging decision or a conviction; to obtain a stay of trial; or to compel a new trial. Nothing in this article shall give rise to a claim for damages against the United States, a State, a political subdivision, or a public official, nor provide grounds for the accused or convicted offender to obtain any form of relief.

Section 3. The Congress and the States shall have the power to enforce this article within their respective jurisdictions by appropriate legislation, including the power to enact exceptions when required for compelling reasons of public safety or for judicial efficiency in mass victim cases.

Section 4. The rights established by this article shall apply to all proceedings that begin on or after the 180th day after the ratification of this article.

Section 5. The rights established by this article shall apply in all Federal and State proceedings, including military proceedings to the extent that Congress may provide by law, juvenile justice proceedings, and collateral proceedings such as habeas corpus, and including proceedings in any district or territory of the United States not within a State.

Court Cases

The court case summaries presented below are organized thematically in sections covering the exclusionary rule; the Fourth, Fifth, Sixth, Eighth, and Fourteenth Amendments; and habeas corpus review cases. Many of the summaries make reference to other cases that appear as their own entries elsewhere in this chapter, and readers may consult the general index at the end of the book to guide them in locating entries.

Cases Concerning the Exclusionary Rule

The exclusionary rule is the principle that evidence seized by government officials in violation of a defendant's constitutional protection against unlawful searches and seizures is not admissible at trial. The term itself refers to suppression of physical evidence obtained in violation of the Fourth Amendment.

Weeks v. United States, 232 U.S. 383 (1914)

Authorities seized documents relating to the transfer of lottery tickets through the mail from Weeks's home. They did not have a warrant for the search. The Supreme Court unanimously decided that the trial court's admission of the documents violated Weeks's constitutional rights. As the Fourth Amendment does not outline the consequences of illegal searches and seizures, the justices essentially were writing search and seizure law. Prior to *Weeks*, such a violation was trivial and defendants had no reason to challenge the legality of a police search. The thinking behind *Weeks* is the principle of limited government power, and the fruits of any search that goes beyond law enforcement officials' constitutional authority must be invalidated. If police did not have authority to seize something, then judges have no right to use it in a trial. The *Weeks* decision, however, applied only to federal government authorities, not to states. Some states amended their search and seizure rules, but many did not. The ruling set the stage for future debates on applicability of the Bill of Rights to the states via the Fourteenth Amendment's Due Process Clause.

Wolf v. Colorado, 338 U.S. 25 (1949)

Convicted of conspiracy to commit abortion in Colorado, Wolf's conviction was upheld by the state supreme court when he challenged the constitutionality of the seizure and the use of evidence at trial. In a 6–3 decision, Supreme Court justices ruled that the Fourth Amendment's protections against illegal searches and seizures limit state governmental authority through the Fourteenth Amendment's Due Process Clause. The Court did not, however, extend the exclusionary rule to state courts; therefore, Wolf's conviction was upheld. Justice Felix Frankfurter stated that protection against arbitrary intrusion by police is inherent in the "concept of ordered liberty" and passes through the Fourteenth Amendment to restrict states. Frankfurter agreed that the exclusionary rule could restrict police from committing unreasonable searches but emphasized that other means of enforcing the Fourth Amendment existed.

In dissenting opinions, Justice William O. Douglas stated that the Fourth Amendment is not effective when illegally seized evidence is not excluded, and Justice Frank Murphy stated that few states would develop efficient ways of redressing violations of the Fourth Amendment. Justice Wiley B. Rutledge agreed with Murphy's dissent.

Mapp v. Ohio, 367 U.S. 643 (1961)

When seven police officers broke into and searched Dolly Mapp's house in Cleveland, Ohio, they claimed to have a warrant but never showed it. According to the police, an informant had told them a bombing suspect was hidden in Mapp's house along with gambling paraphernalia. Their search turned up neither. Instead, they discovered several allegedly obscene books and pictures. Mapp was convicted of possession of obscene literature and imprisoned. Despite the fact that Mapp's prosecutors neither produced a warrant used in the search of her home, nor an explanation for the failure to secure one, the Ohio Supreme Court determined that the state was not prevented from using unconstitutionally seized evidence based on *Wolf v. Colorado*.

In a 5–3–1 decision, Justice Hugo Black cast the breaking vote and he alone wrote that the exclusionary rule is required only by the Fourth and Fifth Amendments in combination. The ruling opinions therefore represented those of four justices concerning the basis for the exclusionary rule and of five justices for its applicability to states. Justice Tom Clark, who wrote the majority opinion, stated the rule was a "deterrent safeguard" and that without it, the Fourth Amendment would be, borrowing from Justice Oliver Wendell Holmes, "a form of words." Clark repeated then-Judge Benjamin Cardozo's complaint about the rule that "the criminal is to go free because the constable has blundered," and he answered, "The criminal goes free if he must, but it is the law that sets him free."

Clark backed up his reasoning with practical concerns: states lacking exclusionary rules had not developed effective alternatives for handling unlawful police searches. In fact, Clark stated that prior to Wolf, about two-thirds of states opposed using the exclusionary rule as a way of complying with constitutional provisions. But since the *Wolf* decision in 1949, about half the U.S. states, including California, have had to adopt its use because no other remedies for lack of constitutional compliance work. Clark likened the right to privacy, upon which the constitutional search and seizure provision is drawn, to other rights, such as free speech and press, the right to a fair, public trial, and "the right not to be convicted by use of a coerced confession, however logically relevant it be, and without regard to its reliability. . . . Why should not the same rule apply to what is tantamount to coerced testimony by way of unconstitutional seizure of goods, papers, effects, documents, etc.?"

Cupp v. Murphy, 93 S. Ct. 2000 (1973)

Supreme Court justices in this case ruled 7–2 that police, in certain situations, may obtain "disposable" evidence from criminal suspects without first getting a search warrant. The case concerned Daniel P. Murphy, an Oregon resident, who was a suspect in the strangulation of his wife and who voluntarily went to a police station to be questioned. At the station, although he protested, police scraped his fingernails for evidence, which was later used to convict him of second-degree murder.

Writing for the majority, Justice Potter Stewart stated that police were justified when they conducted a "very limited search necessary to preserve the highly evanescent evidence they found under his fingernails." Justice William J. Brennan, Jr., dissented: "In upholding this search, the court engrafts another, albeit limited, exception on the warrant requirement. Before we take this serious step of legitimating even limited searches merely upon probable cause—without a warrant or as incident to an arrest—we ought first be certain that such probable cause in fact existed." Justice William O. Douglas also dissented in the case.

Stone v. Powell and *Wolff v. Rice,* 96 S. Ct. 3037 (1976)

Supreme Court justices held 6–3 in *Stone v. Powell* and *Wolff v. Rice* that federal courts are not allowed to overturn state convictions based on illegally obtained evidence if defendants had a "full and fair" chance to question the evidence in state courts. Justice Lewis F. Powell, Jr., wrote that "application of the (exclusionary) rule . . . deflects the truthfinding process and often frees the guilty." He notes that "the disparity in particular cases between the error committed by the police officer and the windfall afforded a guilty defendant by application of the rule is contrary to the idea of proportionality that is essential to the concept of justice."

In a dissenting opinion, Justice William J. Brennan, Jr., wrote that the use of illegally seized evidence creates a "constitutional deprivation" and that it is up to federal courts in such cases to allow habeas corpus relief.

United States v. Havens, 100 S. Ct. 1912 (1980)

In *United States v. Havens*, the Supreme Court ruled 5–4 that illegally seized evidence may be presented in a criminal case to void the testimony of a defendant. In the case, John McLeroth and J. Lee Havens were arrested at a Miami airport for smuggling cocaine. Their luggage was taken and searched despite authorities' lack of a warrant. McLeroth carried the drug in makeshift pockets sewn into his T-shirt. He pleaded guilty and implicated Havens, who was not carrying any cocaine and maintained his innocence. Authorities found a cut-up T-shirt in his luggage that matched the pieces used to make McLeroth's pockets.

The exclusionary rule did not permit prosecutors to use the cut-up shirt as evidence against Havens, but they did use it to impeach Havens's testimony during cross-examination. He was convicted of drug smuggling. An appeals court overturned the conviction based on the use of the shirt, which should have been excluded.

The Supreme Court ruling reversed the decision. Justice Byron R. White in the majority opinion stated, "There is no gainsaying that arriving at the truth is a fundamental goal of our legal system. When defendants testify, they must testify truthfully or suffer the consequences."

United States v. Payner, 100 S. Ct. 2439 (1980)

The Supreme Court ruled 6–3 in *United States v. Payner* that federal judges are not allowed to suppress illegally obtained evidence unless taking such evidence directly violates the defendant's constitutional rights. In the case, the Internal Revenue Service (IRS) used an informant to conduct an illegal search and obtained a document used to convict Jack Payner, an Ohio businessman, of falsifying a federal income tax return. The document, found in the briefcase of a Bahamian bank officer, revealed that Payner had a secret bank account in the Bahamas. The federal district court used its supervisory power to overturn Payner's conviction. The reversal was based on the tainted evidence used against Payner.

Writing the majority opinion, which upheld Payner's conviction, Justice Lewis F. Powell, Jr., stated, supervisory powers do not "authorize a federal court to suppress otherwise admissible evidence on the ground that it was seized unlawfully from a third party not before the court." Powell and Chief Justice Warren E. Burger chided the IRS for what it did, but agreed the exclusionary rule did not apply in cases like Payner's. Justice Thurgood Marshall criticized the majority for letting the government "invade one person's Fourth Amendment rights in order to obtain evidence against another person."

United States v. Salvucci, 100 S. Ct. 2547 (1980)

In *United States v. Salvucci*, the Supreme Court ruled 7–2 that people charged with illegal possession do not have a right to automatically challenge police searches. In the case, two Massachusetts residents were convicted of mail theft when police searched an apartment rented by one of the men's mothers and discovered stolen checks. The men got their convictions overturned on the grounds that the search was not legal. They based their challenges on a 1960s ruling that granted defendants "automatic Fourth Amendment standing" to question the legality of searches leading to their arrest.

Justice William H. Rehnquist stated the defendants in *Salvucci* could challenge the search's legality only if they could show "an expectation of privacy in the premises searched."

Illinois v. Gates, 103 S. Ct. 2317 (1983)

In *Illinois v. Gates*, Lance and Susan Gates of Bloomingdale, Illinois, were accused of drug trafficking after police followed an anonymous tip and obtained a search warrant for the Gates residence. They found marijuana, cocaine, drug paraphernalia, and firearms. State courts did not admit the evidence on the grounds that police lacked enough probable cause to get a search warrant.

The Supreme Court ruled 6–3 to allow police to get search warrants based on anonymous tips, but did not consider whether there is a good faith exception to the exclusionary rule. The decision overturned precedents from 1964 and 1969 that required judges to make sure anonymous tips were valid prior to issuing search warrants. Justice William H. Rehnquist, who wrote the majority opinion, said the issue of admissibility when police act in good faith should first come up in state courts.

Justices William J. Brennan, Jr., Thurgood Marshall, and John Paul Stevens dissented. Brennan and Marshall joined to criticize the majority's "overly permissive attitude towards police practices in derogation of the rights secured by the Fourth Amendment." Stevens in a separate dissent stated that the police in *Gates* presented flawed information. He wrote, "No one knows who the informant in this case was, or what motivated him or her to write the note."

Nix v. Williams, 104 S. Ct. 2501 (1984)

In *Nix v. Williams*, the Supreme Court unanimously determined there is an "inevitable discovery" exception to the exclusionary rule.

In 1977, Robert Anthony Williams was the defendant in the *Brewer v. Williams* case, in which the justices voted 5–4 to overturn Williams's conviction for the murder of a ten-year-old Iowa girl. They deemed the conviction invalid because police had illegally questioned Williams about the location of the girl's body. Williams sat through a second trial and was convicted again. Defense attorneys challenged the second conviction based on the idea that police would not have found evidence (the girl's body and clothes) without their earlier interrogation. A federal appeals court overturned the second conviction.

In *Nix v. Williams*, the Supreme Court reversed that decision with Chief Justice Warren E. Burger, who dissented in the earlier case, writing the opinion. He maintained that since searchers had been close to the girl's body when Williams told police where she was, the evidence was valid. "If the prosecution can establish by a preponderance of the evidence that the information ultimately or inevitably would have been discovered by lawful means—here the volunteers' search—then the deterrence rationale has so little basis that the evidence should be received. Anything less would reject logic, experience and common sense."

United States v. Leon, 468 U.S. 981 (1984) and Massachusetts v. Sheppard, 468 U.S. 897 (1984)

In two cases, Supreme Court justices decided that there is a good faith exception to the exclusionary rule. In the 6–3 *United States v. Leon* case, a magistrate issued a warrant to allow narcotics agents to raid Antonio Leon's Sunset Canyon, California, home. They found cocaine, and Leon and four others were indicted on charges of drug-trafficking conspiracy. A federal judge threw out the indictment because the magistrate had issued the warrant without enough probable cause, as required by the Fourth Amendment.

In the 7–2 *Massachusetts v. Sheppard* case, Roxbury, Massachusetts, police searched Osborne Sheppard's apartment. Sheppard was the chief suspect in a murder case, and police discovered enough evidence to score a conviction. The Massachusetts Supreme Judicial Court, however, reversed the conviction as the search warrant was the type used for drug searches and did not correctly identify Sheppard's apartment as the one to be searched.

The high court justices used *Leon* to express their opinions about both cases. They held that the exclusionary rule was "judge-made" and not intrinsic to the Fourth Amendment. The magistrate, not police, made the mistake. "When an officer acting with objective good faith has obtained a search warrant from a judge or magistrate and acted within its scope," wrote Justice Byron R. White for the majority, there is "no police illegality and thus nothing to deter. Particularly when law enforcement officers have acted in objective good faith or their transgressions have been minor, the magnitude of the benefit conferred on such guilty defendants offends basic concepts of the criminal justice system."

In the main dissent in *Leon*, Justice William J. Brennan criticized the majority for their "gradual but determined strangulation" of the exclusionary rule. He considered the decision an expedient solution to the public demand to fight crime. "In the long run, however, we as a society pay a heavy price for such expediency."

Maryland v. Garrison, 107 S. Ct. 1013 (1987)

In a 6–3 decision in *Maryland v. Garrison*, the Supreme Court ruled that although improper, evidence obtained by law enforcement through an "honest" mistake is admissible in court. In the case, police had a warrant to search an apartment but did not realize there were two apartments. Not until after they found drugs and drug paraphernalia did they discover there were two apartments and they had unknowingly searched the wrong one. The Supreme Court's decision reinstated the conviction and 15-year prison term of the defendant, Harold Garrison.

Ornelas v. United States, 116 S. Ct. 1657 (1996)

The Supreme Court ruled 8–1 in *Ornelas v. United States* that defendants challenging convictions on the grounds that they were victims of improper police searches are entitled to new reviews of their cases by appellate court judges. In doing so, the justices ordered a new hearing for two California men, Saul Ornelas and Ismael Ornelas-Ledesma, who were convicted of drug possession in 1993.

Acting without a warrant, police discovered several pounds of cocaine hidden in the door panel of the men's car in a hotel parking lot in Milwaukee, Wisconsin. Police are allowed to search without warrants if they have probable cause to believe a crime is occurring. The officers in this case insisted their search was valid because the two men fit a police profile of drug traffickers they obtained through the Drug Enforcement Administration, which they believed gave them probable cause.

The men appealed the conviction because they said their Fourth Amendment protection against unreasonable searches was violated when they were detained, and they requested that the drug evidence be suppressed. A trial judge rejected the appeal. The Seventh U.S. Circuit Court of Appeals in Chicago upheld the trial judge's opinion because it did not believe the judge made a "clear error," which would have required the appellate court to set aside the trial judge's ruling. In using the "deferential standard," the appellate court judges did not need to conduct their own review of the facts of the case.

In writing the majority opinion of the Supreme Court, Chief Justice William H. Rehnquist asserted that the appellate judges must conduct a new review of the facts. A "de novo (new) review tends to unify precedent and will come closer to providing law enforcement officers with a defined set of rules" to follow in what Rehnquist called a "fluid" area of law. When determining reasonable suspicion or probable cause, reviewers should learn the historical facts preceding a stop and search and whether, accounting for law and fact, an objectively reasonable police officer would consider these historical facts to justify reasonable suspicion or probable cause. Also, ordering appellate courts to thoroughly scrutinize improper search claims would encourage law enforcement to obtain warrants before conducting searches. Justice Antonin Scalia wrote the sole dissenting opinion in the case.

Fourth Amendment Cases

Rooted in American history, the Fourth Amendment guards against unreasonable searches and seizures and specifies the conditions for issuing warrants. It may be looked at in conjunction with the exclusionary rule cases mentioned previously, as many of those cases grew out of what the Court deemed inconsistent following of the Fourth Amendment.

Dunaway v. New York, 99 S. Ct. 2248 (1979)

The Supreme Court decided 6–2 in *Dunaway v. New York* that police cannot detain criminal suspects for questioning unless they have the probable cause to justify an arrest. In the case, a New York state court upheld Rochester resident Irving Dunaway's murder conviction. Police, who suspected him to be the murderer, detained him for questioning although they did not have enough evidence to arrest him. Dunaway waived his right to an attorney and his right to remain silent and said things that linked him to the murder.

The Supreme Court decided that police had respected Dunaway's Fifth Amendment rights but violated his Fourth Amendment rights via the unreasonable searches and seizures ban when they brought him to the police station to question him. On behalf of the majority, Justice William J. Brennan, Jr., compared police taking Dunaway to the police station to a seizure "in the Fourth Amendment sense. . . ."

Chief Justice Warren E. Burger and Justice William H. Rehnquist dissented. Rehnquist argued that Dunaway was not detained involuntarily and that, based on the specifics of the case, the murder conviction was justified. Justice Lewis F. Powell, Jr., did not participate in the ruling.

Hudson v. Palmer, 104 S. Ct. 3194 (1984) and Block v. Rutherford, 104 S. Ct. 3227 (1984)

In the 5–4 *Hudson v. Palmer* and 6–3 *Block v. Rutherford* cases, Supreme Court justices ruled that prison inmates have no constitutional right to privacy in their cells and that prison officials may limit physical contact between prisoners and visitors. The majority in the first case wrote that Fourth Amendment unreasonable searches and seizures protections do not extend to prisoners and in the second that jail administrators may consider security as a reason for not allowing inmates contact with family or friends.

Fifth Amendment Cases

Included in the Bill of Rights in 1791, the Fifth Amendment contains several principles overseeing the prosecution of cases. As with other amendments, the Supreme Court's interpretation of the Fifth Amendment has evolved, as the following cases illustrate.

Malloy v. Hogan, 378 U.S. 1 (1964)

The Supreme Court ruled 5–4 that states are bound by the Fifth Amendment to respect an accused person's privilege against self-incrimination. In the case, Malloy pleaded guilty to participating in an illegal gambling operation in Connecticut. The Connecticut Superior Court sentenced him to a year in jail. After 90 days, his term was suspended and he was put on probation for two years. During this time, Malloy was called to testify in a state inquiry regarding gambling and other crimes. Malloy did not answer questions concerning his earlier arrest and conviction and cited his Fifth Amendment protection against self-incrimination. He was held in contempt and put in jail until he was willing to answer. State courts rejected his habeas corpus petition, so the Supreme Court took up the case.

Rejecting a long-held view, the justices ruled that Fifth Amendment protections against self-incrimination extend to states via the Fourteenth Amendment's Due Process Clause. The majority held that it was time to realize that "the American system of criminal prosecution is accusatorial, not inquisitorial, and that the Fifth Amendment privilege is its essential mainstay."

The decision overturned *Twining v. New Jersey*, a 1908 case in which a trial judge instructed the jury that the defendants' refusal to testify on their own behalf could be taken into account when finding guilt or innocence. The Supreme Court then held that such instructions infringed on the privilege against self-incrimination but that it was a federal provision and did not apply to the states.

The ruling also overturned *Adamson v. California*, a 1947 case in which justices again decided that the Bill of Rights did not apply to the states and that a prosecutor who called the jury's attention to the defendant's refusal to testify did not violate the Fifth Amendment's privilege against self-incrimination.

Miranda v. Arizona, 384 U.S. 436 (1966)

Considered the peak of the Warren Court's period of outlining defendants' rights, *Miranda v. Arizona* considered the admissibility of a suspect's confession when that confession is obtained without the suspect's being informed of his rights. Prior to *Miranda*, state courts based a confession's admissibility on whether it was secured voluntarily (which might involve some pressure from the police) or whether it was coerced (which involved heavy-handed tactics by the police). But those definitions were too vague, and *Miranda* presented a good platform for the Court to set down across-the-board standards for confessions.

In the case, 23-year-old Ernesto Miranda, a poor high school dropout, was arrested at his home and taken to a Phoenix, Arizona, police station, where he was identified by the victim of a rape-kidnapping. He was taken to an interrogation room and questioned about the crime. He initially professed innocence but, after two hours of questioning, signed a written confession. The confession was accepted as evidence at his trial, and he was convicted of kidnapping and rape. Police admitted they did not advise Miranda of his rights to counsel with an attorney before answering any questions or to have an attorney present during questioning.

In deciding the case and developing the Miranda warnings, the Supreme Court considered three issues:

1. The Fifth Amendment privilege against self-incrimination is present outside of court and other formal proceedings and protects citizens from being compelled to incriminate themselves. Therefore, it applies to police interrogations after a person has been taken into custody.
2. A person taken into police custody and subjected to the persuasive techniques described in police interrogation manuals can only be under coercion to speak. Such coercive tactics are at odds with the privilege against self-incrimination. Unless steps are taken to dispel the inherent coercion involved in police questioning, no statement obtained from a person under such circumstances is admissible.
3. While the Constitution does not require use of any particular method to dispel such coercion, the government must use a method at least as effective as the Miranda warnings before questioning a suspect, and the suspect must effectively waive his rights for his statement to be allowed as evidence.

The Miranda warnings are as follows: you have the right to remain silent; anything you say can and will be used against you; you have the right to talk to a lawyer before being questioned and to have him present while being questioned; and if you cannot afford a lawyer, one will be provided for you before questioning if you would like. Miranda does not demand that a person taken into custody first speak with a lawyer or have a lawyer present for his waiver of constitutional rights to be valid. At least theoretically, the waiver must be knowing and voluntary. The police need not give the warnings or secure waivers with a disinterested person present. They do not need to tape-record the process either. Finally, Miranda permits police to question people at the scene of a crime without providing warnings. They also may interview a suspect at home or at his workplace as long as the context of the questioning does not restrict the person's ability to end the meeting.

Whalen v. United States, 100 S. Ct. 1432 (1980)

By a 7–2 margin in *Whalen v. United States*, the Supreme Court decided courts are not allowed to impose consecutive prison sentences for different violations in a single crime unless authorized specifically by law to do so. The ruling overturned multiple sentences given to a man convicted in a rape-related murder. The sentences were based on the District of Columbia code, which does not permit multiple punishments for this kind of crime, according to the majority opinion.

In the rape-murder case, the defendant received sentences both for the rape (15 years to life) and the murder (20 years to life)—the end result. The sentences were to run consecutively. Supreme Court justices said that sentences in this type of crime should only account for the end result. Multiple sentences violate the Fifth Amendment's protections against double jeopardy.

Jenkins v. Anderson, 100 S. Ct. 2124 (1980)

In a 7–2 decision in *Jenkins v. Anderson*, the Supreme Court upheld the murder conviction of Dennis Jenkins, a Michigan resident, when the justices ruled that he had to answer questions in court regarding his failure to talk voluntarily to police before his arrest. The majority opinion stated that a defendant testifying on his own behalf throws off "the cloak of silence" and must help to advance "the truth-finding function of the criminal trial." The majority contrasted this with the post-Miranda period following arrest when, if a defendant refuses to answer questions for the police, he is not allowed to be cross-examined about his refusal.

Estelle v. Smith, 101 S. Ct. 1866 (1981) and Edwards v. Arizona, 101 S. Ct. 1880 (1981)

In *Estelle v. Smith* and *Edwards v. Arizona*, the Supreme Court voted unanimously to expand Fifth Amendment protections against self-incrimination. In *Estelle*, the justices ruled that defendants suspected of a capital crime may refuse a psychiatric exam if the examining psychiatrist's testimony could be used against them during the sentencing phase of the trial. The decision does not apply to cases in which defendants' mental competency is questionable.

In *Edwards*, the justices ruled that once the accused invokes the right to counsel, any further comments made to police are not to be considered a waiver of that right.

Tibbs v. Florida, 102 S. Ct. 2211 (1982)

In *Tibbs v. Florida*, the Supreme Court decided 5–4 that criminal defendants whose convictions are overturned on appeal may be retried when the appeals court bases its decision on the "weight of the evidence." In the majority opinion, Justice Sandra Day O'Connor wrote that when appellate courts use the "weight of evidence" reasoning to overturn a guilty verdict, defendants may be retried without violation of their double jeopardy protections. "A reversal on this ground, unlike a reversal based on insufficient evidence, does not mean that acquittal was the only proper verdict . . .," she wrote. "Instead, the appellate court sits as a '13th juror' and disagrees with the jury's resolution of the conflicting testimony. This difference of opinion no more signifies acquittal than does a disagreement among the jurors themselves."

For the dissent, Justice Byron R. White wrote, " . . . The state failed to prove the defendant guilty in accordance with the evidentiary requirements of state law"; therefore, there should not be a new trial. White was joined by Justices Thurgood Marshall, Harry A. Blackmun, and William J. Brennan, Jr.

New York v. Quarles, 104 S. Ct. 2626 (1984)

In *New York v. Quarles*, the Supreme Court ruled 5–4 that police do not have to issue Miranda warnings to criminal suspects if, by doing so, they would compromise public safety. In the case, officers cornered a New York City rape suspect, Benjamin Quarles, in a supermarket and saw that he wore an empty gun holster. The police asked Quarles about the location of his gun without telling him of his Miranda rights. Quarles answered their questions. Three New York state courts ruled that the gun and Quarles's answers could not be used as evidence to convict him of weapons violations.

The Supreme Court majority decided that "concern for public safety must be paramount to adherence to the literal language of the prophylactic rules enunciated in *Miranda*" in such situations. Justice Sandra Day O'Connor dissented on the grounds that a "public safety exception unnecessarily blurs the edges of the clear line heretofore established, and makes Miranda's requirements more difficult to understand." In another dissent, Justice Thurgood Marshall wrote that the majority ignored the Fifth Amendment by allowing "the introduction of coerced self-incriminating statements in criminal prosecutions."

Oregon v. Elstad, 105 S. Ct 1285 (1985)

In a 6–3 decision in *Oregon v. Elstad*, the Supreme Court ruled that courts may admit confessions even when suspects confess before they are read their rights and then voluntarily and knowingly confess a second time after they are given Miranda warnings. In the case, the suspect told police of his presence during a burglary before they advised him of his rights. After they told him of his rights, the suspect confessed a second time in writing. Although the second, written confession was allowed as evidence at the trial and the suspect was convicted, a state appeals court reversed the decision on the grounds that authorities could use the initial confession to coerce the suspect into a second confession.

Writing for the majority, Justice Sandra Day O'Connor stated that "it is an unwarranted extension of *Miranda* to hold that a simple failure to administer the warnings, unaccompanied by any actual coercion or other circumstances calculated to undermine the suspect's ability to exercise his free will, so taints the investigatory process that a subsequent voluntary and informed waiver is ineffective for some indeterminate period." O'Connor agreed that the first, pre–Miranda warnings confession should not be allowed and based admission of the second one "on whether it is knowingly and voluntarily made."

Baltimore v. Bouknight, 110 S. Ct. 900 (1990)

The Supreme Court ruled 7–2 in *Baltimore v. Bouknight* that Jacqueline Bouknight could not use her Fifth Amendment right against self-incrimination to resist telling authorities the location of her son, who was abused and believed to be dead. In the majority opinion, Justice Sandra Day O'Connor wrote that the government authority in the case involved "noncriminal regulatory powers," not the issue of criminal activity. If Bouknight were to be prosecuted on criminal charges, the prosecutor's use of any self-incriminating comments could be limited.

Arizona v. Fulminante, 111 S. Ct. 1246 (1991)

The Supreme Court in *Arizona v. Fulminante* ruled 5–4 that using a coerced confession in a criminal case does not automatically suspend a conviction. The ruling changed the Court's stance set forth in the 1967 *Chapman v. California* case—that a coerced or involuntary confession is never a "harmless error" and always acts as a basis for negating a criminal conviction. *Arizona* states that such confessions are "harmless errors" as long as a guilty verdict can be obtained through other evidence at the trial.

Sixth Amendment Cases

These Sixth Amendment cases examine how aspects of criminal cases have been handled and how the Supreme Court has decided problems that have arisen with their handling.

Brewer v. Williams, 97 S. Ct. 1232 (1977)

In *Brewer v. Williams*, Supreme Court justices ruled 5–4 to affirm the overturned conviction of Robert Anthony Williams based on Williams's lack of counsel when he incriminated himself to police. In the case, ten-year-old Pamela Powers disappeared on Christmas Eve 1968 from the Des Moines, Iowa, YMCA, where she was watching a wrestling tournament with her parents. Williams had been staying at the YMCA and was arrested in Davenport, Iowa, after witnesses told police they had seen him leave with a large bundle. At his arrest, police informed him of his Miranda rights. After his arraignment on abduction charges, he had to be returned to Des Moines. Williams's Davenport attorney repeatedly asked police to allow him to accompany them on the 160-mile drive back to Des Moines. Although police refused the attorney's requests, they promised that they would not try to question Williams during the trip.

Cletus Leaming, a Des Moines detective traveling with Williams, started a conversation with him. Leaming said that a heavy snowfall had been forecast and, knowing Williams's professed religious leanings, added that the snow might cover up Powers's body so that even Williams would not be able to find it and that she deserved a "Christian burial." Williams then took police to a place near Mitchellville where Powers was concealed. An autopsy showed she had been sexually abused and asphyxiated.

Williams's attorneys objected to the introduction of evidence about how the body had been found, and prosecutors agreed that Det. Leaming's "burial speech" was the equivalent of an interrogation.

Although Williams's conviction was affirmed by the Iowa Supreme Court, a federal district court and the Eighth U.S. Circuit Court of Appeals decided the conviction was not valid and ordered a second trial. The upper courts based their rulings on a violation of Williams's Miranda rights and his right to an attorney after a judicial proceeding had started.

Iowa appealed to the U.S. Supreme Court, which sided with the upper courts. The justices did not base their decision on the Miranda issues but rather looked at the violation of Williams's Sixth Amendment right to counsel. Justice Potter Stewart cited a 1938 decision that the right to an attorney continues until the accused "intentionally" relinquishes it. Justices William J. Brennan, Jr., John Paul Stevens, and Lewis F. Powell, Jr., joined Stewart.

Justice Thurgood Marshall wrote a concurring opinion. Regarding the issues in the case, he stated that "given the ingenuity of the Iowa prosecutors," he did not believe "very much that there (was) any chance a dangerous criminal (would) be loosed on the streets." He also stated that "the heinous nature of the crime (was) no excuse, as the dissenters would have it, for condoning knowing and intentional police transgressions of constitutional rights of a defendant."

Chief Justice Warren E. Burger and Justices Byron R. White, Harry A. Blackmun, and William H. Rehnquist filed dissents, denouncing the majority's take as "utterly senseless" and stating that police had done "nothing 'wrong.'"

Gannett Co. v. DePasquale, 443 U.S. 368 (1979)

In *Gannett Co. v. DePasquale*, Supreme Court justices decided 5–4 that the public and press do not have a constitutional right to be present at pretrial criminal hearings, thereby giving judges leeway to close their courtrooms if they believe the accused's due process rights would be harmed by the publicity.

Rhode Island v. Innis, 99 S. Ct. 1277 (1980)

Thomas J. Innis was convicted on kidnapping and murder charges in the death of a taxi driver. Police picked up Innis who heard the officers talking about a sawed-off shotgun, the weapon with which the taxi driver was shot. They mentioned that it was probably in an area where handicapped children were playing. Innis then led the officers to the gun. The Rhode Island Supreme Court considered the officers' conversation tantamount to an interrogation. The Supreme Court voted 5–3 to reverse the decision, stating that Innis volunteered to show the officers where the gun was because he did not want any children to find it and injure themselves. The officers' conversation regarding the whereabouts of the gun could be considered work-related, not an attempt to extract information from Innis.

Strickland v. Washington, 466 U.S. 668 (1984)

For the first time, the Supreme Court ruled on the definition of ineffective counsel. In *Strickland v. Washington*, the 8–1 vote reversed a Florida appeals court that had overturned the death sentence of a confessed murderer. The appeals court found that the defense attorney had not examined all the ways of defending the accused against a capital sentence, but the high court determined the attorney's efforts to be reasonable.

Writing for the majority, Justice Sandra Day O'Connor stated, "The benchmark for judging any claim of ineffectiveness must be whether a counsel's conduct so undermined the proper functioning of the adversarial process that the trial cannot be relied on as having produced a just result." In successful appeals based on ineffective counsel, defendants must show that their attorneys' performance "fell below an objective standard of reasonableness" linked to "identified acts or omissions." Defendants must look at the overall circumstances and not just "second-guess" defense strategy. Secondly, defendants must demonstrate "a reasonable probability that, but for counsel's unprofessional errors, the result of the proceeding would have been different." A reasonable probability, according to O'Connor, is "a probability sufficient to undermine confidence in the outcome."

Justice William J. Brennan, Jr., concurred with O'Connor's analysis but dissented because he opposes the death penalty.

Ake v. Oklahoma, 105 S. Ct. 1087 (1985)

In an 8–1 decision, the Supreme Court ruled that states must provide free psychiatric care to defendants who invoke the insanity defense in their guilty pleas. Justice Thurgood Marshall, who wrote the majority opinion in *Ake v. Oklahoma*, viewed the decision as an extension of *Gideon v. Wainwright*, the 1963 Supreme Court case that established entitlement to competent counsel for poor defendants. In the current case, Glen Burton Ake was convicted of murdering a minister and his wife. After undergoing a court-ordered psychiatric examination, he was diagnosed as a paranoid schizophrenic. He was treated and deemed competent to stand trial. Oklahoma courts did not, however, provide Ake with a psychiatrist—someone he did not have the money to hire—to help him present his insanity defense, although he did have a court-appointed attorney.

In the majority opinion, Justice Marshall wrote that 41 states already provide psychiatric expertise to defendants who cannot afford such witnesses. Making such expertise available is as elementary as supplying an indigent defendant with counsel. The basic element is that "when a state brings its judicial power to bear on an indigent defendant in a criminal proceeding, it must take steps to assure that the defendant has a fair opportunity to present his defense."

Holbrook v. Flynn, 106 S. Ct. 1340 (1986)

In a unanimous decision in *Holbrook v. Flynn*, the Supreme Court ruled that during a trial, the presence of armed, uniformed guards sitting near defendants does not circumvent defendants' right to a fair trial by giving the impression to jurors that the defendants are dangerous criminals. In their opinion, the justices stated that the "conspicuous" presence of security agents during a trial is not "inherently prejudicial" to defendants. The Court held that although the accused is entitled to a determination of guilt or innocence based solely on the evidence introduced, this doesn't mean every practice tending to single out the accused must be struck down. The noticeable presence of guards needn't be construed as a sign of the defendant's guilt or culpability. The only question concerning something inherently prejudicial is whether there was an unacceptable risk of prejudice. In this case, even if a slight degree of prejudice could be attributed to the troopers' presence, the Court maintained that the state had a legitimate interest in keeping custody over the defendants.

Michigan v. Jackson, 106 S. Ct. 1404 (1986)

The Supreme Court ruled in a 6–3 decision in *Michigan v. Jackson* that law enforcement authorities are not allowed to question defendants at their arraignments once they have asked for legal representation when their attorney is not present. The ruling broadens the 1981 *Edwards v. Arizona* case that prohibits police from interrogating suspects once they invoke their Fifth Amendment rights to remain silent and have an attorney present at questioning. "The Sixth Amendment right to counsel (at arraignment) requires at least as much protection as the Fifth Amendment right to counsel at any custodial interrogation," Justice John Paul Stevens wrote for the majority.

Lockhart v. McCree, 106 S. Ct. 1758 (1986)

In *Lockhart v. McCree*, the Supreme Court ruled 6–3 that strict death penalty opponents may be prohibited from judging capital cases.

The decision overturned the ruling of the federal district court and the U.S. Court of Appeals for the Eighth Circuit that a jury's "death qualification" infringes on a defendant's right to trial by an impartial jury chosen from a cross section of community residents. The courts used studies demonstrating that "death qualified" jurors are more likely to convict.

The *Lockhart* decision narrowed a precedent. In the 1968 case of *Witherspoon v. Illinois*, the court ruled to allow exclusion from a jury only those people who said they could never vote for the death penalty or those with opinions that prevented them from fairly determining guilt or innocence. The ruling applied only to sentencing, not to judging guilt or innocence, in cases in which separate juries were chosen for verdicts and sentencing.

Wheat v. United States, 108 S. Ct. 1692 (1988)

The Supreme Court ruled 5–4 in *Wheat v. United States* that trial judges have "broad latitude" in denying criminal defendants their chosen attorney when the attorney's representation may be a conflict of interest. The defendant in the case was a California drug dealer who wanted to replace his attorney with one who was representing two others connected to the drug ring.

Duckworth v. Eagan, 109 S. Ct. 2875 (1989)

In *Duckworth v. Eagan*, the Supreme Court ruled 5–4 that it is acceptable for police to tell a suspect they cannot provide him an attorney and that if he cannot afford one, one would be appointed "if and when you go to court." The ruling overturned a federal appeals court decision that the warning did not meet the requirements of the 1966 *Miranda v. Arizona* case. The majority viewed the police statement as an invitation for the suspect to ask when he would receive counsel, while those who dissented wrote that the statement leads the suspect to believe that an attorney will not be appointed "until some indeterminate time in the future after questioning."

Michigan v. Lucas, 111 S. Ct. 1743 (1991)

In *Michigan v. Lucas*, the Supreme Court ruled 7–2 that states are allowed at certain times to restrict an accused rapist's ability to provide evidence about his previous sexual relationship with the alleged victim. In the case, the trial court excluded evidence of a past sexual relationship between the defendant, Nolan K. Lucas, and his ex-girlfriend, whom he allegedly raped. Michigan's rape shield law gave defendants ten days after arraignment to tell the court whether they plan to use evidence of past sexual relations with the alleged victim. Lucas had not notified the court about his previous relationship. While the Michigan Court of Appeals ruled in favor of Lucas, citing his Sixth Amendment right to confront his accuser, the Supreme Court sent the case back for more consideration. Justice Sandra Day O'Connor said the Michigan law was "a valid legislation determination that rape victims deserve heightened protection against surprise, harassment and unnecessary invasions of privacy." She added that the deadline might have been too restrictive.

Mu'Min v. Virginia, 111 S. Ct. 1899 (1991)

The Supreme Court holds 5–4 in *Mu'Min v. Virginia* that a judge in a high-profile criminal case need not ask jurors specifically about their knowledge of the crime based on print or broadcast reports. The judge had asked potential jurors whether they had heard about Mu'Min. Eight of 12 jurors in the case said they had heard or read about Dawud Majid Mu'Min, a Virginia prisoner who escaped from a work detail in 1988 and killed a store owner. The judge also asked them whether they had formed an opinion on the case. As a result, two said they could not serve as unbiased jurors, so the judge dismissed them. For the majority, Chief Justice William H. Rehnquist stated: "Whether a trial court decides to put questions about the content of publicity to a potential juror or not, it must make the same decision at the end of the questioning: is this juror to be believed when he says he has not formed an opinion about the case? Questions about the content of publicity to which jurors have been exposed might be helpful in assessing whether a juror is impartial. To be constitutionally compelled, however, it is not enough that such questions might be helpful. Rather, the trial court's failure to ask these questions must render the defendant's trial fundamentally unfair." Justice Thurgood Marshall wrote in his dissenting opinion that the majority decision made the Sixth Amendment's guarantee to a fair trial "a hollow formality."

Eighth Amendment Cases

While the Eighth Amendment covers bail, fines, and cruel and unusual punishment, the bulk of the Supreme Court's activities has come under the third principle. The following cases are examples of the Court's evolving stance on capital punishment.

Furman v. Georgia, 92 S. Ct. 2726 (1972)

The Supreme Court heard four appeals to decide whether the death penalty is cruel and unusual punishment for people who receive murder or rape convictions. The high court also lifted death sentences, but not convictions, of 39 death-row inmates on the basis of automatic exclusion from the juries of people who oppose capital punishment. Justices linked this decision to the 1968 *Witherspoon v. Illinois* case, in which the high court decided that death sentences are unconstitutional when set by juries from which people who broadly oppose capital punishment are excluded.

The case of one of the appellants, John Henry Furman of Savannah, Georgia, who was sentenced to death for the 1968 burglary-related murder of William J. Micke Jr., became the basis for striking down the death penalty under the Eighth Amendment's Cruel and Unusual Punishment Clause. The jury in Furman's case and those of two others convicted of rape had imposed the death penalty without guidelines. The juries, the justices found, had acted randomly, and this randomness was cruel and unusual. Justice William O. Douglas said that juries imposed death mainly on the poor and socially disadvantaged and concluded that the Eighth Amendment could be equated with equal protection principles. Other justices argued that without mandatory death penalties for specific crimes defined by legislatures, execution was cruel and unusual and that its infrequent application usurped the penalty's effectiveness as a deterrent. Justices William Brennan and Thurgood Marshall wrote that the penalty itself is cruel and unusual, as it degrades human dignity and is arbitrarily severe, unnecessary, and offensive to contemporary values.

Gregg v. Georgia, 428 U.S. 153 (1976)

Supreme Court justices affirmed 7–2 the constitutionality of capital punishment in *Gregg v. Georgia*. The ruling upheld the murder conviction of a Georgia man sentenced under a 1972 statute. The justices also decided 7–2 that death penalty provisions in Florida and Texas were acceptable, while striking down 5–4 capital punishment laws in Louisiana and North Carolina, two states that made the death penalty mandatory for certain crimes.

Regarding the Georgia case, Justice Potter Stewart wrote that the fact that several state legislatures (35) had again enacted death penalty laws since the 1972 Supreme Court decision in *Furman v. Georgia* undercuts the argument that "standards of decency had evolved to the point where capital punishment no longer could be tolerated." Capital punishment is "an expression of society's moral outrage at particularly offensive conduct," he stated, and as such it is "essential" to a society in which citizens "rely on legal processes rather than self-help to vindicate their wrongs."

In answering the high court's concerns about the death penalty's application, Stewart stated that in *Gregg*, Georgia's new procedures "focus the jury's attention on the particularized nature of the crime and the particularized characteristics of the individual defendant." Under Georgia's capital punishment law, juries must determine "at least one statutory aggravating factor before it may impose a penalty of death." This means juries cannot arbitrarily sentence a defendant to death. The law also requires the Georgia Supreme Court to review death sentences, an "additional assurance that the concerns that prompted our decision in *Furman* are not present to any significant degree in the Georgia procedure applied here."

Justices Lewis F. Powell and John Paul Stevens subscribed to Stewart's opinions, and Justices Byron R. White, William H. Rehnquist, and Harry A. Blackmun and Chief Justice Warren E. Burger concurred to sustain the Georgia law. Justices Thurgood Marshall and William J. Brennan, Jr., dissented, holding that the death penalty is excessive.

Wainwright v. Witt, 105 S. Ct. 844 (1985)

In *Wainwright v. Witt*, Supreme Court justices voted 7–2 to reverse an appeals court ruling and to approve the exclusion of a potential juror who had doubts about the death penalty in a murder case. Basing its decision on a 1968 Supreme Court ruling that allowed prosecutors to dismiss jurors if it was "unmistakably clear" that they would not hesitate to rule out death sentences, the Eleventh U.S. Circuit Court of Appeals overturned the death penalty for a child murderer, as the sentence did not meet the standard set forth in the high court's previous decision.

In *Wainwright v. Witt*, the majority of justices deemed the 1968 requirement too rigid, demanding that prosecutors keep jurors who may be against capital punishment and in favor of defendants. Justices William J. Brennan, Jr., and Thurgood Marshall based their dissent on the idea that the state, not defendants, "bear[s] the risk of a less than wholly neutral jury when perfect neutrality cannot, as in this situation it most assuredly cannot, be achieved."

Ford v. Wainwright, 477 U.S. 399 (1986)

The Supreme Court ruled 5–4 in *Ford v. Wainwright* that executing an insane criminal violates the Eighth Amendment's ban on cruel and unusual punishment. As part of the same case, the justices decided 7–2 that Florida's procedure of having three state-selected psychiatrists assess a death-row prisoner's sanity and report their conclusions to the governor, who makes a final decision, was inadequate. In another 7–2 vote, they ruled that the prisoner's attorney must be allowed to present evidence to the official charged with making the last assessment.

Booth v. Maryland, 182 U.S. 496 (1987)

The Supreme Court rules 5–4 in *Booth v. Maryland* that "victim impact statements" during the sentencing phase of capital cases violate the Eighth Amendment's protection against cruel and unusual punishment. (Victim impact statements describe the effect of a crime on the victim and the victim's family.) In the case, John Booth was convicted of killing Irvin and Rose Bronstein during a robbery in their home. The prosecutor called for the death penalty, and under Maryland law, Booth decided to have the jury rather than the judge determine the sentence. The presentence report contained information about Booth and about the victims and how their death affected their surviving family.

Given to the jury, the written statement emphasized the Bronsteins' "outstanding characteristics," their close relationship, their number of friends, and the size of the funeral, as well as the emotional and personal problems family members had suffered since the murders. Many family members believed that Booth could not be rehabilitated or forgiven. Booth's defense counsel rejected the impact statement based on its irrelevance, inflammatory nature, and violation of the Eighth Amendment.

Booth was sentenced to die for Irvin Bronstein's murder and sentenced to life in prison for Rose Bronstein's murder. The state court of appeals upheld the sentence based on the impact statement's factual account of the effects of the murders on the Bronstein family. But the Supreme Court reversed the decision based on its violation of the Eighth Amendment. In the Court's view, the victim impact statement was not relevant to Booth's culpability and injected arbitrariness into the jurors' decision. The family's opinions inflamed the jurors who already knew about the anger and grief a murder victim's family feels.

The dissenting justices believed defendants could be liable for the harm they cause, including the effects of murder on the victims' family. They also believed that victims should be viewed as individuals whose death is a loss to society and particularly to the victims' family.

Sumner v. Shuman, 107 S. Ct. 2716 (1987)

The Supreme Court ruled 6–3 that mandatory death sentences violate the Eighth and Fourteenth Amendments. In *Sumner v. Shuman*, the defendant, who was serving time for a murder conviction when he killed a fellow inmate, was sentenced to death under a Nevada law requiring such a sentence for those who murder someone while serving a life term without parole. Nevada repealed the law in 1977. Raymond W. Shuman was one of three death-row inmates in the United States to be sentenced under such a law. The majority of justices stated that defendants facing a death sentence have the right to cite any relevant mitigating evidence and that this right is circumvented by a mandatory sentencing law.

South Carolina v. Gathers, 109 S. Ct. 2207 (1989)

In *South Carolina v. Gathers*, the Supreme Court ruled 5–4 to uphold its stance on the inadmissibility of victim impact remarks. In the case, a prosecutor said capital punishment was acceptable because the victim was "a religious man and a registered voter," but the majority opinion stated that "a sentence of death must be related to the moral culpability of the defendant." The decision upheld the 1987 *Booth v. Maryland* ruling.

In *South Carolina v. Gathers*, a majority of justices again ruled that information about the victim had no connection with the defendant's moral culpability and expanded victim information to include information presented by prosecutors. The prosecutor in the case had been allowed to read from religious tracts and prayer cards the victim was carrying at the time of the murder. The prosecutor had also inferred that the victim was a registered voter. The majority determined that this information amounted to a victim impact statement and disallowed it at sentencing. The dissenting justices again would have admitted such victim impact comments.

Penry v. Lynaugh, 109 S. Ct. 2934 (1989) and Stanford v. Kentucky, 109 S. Ct. 2969 (1989)

The Eighth Amendment's protection against cruel and unusual punishment does not stop execution of mentally retarded murderers or murderers who were minors when they committed murder, the Supreme Court rules in separate 5–4 decisions in *Penry v. Lynaugh* and *Stanford v. Kentucky.*

In *Penry*, justices upheld the death sentence of Johnny Paul Penry, a 22-year-old in 1979 when he committed murder. Penry had an intelligence quotient of 54 and the mental age of a six-and-one-half-year-old child. By a second 5–4 vote, however, justices decided that mental retardation must be taken into account as a mitigating factor when imposing death. They sent the case back for resentencing.

In *Stanford*, Kevin Stanford was 17 when he committed murder in 1981. Justice Antonin Scalia, who wrote the majority opinion, stated that "neither a historical nor a modern societal consensus" exists to prohibit capital punishment for crimes committed when convicts are juveniles.

Payne v. Tennessee, 111 S. Ct. 2597 (1991)

In a 6–3 decision in *Payne v. Tennessee*, the Supreme Court ruled that victims or their families may make victim impact statements during the sentencing phase of capital cases. The Court—with a new makeup of justices—overturned two precedents, the 1987 *Booth v. Maryland* case and the 1989 *South Carolina v. Gathers* case.

In *Payne*, Charisse Christopher, 28, and her two children, Nicholas, 3, and Lacie, 2, were stabbed several times by Pervis Tyrone Payne, who used a butcher knife. Payne's girlfriend lived across the hall from the Christophers. Without invitation, Payne came into the Christophers' apartment after he had been drinking for several hours, using cocaine, and reading pornography. Charisse Christopher's refusal of his sexual advances sparked his violent outbreak. The apartment was covered with blood when police arrived. Charisse and Lacie were dead, but Nicholas, whose wounds extended from the front to the back of his body, survived.

Payne was convicted on two counts of first-degree murder and one count of assault with intent to commit murder. During sentencing, four witnesses testified to Payne's good character, lack of criminal history, abstinence from drinking and using drugs, and mental handicap based on a low IQ score. Charisse Christopher's mother, in violation of *Booth* and *Gathers*, testified to Nicholas's reaction to the crime. She said Nicholas "missed his mother and sister, worried about them, and did not understand why they did not come home." The prosecutor included this testimony in the closing argument and asked jurors to concentrate on the victims, not the "alleged good reputation of the defendant." The jury sentenced Payne to death.

The state supreme court ruled that while Nicholas's grandmother's testimony was not relevant, it did not serve as a basis for unconstitutional sentencing of the death penalty. However, the court also ruled that Nicholas's physical and mental condition when he was left to die were relevant to Payne's culpability.

The U.S. Supreme Court upheld the ruling of the Tennessee Supreme Court, citing dissenting opinions from *Booth* and *Gathers*. The ruling opinion quoted Justice Byron White's dissent in *Booth*: "The State has a legitimate interest in counteracting the mitigating evidence which the defendant is entitled to put in, by reminding the sentencer that just as the murderer should be considered as an individual, so too the victim is an individual whose death represents a unique loss to society and in particular to his family."

The justices left it up to state legislatures to decide the bases upon which a death sentence may be imposed and stated that defendants would have recourse through the Fourth Amendment Due Process Clause if highly prejudicial evidence resulted in an unfair trial. A lot of the evidence questioned in *Booth* would already have been heard during the trial's guilt phase. The high court also stated that juries do not have to determine the worth of different victims, that the purpose of victim impact statements is not to promote comparisons between victims' worth.

In his dissent in *Payne*, Justice John Paul Stevens stated the Court "ventures into uncharted seas of irrelevance" when it concludes that prosecutors "may introduce evidence that sheds no light on the defendant's guilt or moral culpability, and thus serves no purpose other than to encourage jurors to decide in favor of death rather than life on the basis of their emotions rather than reason."

Harmelin v. Michigan, 111 S. Ct. 2680 (1991)

Ruling 5–4, the Supreme Court decided that a Michigan law mandating life imprisonment with no chance of parole for possession of 650 grams of cocaine did not violate the Eighth Amendment's guarantee against cruel and unusual punishment. In the case of *Harmelin v. Michigan*, Chief Justice William H. Rehnquist wrote for the majority that the Eighth Amendment's "proportionality principle" applies only in capital punishment cases. In a second opinion, Justice Anthony M. Kennedy wrote that the Eighth Amendment does guard against "grossly disproportionate" sentences, but that given the amount of cocaine (about one and a half pounds), applying the safeguard is "false to the point of absurdity."

Fourteenth Amendment Cases

The Fourteenth Amendment grew out of the aftermath of the Civil War. It was passed to ensure that all citizens be afforded equal protection of the law. In the realm of criminal justice, it has been used by the Supreme Court to gradually impose the same restrictions that traditionally applied to the federal government—under the Fourth, Fifth, and Sixth Amendments—to the states.

Bordenkircher v. Hayes, 98 S. Ct. 663 (1978)

The Supreme Court ruled 5–4 in *Bordenkircher v. Hayes* that prosecutors are allowed to threaten defendants with second, more serious indictments if they refuse to plead guilty to a lesser charge. In the case, Paul L. Hayes, who had two prior felony convictions, was indicted for forging an $88.30 check in 1973 in Lexington, Kentucky. A prosecutor gave him two choices—plead guilty or be charged under the state's Habitual Criminal Act. Pleading guilty on the charge, Hayes could face two to ten years in prison (the prosecutor would recommend a five-year sentence). But under the Habitual Criminal Act, anyone over 18 who is deemed guilty of a third felony after two previous felony convictions automatically is sentenced to life in prison. At the trial, Hayes was found guilty and received a life sentence.

An appeals court reversed the conviction, basing its judgment on the prosecutor's deprivation of Hayes's due process rights. But the Supreme Court sustained Hayes's conviction, as the prosecutor had been open with Hayes regarding the alternatives of foregoing trial and facing the charges. Plea bargaining is acceptable as long as the accused is free to take or leave the prosecutor's offer.

Schall v. Martin, 104 S. Ct. 2403 (1984)

In *Schall v. Martin*, the Supreme Court ruled 6–3 that states may detain juvenile criminal suspects before trial without violating the Constitution. Detainment is used to prevent suspects from committing more crimes while awaiting trial. *Schall* originated in New York where state law permits judges to order juveniles 15 years old or under to be held up to 17 days if they have been charged with a serious crime and up to 6 days if charged with a minor crime. Three juveniles charged with robbery initiated a class action suit based on the idea that the preventive detention law violated the Fourteenth Amendment's Due Process Clause. The appeals court in the case ruled that the law punished the accused without a trial.

The Supreme Court reversed the decision. Writing for the majority, Justice William H. Rehnquist stated that preventive detention serves a legitimate regulatory purpose and is "compatible with the 'fundamental fairness'" that the Due Process Clause demands in juvenile proceedings.

Batson v. Kentucky, 106 S. Ct. 1712 (1986)

In *Batson v. Kentucky*, the Supreme Court ruled 7–2 that prosecutors' exclusion of blacks and other minorities from juries violates the Fourteenth Amendment provision of "equal protection of the laws." The decision expanded on the 1965 *Swain v. Alabama* ruling, which prohibits racial exclusion only if the defendant demonstrates that the prosecutor uses such exclusion "in case after case." Under *Batson*, if a minority defendant objects to a prosecutor's peremptory challenge, the prosecutor must convince the court that his reasons for exclusion are not motivated by race.

Habeas Corpus Review Cases

Attributed to the Magna Carta, the writ of habeas corpus was passed through the common law to the colonies. The writ allows judges to review the legality of any loss of personal freedom. Habeas corpus is a fundamental part of any civilized society in which, as Justice William J. Brennan stated, "government must always be accountable to the judiciary for a man's imprisonment; if the imprisonment cannot be shown to conform with the fundamental requirements of law, the individual is entitled to his immediate release."

Fay v. Noia, 372 U.S. 391 (1963)

In the case, Noia, who was convicted of murder in New York, sought relief based on the inadmissibility of two coerced confessions. Although Noia's codefendants appealed, he did not. Eventually, they were successful in proving their confessions were coerced and they were released. Following their release, Noia appealed his conviction, but the state court denied the appeal because it did not meet the time frame in which he had to appeal.

The U.S. District Court for the Southern District of New York acknowledged that his confession had been coerced but denied him relief for failure to exhaust all state remedies. The time in which he needed to file for review of his sentence in a state appellate court had lapsed, and prisoners who sought habeas corpus relief typically had to exhaust all state appeals first before applying to federal courts. The U.S. District Court for the Southern District of New York denied Noia relief, but the federal appeals court reversed. The Supreme Court in a 6–3 vote affirmed the relief. Justice William Brennan wrote that courts must maintain the highest duty to not encumber habeas petitioners, as the writ's "root principle is that in a civilized society, government must always be accountable to the judiciary for a man's imprisonment. . . ."

Moody v. Dagget, 97 S. Ct. 274 (1976)

In *Moody v. Dagget*, the Supreme Court ruled 7–2 that parolees who are convicted for a second crime they commit while on parole do not have a constitutional right to an immediate parole revocation hearing. Convicts seek immediate hearings so that if the parole board rules they must serve out the time from the first sentence, they can try to have the sentences run concurrently. Justices John Paul Stevens and William J. Brennan, Jr., dissented.

United States v. Frady, 102 S. Ct. 1584 (1982) and Engle v. Isaac, 102 S. Ct. 1558 (1982)

In two cases, the Supreme Court limited convicted criminals' use of habeas corpus petitions. In *United States v. Frady*, the justices voted 6–1 (with Justices Burger and Marshall taking no part in the decision) and reversed a decision by the U.S. Court of Appeals for the District of Columbia. In 1980, that Court overturned Joseph C. Frady's conviction stemming from murder charges in 1963. Frady spent 17 years in prison and appealed numerous times, but he did not challenge the jury instructions at his trial. The Court used the "plain error" standard that allows higher courts to correct alleged errors by lower courts even when defendants have not appealed the errors. Frady sought to vacate his sentence by alleging that the jury instructions were defective. He based this on the instruction given by the trial judge who "had improperly equated intent with malice by stating that 'a wrongful act . . . intentionally done . . . is therefore done with malice aforethought.'" Writing the ruling opinion for the Supreme Court, Justice Sandra Day O'Connor stated the appeals court should have used the "cause and actual prejudice" standard, judging whether the alleged error hampered Frady's ability to get his conviction overturned through standard appeals.

The justices voted 7–2 in *Engle v. Isaac* to reverse the Sixth U.S. Circuit Court of Appeals decision that overturned the convictions of three Ohio men who questioned their attorney's understanding of the Ohio Rules of Criminal Procedure. The attorney did not challenge the jury instruction at their trial. Again for the majority, O'Connor wrote that the Constitution does not guarantee that defense attorneys "will recognize and raise every conceivable constitutional claim." Habeas corpus petitions offer protection against fundamentally unfair convictions. "Liberal allowance of the writ also degrades the prominence of the trial and costs society the right to punish admitted offenders. Moreover, the writ imposes special costs on the federal system, frustrating both the states' sovereign power to punish offenders and their good-faith efforts to honor constitutional rights."

Barefoot v. Estelle, 103 S. Ct. 3383 (1983)

In *Barefoot v. Estelle*, Supreme Court justices decided 5–4 to allow federal courts to expedite death penalty appeals, thereby making it harder for death-row prisoners to lengthen the appeals process. The ruling was against Thomas Andy Barefoot who was on death row in Texas for the 1978 murder of a police officer. Until *Barefoot*, state prison inmates were allowed to challenge their convictions and sentences by direct appeal or habeas corpus writs in federal courts. Federal appeals courts had not been permitted to review a habeas application before a U.S. district judge issued a "certificate of probable cause" that the writ was not frivolous. Barefoot lost direct state and federal appeals and objected to the expedited review of his habeas writ by the Fifth U.S. Circuit Court of Appeals, which refused his plea for a stay of execution. By upholding the appeals court ruling, the Supreme Court ruled that federal habeas applications need not be accorded the full formal procedures of direct appeals.

In the majority opinion, Justice Byron R. White stated "that direct appeal is the primary avenue for a review of a conviction or sentence, and death penalty cases are no exception. . . . [The] role of federal habeas corpus proceedings, while important in assuring that constitutional rights are observed, is secondary and limited. Federal courts are not forums in which to relitigate state trials. Even less is federal habeas a means by which a defendant is entitled to delay an execution indefinitely."

White set forth guidelines concerning habeas death penalty appeals in federal courts:

- A death or other severe sentence does not warrant the automatic issuing of a probable cause certificate, which requires the petitioner "to make a substantial showing of the denial of a federal right."
- Federal appeals courts are free to hear arguments on the merits of and on a motion for a stay of execution at the same time. They also may issue a single opinion on both matters.
- Appeals courts are allowed to automatically expedite the processing of repeated habeas petitions by the same defendant.
- Defendants are entitled to stays of execution when they are "necessary to prevent the case from becoming moot by the petitioner's execution."

Also in *Barefoot*, the justices ruled 6–3 to uphold the prosecution's use of a psychiatrist during sentencing. The doctor's testimony persuaded the jury that the defendant would be a threat to society if he received anything less than a death sentence.

United States v. Jakobetz, 955 F.2d 786 (1992)

The Second U.S. Circuit Court of Appeals issued a ruling making it easier for prosecutors to introduce DNA "fingerprint" evidence in criminal cases. While the court is based in New York City and covers New York, Connecticut, and Vermont, the ruling, applicable only in federal courts, is expected to greatly influence court proceedings in other states.

DNA fingerprinting links patterns in a suspect's DNA (deoxyribonucleic acid) with patterns of genetic material, such as blood or semen, found on a victim. Proponents argue the fingerprinting method's reliability, given that everyone's DNA is unique and the likelihood of a mismatch is one in several hundred million. Critics contend that DNA testing is complex and that the reliability of the outcome depends mainly on the skill of technicians who analyze the test and its results. At this time, there are no specific standards to which laboratories must conform.

A three-judge panel of the appeals court concluded unanimously that trial judges need not hold pretrial hearings to determine the admissibility of DNA evidence. "Although scientific and statistical evidence may seem complicated, we do not think a jury will be so dazzled or swayed as to ignore evidence suggesting that an experiment was improperly conducted or that testing procedures haven't been established," the court said.

The ruling is a response to an appeal filed by Randolph Jakobetz, who was convicted in federal court of kidnapping and raping a woman in Vermont. The basis of Jakobetz's conviction stemmed partly from DNA samples taken from semen on the victim.

McCleskey v. Zant, 111 S. Ct. 1454 (1991)

In *McCleskey v. Zant*, the Supreme Court ruled 6–3 that second-round habeas corpus petitions can be considered only when inmates show the constitutional violation being appealed actually harmed their cases and when they show how "some external impediment" prevented earlier discussion of the relevant issue. Also, an inmate who provides evidence that demonstrates his or her probable innocence may file a second petition.

Coleman v. Thompson, 111 S. Ct. 2546 (1991)

Failure to follow a state's requirements for filing writs of habeas corpus may cause prisoners to lose their rights to file such appeals in federal court, according to a 6–3 Supreme Court decision in *Coleman v. Thompson*. The decision overturned *Fay v. Noia*, a 1963 landmark case in which state inmates almost always were guaranteed the right to challenge their convictions in federal courts.

Keeney v. Tamayo-Reyes, 112 S. Ct. 1715 (1992)

In a 5–4 vote, the Supreme Court overturned a 1963 precedent establishing state inmates' access to federal courts. In the case of *Keeney v. Tamayo-Reyes*, the Court decided that federal courts do not have to grant a federal court hearing to a state prisoner who challenges his conviction even if he can demonstrate that his lawyer in the state appeals process did not properly present important facts of the case.

The 1963 *Fay v. Noia* case established a "deliberate bypass standard" by which state prisoners could file for habeas corpus relief through federal courts despite any lack of apparent fault of defense counsel or lack of compliance with procedures on the part of the convicted. Gradually, the Supreme Court has narrowed this direct access, replacing it with a "cause and prejudice" standard both for procedural default cases like *Fay* and for material fact cases like *Keeney*.

In the present case, Tamayo-Reyes, a Cuban immigrant with little education and almost no knowledge of English, alleged after the fact that his plea of no contest to first-degree manslaughter had not been knowing and intelligent because the court-appointed translator had not properly explained the degree of guilt involved in a manslaughter charge. However, since facts about the translation were not developed during the state court proceedings, Tamayo-Reyes must "show cause" for this failure and "actual prejudice resulting from that failure, or . . . show that a fundamental miscarriage of justice" would ensue from failing to hold a federal hearing.

In the majority opinion, Justice Byron White stated that, "applying the 'cause and prejudice' standard in cases like this will obviously contribute to the finality of convictions, for requiring a federal evidentiary hearing solely on the basis of a habeas petitioner's negligent failure to develop facts in state court proceedings dramatically increases the opportunities to relitigate a conviction." This decision, therefore, sought to promote judicial economy by "ensuring that full factual development" takes place in earlier state court proceedings and to reduce the "inevitable friction" arising when federal habeas courts "overturn either the factual or legal conclusions reached by the state court system." Joining White were Chief Justice William H. Rehnquist and Justices Antonin Scalia, David Souter, and Clarence Thomas. Justice Sandra Day O'Connor delivered the dissenting opinion and was joined by Justices Harry A. Blackmun, John Paul Stevens, and Anthony M. Kennedy, who also filed a separate dissent.

Custis v. United States, 114 S. Ct. 1732 (1994)
The Supreme Court decided 6–3 in *Custis v. United States* that repeat offenders who are being sentenced under the strict federal laws for so-called career criminals may not have their earlier convictions reviewed. The high court restricts such review requests to cases in which defendants' right to counsel was violated.

McFarland v. Scott, 114 S. Ct. 2568 (1994)
In a 5–4 ruling in *McFarland v. Scott*, the Supreme Court decided that federal judges are allowed to postpone executions of death-row prisoners who do not have legal counsel and who want to file habeas corpus writs to request federal reviews of their convictions. In the case, Frank B. McFarland, on death row in Texas for a murder conviction, requested a stay of execution from two federal

appeals courts. They refused to grant him the stay, as they did not have the authority because McFarland had not filed a habeas corpus petition. McFarland said he did not have enough time to find an attorney who would file the legally complex petition before he was due to be executed. In November 1993, the Supreme Court stayed the execution one hour before it was set to take place.

In the majority opinion, Justice Harry A. Blackmun noted that federal judges can stay the executions of death-row prisoners when they invoke their constitutional right to counsel representation. The stay would give them time to prepare the habeas corpus writ. Because of the difficulty of filling out the writ, death-row inmates have a hard time finding attorneys who handle them. Justice Sandra Day O'Connor agreed separately that prisoners on death row have a right to counsel, but that federal judges are not allowed to postpone executions. Justice Clarence Thomas, who also dissented, wrote that federal law does not mandate states to provide death-row inmates with free attorneys until a habeas petition is filed. Chief Justice William H. Rehnquist and Justice Antonin Scalia signed Thomas's opinion.

Felker v. Turpin, 116 S. Ct. 2333 (1996)

The Supreme Court ruled unanimously in *Felker v. Turpin* to uphold portions of federal legislation—passed as part of the Antiterrorism and Effective Death Penalty Act of 1996 that was signed by President Clinton in April—that curb the rights of death-row inmates in state prisons to seek federal reviews of their convictions. *Felker* provided the first challenge to the new legislation. In the case, Ellis Wayne Felker, who had been on Georgia's death row for 13 years, challenged a provision that makes it more difficult for inmates to file more than one petition for a writ of habeas corpus—the primary way for states' death-row inmates to challenge the constitutionality of their convictions. Congress placed restrictions on habeas corpus petitions to cut down protracted appeals processes and reduce delays in executions. The Supreme Court considered whether Congress had unconstitutionally stripped the high court of its authority to review a category of appeals. In a majority opinion, Chief Justice William H. Rehnquist wrote that Congress had not eliminated inmates' rights to appeal their convictions directly to the Supreme Court. "We conclude that although the Act does impose new conditions on our authority to grant relief, it does not deprive this Court of jurisdiction to entertain original habeas corpus petitions." However, as Rehnquist noted, the

Supreme Court will grant such reviews only in "exceptional circumstances" without defining the meaning of "exceptional circumstances." The justices ruled that Felker's case did not meet their criteria for granting an original writ of habeas corpus.

Although the Court's ruling is expected to diminish the number of death penalty appeals, legal analysts say that many challenges to other provisions in the legislation are pending in lower courts and are likely to reach the Court.

Directory of Organizations

T he following organizations do not represent all groups that deal with victims of violent crime. Some of the higher-profile state organizations are included, but many important groups exist at the state—and even local—levels that readers may want to look into.

The organizations covered in this chapter, which include Mothers Against Drunk Driving, the National Victim Center, and the National Organization for Victim Assistance, have long been in the practice of assisting victims and compiling research. From that angle, they are very helpful in providing information on the theoretical as well as the practical, such as victim studies and legislative efforts in the victims' rights movement. Additionally, readers may locate several organizations through the Internet—some of which they may not be able to corroborate through a directory of associations.

Aid for Victims of Crime (AVC)
4144 Lindell Boulevard, Suite B-20
St. Louis, MO 63108
(314) 652-3623
Founder: Carol Vittert

Aid for Victims of Crime (AVC) was established in 1972 to help crime victims and continues its mission today. It provides emotional support; guides victims through the criminal justice system; advocates on behalf of victims with their utility companies, employers, and landlords; networks with similar agencies to cut down duplication of services; refers victims to various community agencies that help with food, clothing, and shelter; and assists victims in filing for state victims' compensation for nonreimbursable hospital and medical costs, lost wages, funeral expenses, and counseling. The AVC also has worked through the legislative process to help pass the Missouri Crime Victims Compensation Fund and the Victim Bill of Rights.

American Bar Association (ABA)
Section of Criminal Justice
Victims Committee
740 15th Street, NW
Washington, DC 20005
(202) 662-1503
Staff Liaison to Victims' Committee: Shirleen Pilgrim

The Victims Committee of the Criminal Justice Section of the American Bar Association (ABA) conducts research on crime victims and develops victim-related policies for the entire association. Some of the issues it has explored and continues to explore include fair treatment guidelines for victims and witnesses, policies on intimidation, and trial continuances and delays. While the ABA makes its findings available to interested agencies and jurisdictions, it acts only in an advisory role.

American Civil Liberties Union (ACLU)
Public Education Department
25 Broad Street, 18th Floor
New York, NY 10004
(212) 549-2500, ext. 2666
Fax (212) 549-2646
www.aclu.org

Although the American Civil Liberties Union (ACLU) does not have a specific division devoted to crime victims, it researches constitutional issues involving victims of police brutality and of racial discrimination in the justice system. The ACLU's position on the proposed victims' rights constitutional amendment is one of concern for the potential effects on the rights of defendants. The organization has offices in all 50 states. The ACLU web site provides links to the states.

Bureau of Justice Statistics (BJS)
1110 Vermont Avenue, NW
Washington, DC 20531
(202) 633-3047 (public affairs)
(202) 633-3055
(800) 307-5846
http://www.ojp.usdoj.gov/bjs/
Public Affairs Spokesman: Stuart Smith
Director of Publications: Marilyn Marbrook

The Bureau of Justice Statistics (BJS) publishes crime victim interviews conducted by the Census Bureau. The interviews provide information that slips through the record-keeping cracks of both the *Uniform Crime Reports* and the *National Crime Reports*, the two standard forms of crime reporting. The BJS fax-on-demand service is available by dialing (301) 251-5550.

Criminal Justice Policy Foundation
1899 L Street, NW, Suite 500
Washington, DC 20036
(202) 835-9075
Fax (202) 833-8561
www.ndsn.org

The Criminal Justice Policy Foundation offers expertise in the areas of juvenile justice, drug policies, sentencing reform, gun control, crime prevention, prisons, community policing, and forfeiture. The foundation tracks court cases and state and federal legislation. It also coordinates the National Drug Strategy Network, a database of drug policy information. *NewsBriefs*, its monthly publication containing summaries of drug-related news, is available to subscribers.

Independence Institute
14142 Denver West Parkway, Suite 185
Golden, CO 80401
(303) 279-6536
Research Director: David Kopel

The Independence Institute researches several current hot-button topics, including gun issues, mandatory sentencing, terrorism, and juvenile crime. It makes the information available to researchers, public policymakers, and the media.

Mothers Against Drunk Driving (MADD)
511 East John Carpenter Freeway, #700
Irving, TX 75062-8187
(214) 744-6233
(800) GET-MADD (Victim hotline)
Fax (214) 869-2206
Assistant Director, Victim Advocacy and Research: Regina Sobieski

Mothers Against Drunk Driving (MADD) was founded by Candy Lightner in 1980 in California after her daughter was killed by a hit-and-run repeat drunk driving offender. The organization was established to halt drunk driving and support its victims. It now has about 3 million members in 500 chapters, community action teams, and offices throughout the United States. MADD tries to achieve the goal of stemming drunk driving through publicity campaigns, including MADD's PosterESSAY Contest, the "Tie One on for Safety" Campaign, and National Sobriety Checkpoint Week. True to its original purpose, MADD offers the following victims' services: emotional support, guidance through the criminal justice system, court accompaniment, and victim support groups. Members receive a newsletter, *MADD in Action*, which includes articles on what the organization is doing, legislation in the states, studies, and victims' advocacy. MADD also publishes *MADDvocate*, a victim magazine. Both are published twice per year.

National Center for State Courts
300 Newport Avenue
Williamsburg, VA 23187
(757) 253-2000
Fax (757) 220-0449
http://ncsc.dni.us

Founded in 1971 at the urging of Chief Justice Warren E. Burger, the National Center for State Courts is responsible for developing policies to improve state courts. This includes securing resources and forming a model for organizational administration. While the center cannot offer specific information about victims, it can provide information on the links between treatment and social services for domestic violence and child victims. The center examines the way courts treat a variety of people, including litigants, attorneys, and victims, and can offer basic information about the operation of courts. Callers to the center are directed to the person who is an expert in the area in which they are interested.

National Council on Crime and Delinquency (NCCD)
685 Market Street, Suite 620
San Francisco, CA 94105
(415) 896-6223
Fax (415) 896-5109
Vice President: Barry Krisberg

1325 G Street, Suite 770
Washington, DC 20005
(202) 638-0556
Fax (202) 638-0723
Senior Researcher: Michael Jones

The National Council on Crime and Delinquency (NCCD) conducts criminal and juvenile justice research, advises state and local agencies, and educates the public. The staff can provide analyses
of alternatives to imprisonment and information about juvenile
detention, the way child abuse affects crime, and juvenile justice
and statistics regarding juveniles, such as crime and arrest rates
and trends.

National Criminal Justice Reference Service (NCJRS)
P.O. Box 6000
Rockville, MD 20849-6000
(301) 251-5500
(800) 851-3420
e-mail: look@ncjrs.org
http://www.ncjrs.org

Operators of the National Criminal Justice Reference Service
(NCJRS) 800 number assist callers by running an information search
to bring up a cluster of publications in the caller's specific area of
interest. The NCJRS handles information for issues related to the
Office of Juvenile Justice and Delinquency Protection, the Bureau
of Justice Statistics, the Bureau of Justice Assistance (established
by the Omnibus Crime Control and Safe Streets Act of 1968, it
handles funding, evaluation, training, technical assistance, and
information for state and community criminal justice programs),
and the Office of National Drug Control Policy. The Office for Victims of Crime (OVC) also is accessible via the NCJRS. The OVC
was formed in 1985 to administer Victims of Crime Act money
and to supplement, reinforce, and promote expansion of state compensation and assistance programs throughout the country. It

sponsors grants and works with victims' advocates and criminal justice system personnel who regularly interact with victims. The OVC Resource Center, a component of the NCJRS, provides victim-related information on domestic violence, child abuse, elderly victims, bias-related violence, victims' rights, and compensation. The NCJRS offers links to the above agencies. Callers may request a booklet, *Office for Victims of Crime Resource Center Products, Publications, and Online Services,* which offers several victim-related titles and their price—many are free—along with an order form and online information.

National Institute of Justice (NIJ)
U.S. Department of Justice
633 Indiana Avenue, NW
Washington, DC 20531
(202) 307-2958
e-mail: hillsman@justice.usdoj.gov
Director: Jeremy Travis
Deputy Director: Sally Hillsman

The National Institute of Justice (NIJ) is the research and development arm of the U.S. Department of Justice. It is charged with reducing and preventing crime and improving the justice system. Sally Hillsman, the deputy director, has several years' experience as a criminal justice researcher. She is well versed on issues such as court technology, intermediate sanction, pretrial detention, prosecution, and general law and drug law enforcement. Jeremy Travis, the director, develops law enforcement policy and can speak about many issues, including gun control and police.

National Organization for Victim Assistance (NOVA)
1757 Park Road, NW
Washington, DC 20010
(202) 232-6682
Fax (202) 462-2255
Executive Director: Marlene A. Young, Ph.D., J.D.
Deputy Director: John Stein

Founded in 1975, the National Organization for Victim Assistance (NOVA) comprises members among crime victims, criminal justice representatives, professionals from the health and mental health fields, victims' advocates, and the public. The organization devotes itself to four purposes: national advocacy (speaking on behalf of victims in state legislatures and Congress), direct services for crime and crisis victims (24-hour crisis counseling and follow-up assistance to all types of victims from all states, wherever local programs are not available), professional development (establishing new programs, expanding existing services, and training and educating victims' assistance and allied professionals), and membership communication and support (through *The NOVA Newsletter*, the annual conference, and other means, the organization offers timely information on new ideas, programs, and knowledge in the field of victims' assistance).

Some of the organization's successes include being a major player in securing pro-victim legislation in the form of the Victim/Witness Protection Act of 1982, the Victims of Crime Act of 1984, and bills of rights for victims in a majority of states. NOVA not only is the first contact that many undeserved victims have, but it also offers assistance in international crises, such as in Bosnia and Croatia and in Kobe, Japan, after an earthquake there killed several hundred people and destroyed lots of homes.

National Victim Center (NVC)
2111 Wilson Boulevard, Suite 300
Arlington, VA 22201
(703) 276-2880
Fax (703) 276-2889

The National Victim Center (NVC) was established in 1985 in honor of Sunny von Bulow to meet the needs of crime victims and protect their rights. It is a resource center for victims and victims' advocacy and criminal justice organizations. It assists victims involved in a variety of crimes from sexual assault and elder abuse to hate violence and homicide. In addition to fielding requests and questions from crime victims, the organization also offers several publications to professionals in the areas of statistics, technical assistance, and training manuals. The NVC tracks litigation and legislation that affect victims at local, state, and federal levels. It also promotes legislation to aid victims at all levels of government.

The NVC publishes *NETWORKS*, a quarterly newsletter to keep readers up-to-date with legislation and court decisions that affect victims. It is available for $20 annually. It also publishes the *Crime Victims' Litigation Quarterly* in conjunction with its Carrington Victims' Litigation Project, which works on behalf of crime victims who bring civil suits against those who may have contributed, through negligence, for example, to the conditions that assisted a person in carrying out a crime. The publication contains articles on new cases and trends among civil remedies for crime victims, law practice techniques, victims' services, and more.

The NVC set up INFOLINK—(800) FYI-CALL—in February 1993 with the broadcast of *I Can Make You Love Me: The Stalking of Laura Black* as a toll-free source of information and referral for crime victims, concerned citizens, public policymakers, and professionals. It can link callers to assistance organizations near where they live or to national crisis hotlines related to specific areas of victimization. It also provides callers with general information about the criminal justice system, including how it works, local and statewide resources, and local contacts. Other information, including current statistics, legislative overviews, bibliographies, and organization referrals on 68 topics such as crime victims' rights, also is available. Callers can receive up to five Information Bulletins/Resources packages free of charge. Additional copies or multiple copies of the same topic are $1.50 each, including postage and handling.

Parents of Murdered Children (POMC)
100 East Eighth Street, B-41
Cincinnati, OH 45202
(513) 721-5683
Fax (513) 345-4489
Executive Director: Nancy Ruhe-Munch

Parents of Murdered Children (POMC) was founded in 1978 by Charlotte and Bob Hullinger in Cincinnati, Ohio, after the murder of their daughter Lisa. Father Ken Czillinger, a Roman Catholic priest active in leading support groups for the bereaved, directed the Hullingers to others whose children had been murdered. To date, there are more than 100 chapters and 350 contact people in the United States. The organization offers emotional support for survivors through contact with other people who have lost someone to murder and through information on grieving and the criminal justice system. POMC also communicates with professionals about problems faced by people surviving a homicide victim and helps to educate the public about these problems.

POMC directs two programs: Murder Is Not Entertainment (MINE) and the Parole Block Program (PBP). MINE was started in 1993 to alert Americans to their insensitivity toward murder and its consequences. POMC objects to any product, promotion, film, or print media that features graphic photos or illustrations that present scenes of crimes and victims' dead bodies; unauthorized photos of grieving family members and friends of victims; material that focuses solely on murder for entertainment, instruction, promotion, or profit; anything with content related to murder, violence, or stalking that is directed toward children; products that try to entertain by highlighting the lives of infamous killers; anything that shows murderers as heroes or gives them celebrity status; and anything in the guise of entertainment that brings more pain and grief to victims' families and friends. POMC sends a "MINE Alert" describing such products to its representatives and volunteers around the country and asks that they express their concerns by writing letters to those responsible for the products. The organization provides a list of products and addresses. POMC also uses the same procedure in schools when there is a product that glorifies or focuses on murder or violence and is aimed at children.

POMC began the PBP in 1990. Upon the request of survivors, the organization writes and circulates petitions to stop the parole or early release of loved ones' murderers. The petitions are sent to people throughout the United States. The PBP does not lobby for longer sentences, but it requests that sentences imposed by courts be served in full. Since its beginning, the program has protested the early release or parole of more than 500 murderers. According to program literature, the PBP keeps more than one murderer per week behind bars.

POMC publishes *Survivors* on a monthly basis. The newsletter contains information about the organization, its programs, and victims' rights. Survivors of murder victims may receive a one-year complimentary subscription to the newsletter. Otherwise the annual price is $10.

Save Our Sons and Daughters (SOSAD)
2441 West Grand Boulevard
Detroit, MI 48208
(313) 361-5200
Fax (313) 361-0055
President: Clementine Barfield

Clementine Barfield founded Save Our Sons and Daughters (SOSAD) in 1987 after two of her sons were shot. SOSAD works with schools and various community-based groups to form alternatives to violence. It also provides counseling and training in violence prevention and conflict resolution. The organization lobbies for victims' rights. Besides its Detroit headquarters, there are chapters in Fresno, California; Louisville, Kentucky; and Washington, D.C.

Stephanie Roper Committee & Foundation, Inc.
14804 Pratt Street, #1
Upper Marlboro, MD 20772-3002
(301) 952-0063
(301) 952-2319
Director: Roberta Roper

Named for Roberta Roper's daughter Stephanie, who was murdered shortly before she was due to graduate from college in 1982, the organization assists crime victims by providing information about their rights, criminal injury compensation, and legal referrals for civil action; acting as a court companion during a trial; and directing them to counselors and support groups. Foundation employees also help prepare victims for the courtroom experience; for handling newspaper, television, and radio reporters; and for dealing with the Maryland Parole Commission. Roberta Roper also cochairs the National Victims Constitutional Amendment Network (National VCAN). Membership in the Stephanie Roper Committee & Foundation is $10 and includes a subscription to the quarterly newsletter. Half of the newsletter information is about Maryland issues, while the other half is devoted to national issues, such as the proposed constitutional amendment and the progress among states that are amending their constitutions to provide for victims' rights.

Vera Institute of Justice
377 Broadway
New York, NY 10013
(212) 334-1300
http://broadway.vera.org
Director: Christopher Stone

Louis Schweitzer, a successful chemical engineer who became a philanthropist, founded the Vera Institute of Justice in 1961 to find ways to ease crowding in New York City jails. Many who were being held had committed minor offenses and were not able to post bail. With Herbert Sturz, Vera's first director, Schweitzer organized the Manhattan Bail Project to show how people with little money but valid community ties could be released while awaiting trial. The project served as a template for bail and custody decision making throughout the country. Vera has operated similarly since then, creating model projects on which true reforms can be based. Vera pioneered research in criminal justice and currently is exploring violence and youth. The organization also contributed to the ideas of community policing, alternative sentencing, and victims' services.

Victims' Assistance Legal Organization (VALOR)
99 Canal Center Plaza, Suite 510
Alexandria, VA 22314
(703) 684-8310
Fax (703) 836-3195
Executive Director: Jane Nady Burnley, Ph.D.

Founded as the Crime Victims' Legal Advocacy Institute, Inc., in 1979 by the late Frank Carrington, a longtime crime victims' activist, the organization was renamed the Victims' Assistance Legal Organization (VALOR) in 1981. Its purpose is to promote the rights of crime victims in the civil and criminal justice systems. The organization accomplishes this by educating the public about the rights and needs of crime victims; advancing victims' rights through public policy at the federal, state, and local levels; supporting justice reforms that make offenders accountable to both crime victims and communities; enhancing victims' ability to recover damages through civil litigation; improving services for victims to assist in their emotional, financial, and physical recovery; and securing basic rights for victims as articulated in the President's Task Force on Victims of Crime *Final Report* of 1982 throughout the United States. Given its beginnings, VALOR expanded its involvement in victims' issues beyond offender accountability, civil litigation, and rights and services to include juvenile justice reform and college and university campus security. Carrington examined child protection issues, and Dr. Jane Burnley, the executive director, continues to work in that area. She is an executive committee member of the U.S. Advisory Board on Child Abuse and Neglect and serves as a volunteer court-appointed special advocate in child abuse cases in Fairfax County, Virginia. Dr. Burnley's involvement in victims' issues dates to the early 1980s with the establishment of the U.S. Department of Justice Office for Victims of Crime, where she served as director.

Selected Resources 6

Print Resources

Indexes, Abstracts, and Annual Reports

Garoogian, Rhoda, and Andrew Garoogian. **Crime in America's Top-Rated Cities: A Statistical Profile.** Boca Raton, FL: Universal Reference Publications, 1995.

This book profiles the 75 American cities that are considered the best places to live and do business, based on a number of magazine surveys. For each city cited, the handbook provides detailed information about crime for the past two decades. The cities are not compared or ranked, but data include the number of crimes and crime rates for the cities, suburbs, *Metropolitan Statistical Abstract*, and the United States. Statistics are broken down even further to include hate crimes, correctional facilities, the death penalty, law enforcement personnel, gun laws, inmates and HIV/AIDS, anticrime programs, and the chances of becoming a crime victim.

Morgan, Kathleen O., ed. **City Crime Rankings.** Lawrence, KS: Morgan Quitno, 1995.

America's 100 largest cities and 274 metropolitan areas are ranked in all major crime categories reported by the Federal Bureau of Investigation.

Morgan, Kathleen O'Leary, Scott Morgan, and Neal Quitno, eds. **Crime State Rankings 1994: Crime in the 50 United States.** Lawrence, KS: Morgan Quitno, 1994.

In six sections, the editors break down data through 1992 into arrest rates of various crimes ranked by state; corrections statistics, including prison populations; drug and alcohol information; justice-related government spending; and the percentage of change and differences between urban and rural areas concerning conventional offenses, including gun-related crimes. While there is no interpretation of the statistics, readers may find information they can use as a jumping-off point to something more specific.

Sourcebook of Criminal Justice Statistics. Washington, DC: U.S. Department of Justice. Annual.

This resource includes information on the criminal justice system, public attitudes toward crime and criminal justice–related topics, the nature and number of known offenders, and the characteristics and number of persons arrested.

Uniform Crime Reports for the United States. Washington, DC: U.S. Department of Justice. Annual.

This annual report provides a nationwide view of crime based on statistics contributed by state and local law enforcement agencies. Sections include "Crime Index Offenses Reported," "Crime Index Offenses Cleared," "Persons Arrested," and "Law Enforcement Personnel."

Directories

Harvard Law Students. **The Insider's Guide to Law Firms 1993–94.** Washington, DC: Insider's Guide to Law Firms, 1993.

This guide truly is for lawyers and law students who are interested in researching career options. For anyone who is conducting general research, however, the profiles of 200 large U.S. law firms contain information on their development and areas of practice.

Saldana, Richard H. **Crime Victim Compensation Programs: A Reference Guide to the Programs in the U.S.** Bountiful, UT: QuartZite Publishing, 1994.

With an introduction to the history and spectrum of crime victims' compensation programs, this work offers practical information for people considering applying for compensation. Saldana offers a guide to compensation by state and reviews eligibility, the types of losses covered, and the application process with addresses and telephone numbers. The appendix contains a copy of the Victims of Crime Act of 1984 (VOCA) along with amendments and leads readers to other databases, reference sources, and related reading.

Yearbooks, Dictionaries, and Encyclopedias

Epstein, Lee, et al. **The Supreme Court Compendium: Data and Developments.** Washington, DC: Congressional Quarterly, 1994.

This collection is presented mainly in tables with hundreds of topics available. It covers the Supreme Court as an institution, individual justices, and the way in which the high court affects the political process. In addition to personal information, readers can learn about congressional legislation that came before the Court, landmark cases, petitions reviewed, caseload, and voting behavior. The final chapter discusses other courts in the judicial system.

Garner, Bryan A. **A Dictionary of Modern Legal Usage.** 2d ed. New York: Oxford University Press, 1995.

A vast improvement over the first edition, this dictionary has more than double the entries of its predecessor. It is written with clarity and provides word usage and origins, not just definitions. Entries are arranged alphabetically, but the bonus comes from short essays on the subjects of style, grammar and usage, origin and meanings of legal terms, punctuation, and word formation.

Knappman, Edward W., ed. **Great American Trials.** Detroit: Gale Research, 1994.

Spanning 200 cases, *Great American Trials* provides brief summaries based on the cases' historical or constitutional significance. It focuses on those cases that inspired controversy, garnered public attention, showcased legal ingenuity, or attracted writers' pens. Ted Bundy, Mike Tyson, Lizzie Borden, and *Roe v. Wade* all show up here in three- to six-page entries. Readers can review cases by date, trial name, or crime, and other ideas for sources accompany each case.

Patrick, John J. **The Young Oxford Companion to the Supreme Court of the United States.** New York: Oxford University Press, 1994.

Information on 107 justices through Ruth Bader Ginsburg, important cases, concepts, and constitutional information are presented here in an encyclopedic format with accompanying photos, drawings, sidebars, and cartoons. General coverage of the court provides a good overview, but someone looking for more specific information may have to check other sources.

Urofsky, Melvin I., ed. **The Supreme Court Justices: A Biographical Dictionary.** Hamden, CT: Garland Reference Library of the Humanities, 1994.

Essays up to 12 pages are written by highly esteemed American legal scholars who analyze Supreme Court justices by focusing on their legal career and significant cases. The book contains 107 biographical listings for all the justices, from Chief Justice John Jay to Ruth Bader Ginsburg. It also has a bibliography that points to important publications written by the justices as well as where to find personal papers, documents, and more sources. A topical and case index makes pinpointing information easier.

Women in Law: A Bio-Bibliographical Sourcebook. Westport, CT: Greenwood Press, 1996.

This work presents profiles of 43 women, some international, who have made important contributions to law and legal reform.

Books and Monographs

Abramson, Jeffrey. **We, The Jury: The Jury System and the Ideal of Democracy.** New York: BasicBooks, 1994.

Abramson's experience as a law clerk to the California Supreme Court and an assistant district attorney in Massachusetts allowed him to see how juries operate. He uses this knowledge to trace their evolution in the system in both local and higher courts, discuss theories behind why they are needed, and delve into issues such as the death penalty and race. The paperback edition also includes an epilogue on the Simpson trial. Abramson goes beyond pointing out problems, though. He offers proposals on how to improve jury trials and stop discrimination (in spite of *Batson v. Kentucky*).

Abramson, Jeffrey, ed. **Postmortem: The O. J. Simpson Case.** New York: BasicBooks, 1996.

One of the country's foremost social and cultural commentators presents thoughtful and engaging essays about the implications of the so-called trial of the century. The book is broken down into six aspects of the trial: race relations, jury reform, domestic violence, the media, ethics and lawyers, and general postmortems.

Abramson, Leslie, with Richard Flaste. **The Defense Is Ready: Life in the Trenches of Criminal Law.** New York: Simon & Schuster, 1997.

Abramson was a young, single mother while attending UCLA law school. She worked her way through the Los Angeles Public Defender's Office (aka crime central) to become a homicide attorney with a bag of cases including that of Erik Menendez of the Menendez brothers. Through all that she has learned, Abramson writes of the importance of the credo "innocent until proven guilty," and she explains how true justice demands thoughtful contemplation, not snap judgments based on stereotypes and provoked by a desire for quick solutions in especially heinous crimes.

Anner, John, ed. **Beyond Identity Politics: Emerging Social Justice Movements in Communities of Color.** Boston: South End Press, 1996.

This collection of essays, based on 1993–1995 articles from the Center for Third World Organizing's publication *Third Force*, looks at alternatives that get away from waging "middle-class campaigns" in the workplace, classroom, university campuses, and neighborhoods throughout the country. Race, ethnicity, personal and community safety, sexuality, wages, police accountability, and environmental justice are issues explored to lend support to the stand that justice is a multicultural issue.

Arax, Mark. **In My Father's Name: A Family, a Town, a Murder.** New York: Simon & Schuster, 1996.

Arax goes after his ghosts and vanquishes them. The *Los Angeles Times'* investigative reporter was 15 when his father was gunned down by two men in his own nightclub on 2 January 1972. Twenty years later, Arax returns to the scene of the crime, gathering countless interviews with friends, family, witnesses, bar patrons, and members of the local police force. Arax, despite painful memories of his father's death, eventually cracks the mystery, discovering local organized crime was to blame.

Baker, Mark. **Bad Guys: America's Most Wanted in Their Own Words.** New York: Simon & Schuster, 1996.

Those who have chosen the wrong side of the street tell, straight up, their stories. Greed, laziness, contempt for the law, and a means to feel powerful are the predominate justifications given for their choices. The criminals interviewed have backgrounds that range from broken homes to poverty to middle class.

Beccaria, Cesare. **On Crimes and Punishments.** Indianapolis, IN: Hackett Publishing, 1986

Translated by David Young, this compact treatise offers a critique of eighteenth-century European justice as it actually was. Beccaria probes the origins of punishment, the right to punish, interpretation of the law, proportionality errors, public tranquillity, prosecution, the purpose of punishment, and various crimes and punishments, including death, imprisonment, and torture.

Bedau, Hugo Adam, ed. **The Death Penalty in America: Current Controversies.** New York: Oxford University Press, 1997.

Various scholars wrote the articles that are compiled in this book. They provide information about public support of the death penalty, the controversy regarding deterrence and incapacitation, and the constitutionality of the death penalty as well as the proportionality of its application and arguments for and against it.

Bennett, William J., et al. **Body Count: Moral Poverty . . . and How To Win America's War against Crime and Drugs.** New York: Simon & Schuster, 1996.

This work outlines Bennett's personal prescription to the ills of a public that is becoming increasingly apathetic toward an epidemic of violent crime and drug abuse by the nation's youth. His brand of tough love includes coming down hard on lesser crimes to deter those more serious in nature and reversing the "moral poverty" that spreads when easily swayed youth have no parental figures to turn to for guidance.

Bidinotto, Robert James, ed. **Criminal Justice? The Legal System v. Individual Responsibility.** Irvington-on-Hudson, NY: Foundation for Economic Education, 1996.

Another compilation of articles from various contributors, this book addresses crime, plea bargaining, the exclusionary rule, confessions, the insanity defense, and punishment. The overall premise of the book is that it is time for restoration of responsibility in the fight against crime, with specific solutions suggested.

Blackstone, Sir William. **Commentaries on the Laws of England: A Facsimile of the First Edition of 1765–1769.** Chicago: University of Chicago Press, 1979.

Divided into four volumes, *Commentaries* illustrates the foundations and early evolution of Western law and explores the traditions of British common law. The volumes are as follows: I, *On the Rights of Persons* (the structure of the English legal system); II, *On the Rights of Things* (property rights); III, *Of Private Wrongs* (procedures of justice, including the jury trial and the concept of equity); and IV, *Of Public Wrongs* (criminal law and sentencing).

Blasi, Vincent, ed. **The Burger Court: The Counter Revolution That Wasn't.** New Haven, CT: Yale University Press, 1983.

When Chief Justice Warren E. Burger took the helm of the Supreme Court following the leadership of Chief Justice Earl Warren (1953–1969), everyone braced for a conservative backlash sparked by the Warren Court's so-called liberal decisions. But, *The Burger Court* argues, Burger's term from 1969 to 1986 was not as conservative as many think. In the book, legal scholar Yale Kamisar explores the Court's actions in the realm of criminal justice in "The Warren Court (Was It Really So Defense-Minded?) and the Burger Court (Is It Really So Prosecution-Oriented?) and Police Investigatory Practices."

Burnham, David. **Above the Law: Secret Deals, Political Fixes and Other Misadventures of the U.S. Department of Justice.** New York: Charles Scribner's Sons, 1996.

Burnham, who previously wrote in 1990 about the misbehavior of the Internal Revenue Service in *A Law unto Itself*, now takes aim at the U.S. Department of Justice and questions whether it acts in the best interests of the public. He points to constitutional, structural, and bureaucratic roadblocks against those interests and promotes the idea that effective reform lies in vigilance of citizens, the media, public interest groups, and elected officials. Burnham also examines the conflicts of interest inherent when attorney generals serve both the public and their president's goals.

Cabana, Don. **Death at Midnight: The Confession of an Executioner.** Boston: Northeastern University Press, 1995.

Cabana, a criminal justice professor, spent more than 20 years working in corrections in four states. Here, he writes for the ordinary citizen and argues that capital punishment is not the quick fix depicted by politicians and the media. The author weaves three stories: his career, his metamorphosis in terms of his views on capital punishment, and his relationship with convicted murderer Connie Ray Evans, the second man whose execution Cabana supervised as a warden.

Calabro, Marian. **Great Courtroom Lawyers: Fighting the Cases That Made History.** New York: Facts on File, 1996.

Clarence Darrow, Thurgood Marshall, and Sarah Weddington are a few of the nine influential individuals in the American justice system profiled here. Trail-blazing cases, including *Roe v. Wade*, *Brown v. Board of Education*, and the O. J. Simpson murder trial are highlighted. Sexism, Native American claims to constitutional rights, and the elements of a rape case are outlined.

Cardozo, Benjamin N. **The Nature of the Judicial Process.** New Haven, CT: Yale University Press, 1921.

Based on the Storrs Lectures delivered at Yale University, Cardozo, a Supreme Court justice from 1932 to 1938, explores the philosophical methods of determining justice through history, tradition, and society. Cardozo reviews precedent-setting cases and explains how a judge decides a case.

Carlo, Philip. **The Night Stalker: The True Story of America's Most Feared Serial Killer.** Kalamazoo, MI: Kensington Publishing, 1996.

This sordid tale of Richard Ramirez, the "night stalker" rapist and killer who terrorized Los Angeles County in the mid-1980s, is not for the squeamish. The book details Ramirez's violent spree of raping, sodomizing, and stabbing his victims to death. The book also chronicles his capture, arrest, and trial, which drew a bevy of groupies, a few of whom still regularly visit him today.

Carrington, Frank G. **Victims.** New Rochelle, NY: Arlington House Publishers, 1975.

A breakthrough book by one whom many consider the "Father of Victims' Rights." Carrington uses actual cases to show how efforts are made to protect the accused while little is done to secure safety— and justice—for victims of crime. Some of the solutions Carrington recommends have been put into place, while others are still being contemplated. These include making criminals pay restitution to their victims, making judges and parole boards "pay for their softness," and forming a victims' rights commission to represent victims and protect their rights in court. Carrington argues for creating a victim-oriented criminal justice system based on techniques used in Britain, overturning the exclusionary rule, and modifying Miranda.

Chevigny, Paul. **Edge of the Knife: Police Violence in the Americas.** New York: New Press, 1995.

The author analyzes his 1969 study of "police abuse" in New York City, which has been used as a basic guideline for other major American cities. The New York University Law School professor continued his research in the 1980s for Human Rights Watch by studying police forces in New York, Los Angeles, Jamaica, São Paulo, Buenos Aires, Jamaica, and Mexico City. He concluded societal factors account for the varying levels of official police violence that communities are willing to accept or demand. The level of military involvement applied to keep domestic peace, residents' confidence and sense of participation in their law enforcement agencies, and government accountability all contribute to that public threshold.

Dershowitz, Alan M. **Reasonable Doubts: The O. J. Simpson Case and the Criminal Justice System.** New York: Simon & Schuster, 1996.

The celebrity lawyer hired to handle any possible appeal for Simpson instead offers his opinion on how the jury could have properly reached a verdict for the high-profile case. Dershowitz states in his introduction his aim is not to sway public opinion, but it is difficult not to think he has his own agenda. Dershowitz expounds on the strengths of the defendant's case, but fails to talk about the prosecution's case, particularly the "bloody glove" and DNA evidence presented.

Dunn, William. **Boot: An L.A.P.D. Officer's Rookie Year.** New York: William Morrow, 1996.

Dunn dispenses a memoir of his gripping first year as one of "L.A.'s finest." He discusses the highs and lows of the beat, including the city's gang crisis and the fallout from the Rodney King beating in 1991. Dunn also offers some insight into the causes of crime.

Dusky, Lorraine. **Still Unequal: The Shameful Truth about Women and Justice in America.** New York: Crown Publishing, 1996.

An insightful, ironic look at the female lawyer in America's legal system. The roadblocks presented to women, from law school experiences to treatment of the victim, defendant, and plaintiff in the courtroom, are examined here. Dusky pulls no punches, calling our legal system "still the most backward, sexist, offensive set of institutions in the country."

Elias, Robert. **Victims Still: The Political Manipulation of Crime Victims.** Newbury Park, CA: Sage Publications, 1993.

Elias argues that the official shift in criminal justice from crime and criminals to victims and victimization was really a feel-good policy that furthered the law-and-order platforms of Presidents Ronald Reagan and George Bush without actually altering victimization. Instead, offenders' rights have been reduced and police power has increased. Various media have neglected to hold officials accountable and have taken the focus away from crime sources and changes that could diminish victimization. Elias argues that real change lies in developing a more peaceful culture; a victims' movement in which victims take an active, not passive, part; laws that are equal for everyone; sentencing alternatives; policing innovation; and community involvement.

Evans, James. **Law on the Net.** Berkeley, CA: Nolo, 1995.

A plethora of court records can be researched electronically. Evans provides detailed instructions on how to access information through bulletin boards, the Internet, CompuServe, and America Online sites.

Fletcher, George P. **With Justice for Some: Victims' Rights in Criminal Trials.** Reading, MA: Addison-Wesley, 1995.

Criminal trials no longer are forums for determining the guilt of defendants and condemning evil. Instead, they are used to understand criminals' mentality, to obscure the heinousness of crime, and to overshadow the validity of punishment. Fletcher argues that this status quo evolved beginning with the trial of Dan White for the 1978 deaths of San Francisco Mayor George Moscone and Councilman Harvey Milk, in which White was convicted of manslaughter, not first-degree murder. He also points to four disenfranchised groups who, according to him, are helping to establish a new form of American political trial—gays, blacks, Jews, and women. Fletcher also discusses ten principles for providing justice to victims and defendants.

Friedman, Lawrence M. **Crime and Punishment in American History.** New York: BasicBooks, 1993.

The Marion Rice Kirkwood Professor of Law at Stanford University, Friedman traces the evolution—through crimes, criminal cases, and court decisions—of crime and punishment in America from the colonial period through the twentieth century.

Goldman, The Family of Ron, with William Hoffer and Marilyn Hoffer. **His Name Is Ron.** New York: William Morrow, 1997.

That the family of Ron Goldman was in the media for months during the criminal and civil trials of O. J. Simpson does not mean viewers and readers really knew what the family felt. They try to tell readers in this book. The Hoffers' technique of interweaving the viewpoints of various people is sometimes confusing. The book is nonetheless compelling and gives readers an insider's view of the criminal and civil justice systems.

Hagen, Margaret A. **Whores of the Court: The Fraud of Psychiatric Testimony and the Rape of American Justice.** New York: Regan Books, 1997.

Hagen's premise is one few Americans have noticed: the justice system's demand for expert psychiatric witnesses encroaches on the purpose of the system, which is to provide justice. The psychiatric testimony that courts have embraced is a complete fraud, she argues. Hagen offers examples of real people caught in the throes of injustice—and harmed—when the "expert's" testimony is inadequate to diagnose any future behavior when it aims at interpreting criminal behavior. While Americans as a society have relinquished the ideal of absolute good and evil, they still search for reasons as to why people, including criminals, behave the way they do. Hagen points out and dissects examples of these excuses: the battered women syndrome defense, urban psychosis, Post Traumatic Stress Disorder, and the entire spectrum of reasons (374) illustrated in the Diagnostic and Statistical Manual (DSM-IV). Hagen argues that the best way for the system to exact justice is to stop pretending that psychiatry is the be-all and end-all, throw the experts off the payroll, and have them work *for* the courts. Anyone who sees red reading Ann Landers's columns on far-out lawsuits will find Hagen's book to be a "triple whammy," but it's recommended reading for those who care about the state of justice—or injustice—in America's courts.

Hutchinson, Earl Ofari. **Beyond O. J.: Race, Sex and Class Lessons for America.** Los Angeles: Middle Passage, 1996.

On the heels of the O. J. Simpson case, Hutchinson delves into the topics of race, sex, and class in America and offers compelling comparisons of recent cases involving white and black male defendants with similar charges, yet with different outcomes. The author concludes that white males were treated differently than their black counterparts for the same crimes, which included sexual harassment, date rape, domestic violence, and child molestation. Hutchinson builds the case that the black male is looked at as a menace to society, but he then goes lukewarm to discuss young black males and their media image. The result of his study is left open-ended. However, responses from whites and blacks to the O. J. verdict show the deep chasm between race and class in America.

Jackson, Jesse. **Legal Lynching: Racism, Injustice, and the Death Penalty.** New York: Marlowe, 1996.

This is Jackson's eulogy to capital punishment. The preacher, prophet, and former presidential candidate espouses the effects of capital punishment, chronicling its history and impact on the legal system. Jackson raises tough moral questions and provides alternatives.

Jonnes, Jill. **Hep-Cats, Narcs, and Pipe Dreams: A History of America's Romance with Illegal Drugs.** New York: Charles Scribner's Sons, 1996.

Jonnes, a former journalist, examines the infiltration of hard drugs into American society, charting three "epidemics" over the last 125 years, each more severe than the last. She starts with opium, cocaine, and marijuana—when they were once legal—and explores the influence of drugs on Hollywood and jazz. The psychedelic revolution, the cocaine craze of the 1970s, and the introduction of crack are outlined in scathing accounts. Perhaps most disturbing is her tracking of the federal government's support of drug traffickers, including the Sicilian Mafia, the French Connection, and the Colombian cartels. By the end, her revelations are not pretty, as she brings to light the connection between politics and drugs—a hypocrisy that makes the war on drugs a sham.

Keve, Paul W. **Crime Control and Justice in America: Searching for Facts and Answers.** Chicago: American Library Association, 1995.

Crime Control and Justice in America is a comprehensive resource on contemporary crime issues for the student, researcher, and general enthusiast. Keve explores the complex questions citizens and lawmakers must deal with, such as causes of crime and crime control versus civil liberties.

Knight, Alfred H. **The Life of the Law: The People and Cases That Have Shaped Our Society, from King Alfred to Rodney King.** New York: Crown Publishing, 1996.

This tome takes readers on a journey through the evolution of Anglo-American law, spotlighting 20 historical cases that helped shape legislation into today's laws. From the Magna Carta to the

American Bill of Rights to the present, this book describes the growth and development of laws and lawmaking.

Lazare, Daniel. **The Frozen Republic: How the Constitution Is Paralyzing Democracy.** Orlando, FL: Harcourt, Brace, Jovanovich, 1996.

Lazare takes an "in hindsight" look at the Constitution and argues it perhaps does not hold the same power to deal with changes in the present as it did in the past. He describes it as being incapable of being amended, except for technical changes. He looks at Article V as the harbinger of the problem—the guarantee of the state's equality in the Senate.

Magee, Doug. **What Murder Leaves Behind: The Victim's Family.** New York: Dodd, Mead, 1983.

In these real-life stories, which were first published in the heady, dawning days of the victims' rights movement in the early 1980s, Magee brings together interviews with several individual victims and sets of victims. Tapping into their personal experiences, he paints a straightforward picture of what it's like dealing with the aftermath of murder.

Marshall, Joseph, and Lonnie Wheeler. **Street Soldier: One Man's Struggle To Save a Generation—One Life at a Time.** New York: Delacorte Press, 1996.

This book chronicles Marshall's first view of the harsh circumstances of his students' lives. It is based on his experiences teaching high school from the late 1960s to the mid-1980s in a poor section of San Francisco rife with guns and crack. Marshall and his colleague Jack Jacqua decided working within the system was not enough to make a difference. They decided to create the Omega Boys' Club and got results, taking the boys from the street and showing them options for a better life. Many went from serving time to attending college. Marshall's work did not go unnoticed. He garnered the Essence award and a MacArthur Foundation "genius" grant.

Miller, Jerome G. **Search and Destroy: African-American Males in the Criminal Justice System.** New York: Cambridge University Press, 1996.

Miller explores a U.S. prison population that is increasingly disproportionately black and concludes the criminal justice system is a means to control the underclass. One eye-opening statistic: an African-American male between the ages of 18 and 35 has an 80 percent chance of having a run-in with the justice system at some point.

Morris, Norval, and David J. Rothman, eds. **The Oxford History of the Prison: The Practice of Punishment in Western Society.** New York: Oxford University Press, 1995.

The two author-editors, with 12 other recruited scholars, research the history of prisons in the United States, Great Britain, and, to a lesser degree, continental Europe. The result includes eight historical essays and six articles on various prison topics, including detention of juveniles and women and imprisonment for political reasons. For readers still curious and searching for more, each article contains other sources to check.

Nader, Ralph, and Wesley J. Smith. **No Contest: How the Power Lawyers Are Perverting Justice in America.** New York: Random House, 1996.

The two author-attorneys point their fingers at corporate lawyers as the moral threat to the heart of the American justice system. The usual suspects are all here, representing airline and auto safety, tobacco companies, and silicone breast implants. Nader explores the growing double standard between rights and powers of corporations and real persons.

Parloff, Roger. **Triple Jeopardy: How Determined Lawyers Fought To Save One Man's Life.** New York: Little, Brown, 1996.

The rigors of the justice system for death-row inmate John Henry Knapp included three trials to determine whether he deliberately set fire to a bedroom—with his two daughters in the room—on 16 November 1973. Knapp spent 14 of the following 19 years behind bars, 12 of those on death row. Parloff chronicles the trials, including two hung juries and the second trial, in which Knapp was found guilty. Those jurors, however, were not allowed to see fire tests that suggested the blaze could have been an accident. The author looks at Arizona officials' determination to convict Knapp, which included alleged harassment in forcing Knapp into a confession, manipulation of discovery rules, lost evidence, and key testimony Parloff likens more to myth than science.

Pienciak, Richard T. **Mama's Boy: The True Story of a Serial Killer and His Mother.** New York: Dutton, 1996.

The author details the warped relationship between serial killer Nick Napoletano and his mother, Carolyn, who protected him despite his inner rage toward her. Carolyn, an administrative assistant for the NYPD, tampered with police memos, evidence, and witnesses related to three murder investigations in which her son, described as "a sexually sadistic serial killer," was the prime suspect.

Ramsey, Martha. **Where I Stopped: Remembering Rape at Thirteen.** New York: Putnam, 1996.

Twenty-seven years after the fact, Ramsey is able to come to grips with her rape at 13. A tough, smart, strong-willed girl, Ramsey kept her wits about her and cooperated with the investigation and throughout the trial. But in the process of losing her innocence, she lost her support group, including her parents. The event left her sexually warped and estranged from family and friends. She resigned herself to a lonely, internal struggle. As a result of her traumatic experience, she had a series of disastrous relationships with men. She finally met a man who was compassionate and helpful, but it was the process of writing about the experience that ultimately healed her wounds.

Rothwax, Harold J. **Guilty: The Collapse of Criminal Justice.** New York: Warner Books, 1996.

A member of the New York State Supreme Court and a trial judge for 25 years, Justice Rothwax used to be a defense attorney and a member of the American Civil Liberties Union. He reviews the Fourth Amendment, Miranda rights, counsel rights, speedy trials, plea bargains, juries, and discovery laws to show how truth, the purported goal of criminal trials, is subverted.

Schwartz, Bernard. **Decision: How the Supreme Court Decides Cases.** New York: Oxford University Press, 1996.

A behind-the-scenes look at how the Supreme Court makes its decisions, this book depicts how a number of verdicts came to be. Schwartz focuses on how Chief Justice Rehnquist's appointment as chief caused him to take on a more serious and conservative nature than that of his predecessor, Chief Justice Burger. Chief Justice Burger's honing of the good-ol'-boy network and a description of how Judge Felix Frankfurter's voice would squeal when he became upset are other anecdotes.

Schwartz, Bernard, ed. **The Warren Court: A Retrospective.** New York: Oxford University Press, 1996.

Schwartz has compiled articles by legal scholars, including criminal justice profiles of the justices and what the Supreme Court has meant to America. While the book covers various issues that came before the Warren Court, the section called "The Warren Court and Criminal Justice," by legal scholar Yale Kamisar, spans the period from the 1961 Mapp ruling to 1966–1967, the last years Kamisar sees as being representative of the Court's overall handling of cases. Kamisar evaluates the Miranda rule, the exclusionary rule, and police search powers—illustrating the Court's place in the history of American legal thought.

Smith, Jean Edward. **John Marshall: Definer of a Nation.** New York: Henry Holt, 1996.

This is a view of Marshall as a pioneering chief justice who brought major changes to the Supreme Court system in his 35 years on the bench, beginning in 1801. Marshall was instrumental in asserting the Supreme Court as the ultimate legal power in the United States and helping shape and interpret the Constitution.

Sullivan, John J., and Joseph L. Victor, eds. **Annual Editions: Criminal Justice 84/85.** Guilford, CT: Dushkin Publishing, 1984.

This particular edition on criminal justice is interesting because the time in which it was compiled was replete with activity on the criminal justice front. The book comprises articles on crime, victims, police, the judicial system, juvenile justice, punishment, and corrections. Articles on victims include "Victims of Crime Task Force Sends Report to Reagan" and "Fear of Crime: Sources and Responses." Articles on the same topic but from opposing viewpoints make for a more thorough understanding of issues that still are relevant now.

Taylor, Lawrence. **The D.A.** New York: William Morrow, 1996.

A former district attorney, Taylor examines not the gloss of the high-profile cases CNN and other news programs are drawn to, but covers a year-in-the-trenches with Larry Longo, the senior deputy district attorney for Los Angeles. Outside the media's glare or even interest, Longo digs in every day, committed to upholding the law, while staving off the legal grind that wears him down.

Thornton, Hazel. **Hung Jury: The Diary of the Menendez Juror.** Philadelphia: Temple University Press, 1995.

Thornton served on one of the juries for the trial of the Menendez brothers, one of the highest profile murder trials in recent history. As an outlet for what she saw, heard, and felt, Thornton kept a detailed diary of the proceedings. Intended to help her keep track of all the information presented, it also serves as a commentary on the tensions that result among jurors, particularly the disparate feelings between the sexes. Thornton said these tensions began early and contributed to the deadlock and eventually the mistrial.

Uviller, H. Richard. **Virtual Justice: The Flawed Prosecution of Crime in America.** New Haven, CT: Yale University Press, 1996.

Uviller takes readers through a step-by-step analysis of the criminal justice system procedure, from arrest to the courtroom, and shows how the process often fails to deliver true justice for anyone.

White, G. Edward. **The Marshall Court and Cultural Change, 1815–1835.** New York: Oxford University Press, 1991.

Citing decisions made between 1815 an 1835, White shows how the Marshall Court reinterpreted the Constitution and the principles of Republicanism to meet the needs of a changing nation. White also demonstrates how the high court under Chief Justice John Marshall recast language to give certain legal terms a timeless quality and used discretion in doing so to foster the appearance of objectivity.

Wilson, Debra J., J.D. **The Complete Book of Victims' Rights.** Highlands Ranch, CO: ProSe Associates, 1995.

Debra Wilson offers a comprehensive state-by-state look at victims' rights in action in the criminal justice process. Chapters are devoted to decisions made after the crime; going to court; sentencing participation; postconviction hearings; victims' compensation funds; restitution; privacy rights; and specifics for rape victims, victims of domestic violence, and child victims.

Wilson, James Q. **Thinking about Crime.** New York: Vintage Books, 1985.

Thinking about Crime made its first appearance in 1975. Its premise is to show how society's responses to crime should be used to minimize criminal activity by incorporating a system of penalties and rewards. Wilson looks at heroin, gun control, police, and the nature of crime and punishment.

Articles

Albrecht, J. **"Rights and Needs of Victims of Crime: The Judges' Perspective."** *Judges' Journal* 34, no. 1 (1995).

As victims' rights become more commonplace and are handled through agencies or prosecutors' offices, some judges believe their own involvement should be limited to resolving disputes over victims' rights between defense and prosecuting attorneys. Many say, however, that this casts a negative light on the judiciary and that judges should be active in ensuring the consideration of victims and their needs during criminal trials.

Aynes, Richard L. **"Constitutional Considerations: Government Responsibility and the Right Not To Be a Victim."** *Pepperdine Law Review* 11, no. 63 (1984).

In this article, Richard Aynes examines the government's duty to protect its citizens through historical references to legislation and decisions from the nation's highest court. Aynes argues that from the beginning of the founding of the United States, there has been a governmental duty to protect citizens who offer their allegiance— and pay taxes. Aynes scrutinizes the criminal justice process from the time police become involved through prosecution and release and discusses officials' civil liability. The article also is relevant as the debate to amend the Constitution to enshrine victims' rights rages on.

Dolliver, James M. **"Victims' Rights Constitutional Amendment: A Bad Idea Whose Time Should Not Come."** *Wayne Law Review* 34, no. 69 (1987).

Washington Supreme Court Justice James Dolliver likens the proposed victims' rights amendment to "the private blood feud."

A return to this mentality would serve only to lessen civility by "emphasizing the conflict between the victim and the accused. . . ." Dolliver raises several questions regarding amendment proponents' reasoning regarding uniformity, increased victim involvement, civil liability, and caseload.

Steele, M., and T. J. Quinn. **"Including Victims in the Criminal Justice Equation: Community Justice in the Next Century."** *Perspectives* 18, no. 3 (1994): 31–36.

As justice has come to mean the same thing as punishment, victims and the communities in which they live increasingly have been left out of the process. Steele and Quinn argue the merits of the restorative model of justice, which makes the victim the principal player in the judicial process. As such, the emphasis of the system is on making victims whole, using offenders as the means when possible. Restorative justice, the authors state, brings victims back into the fold, as was the case through the mid–seventeenth century, when the focus was on the harm done to victims, not society as a whole.

Toobin, Jeffrey. **"The Marcia Clark Verdict."** *The New Yorker* (9 September 1996): 58–71.

"The Marcia Clark Verdict" illustrates the issues that come into play when attorneys select verdicts as well as how they act in front of a jury. Toobin explains how Clark developed strategies from cases she successfully prosecuted before the O. J. Simpson case and how those strategies worked against her. In the old style-over-substance argument, the article shows just how little the facts have to do with a trial and how much presentation plays a role in the outcome.

Nonprint Resources

CD-ROMs

Encyclopedia of the American Constitution. New York: Macmillan, 1996.

This CD-ROM product is a user-friendly package of five volumes cross-referenced to provide quick access to an array of names, U.S. Supreme Court cases, historical periods, and public acts. A warning, though: the material has not been updated since 1991, making it more useful for historical purposes than current research.

Encyclopedia of World Crime. Dallas: Stemmons, 1996.

This techno-bible is aimed at true crime buffs, with more than 50,000 entries, from Jeffrey Dahmer to David Koresh. Besides information on criminals, there is plenty of information on notable law enforcement figures, well-known trials, and historical events and a breakdown of types of crimes. Be warned that the O. J. Simpson and Menendez brothers trials are notably absent, and sources are limited to newspapers and periodicals.

Videotapes and Audiotapes

The Conspiracy of Silence
Type: Video
Date: 1995
Length: 50 min.
Cost: $75 rental; $245 purchase
Source: Pyramid Film & Video
           P.O. Box 1048
           Santa Monica, CA 90406-1048
           800-421-2304; Fax 310-453-9083; 310-828-7577

Actress Kathleen Turner hosts this investigation of domestic violence, with comments culled from former victims, police officers, social workers, and writers. The program attempts to educate viewers about the signs of domestic abuse and offers support for abused women to seek professional help and break "the conspiracy of silence." Also, Denise Brown, the sister of Nicole Brown Simpson, highlights the efforts of one organization to help battered women and their children.

Gangs: Turning the Corner
Type: Video
Date: 1994
Length: 60 min.
Cost: $50.00
Source: Arthur Mokin Productions
P.O. Box 1866
Santa Rosa, CA 95402-1866
707-542-4868; Fax 707-542-6182

A cinematic "how-to" focusing on courses of action to help youth at risk. Suppression, intervention, and prevention programs are explored, interspersed with footage of interviews with police and probation officers. Camp, recreation, and mentoring programs and visits to clubs and classrooms are depicted here. Teens talk about their prior experience with gangs and how they have bettered themselves enough to walk away from that destructive lifestyle.

Not Too Young To Die: Capital Punishment for Juvenile Offenders
Type: Video
Date: 1995
Length: 52 min.
Cost: $75 rental; $395 purchase
Source: Filmmakers Library
124 E. 40th
New York, NY 10016
212-808-4980; 800-555-9815; Fax 212-808-4983

This Swedish television production examines America as the only industrialized country that executes juvenile offenders. The video contains some thought-provoking material, including a teen who committed a brutal ax murder in Texas and pleads for sympathy. It is difficult to follow, as there are no captions to identify the speakers and often the location and date of the crimes depicted are omitted.

A Safe Place
Type: Video
Date: 1994
Source: The Production Center for Documentary & Drama
School of Communication
5500 Campanile Drive
San Diego, CA 92182-4561
619-594-4792

Educators and social workers tell why more than 1,000 kids are homeless on the streets of San Diego. The teens themselves also are interviewed and express their vulnerability to their environment.

Index

Above the Law: Secret Deals, Political Fixes and Other Misadventures of the U.S. Department of Justice, 202
Abramson, Jeffrey, 198–199
Abramson, Leslie, 199
Adamson v. California, 8, 39, 156
Aid for Victims of Crime (AVC), 49, 183–184
Aikens, Earnest James, Jr., 48
Ailes, Roger, 93
Ake v. Oklahoma, 70, 163
Albrecht, J., 213
American Bar Association (ABA), 184
American Civil Liberties Union (ACLU), 11, 184–185
American Medical Association (AMA), 67–68
American Psychiatric Association (APA), 65
Anner, John, 199
Annual Editions: Criminal Justice 84/85, 211
Antiterrorism and Effective Death Penalty Act, 106, 144, 180
Appeals
  death penalty, 61, 67, 84, 91, 95, 97, 101, 102, 106, 144, 176–177, 179–180
  poor defendants' right to counsel, 81
  process reform, 46

weight of evidence reasoning, 159
See also Habeas corpus cases
Appeals court, 67
Arave v. Creech, 96
Arax, Mark, 200
Arizona v. Fulminante, 87, 160–161
Arizona v. Hicks, 75
Arizona v. Youngblood, 81
Arkansas v. Sanders, 89
Arms of the Law (Fry), 116
Assault weapons, 143
Attorney General's Task Force on Violent Crime, 132–133
Attorneys' fees, 27
Attorneys general, 36–37
Aynes, Richard L., 213

Bad Guys: America's Most Wanted in Their Own Words, 200
Bail, 11
Bail Reform Act, 76
Baker, Mark, 200
Baltimore v. Bouknight, 83, 160
Barefoot v. Estelle, 67, 176–177
Barker v. Wingo, 9
Barr, William P., 92
Barron v. Baltimore, 12, 37
Batson v. Kentucky, 72, 174
Battered women. *See* Domestic violence
Bay Area Women Against Rape, 49
Beccaria, Cesare, 111–112, 200

Bedau, Hugo Adam, 200
Bell, Griffin B., 55
Bennett, William J., 200–201
Bentham, Jeremy, 112
Berkowitz, David, 92
Beyond Identity Politics: Emerging Social Justice Movements in Communities of Color, 199
Beyond O.J.: Race, Sex and Class Lessons for America, 206
Biden, Joseph R., Jr., 95
Bidinotto, Robert James, 201
Bill of Rights. *See* Constitutional Amendments; Victims' bills of rights
Black, Hugo, 148
Blackmun, Harry Andrew, 43, 44, 98, 180
Blackstone, Sir William, 201
Blasi, Vincent, 201
Block v. Rutherford, 69, 155
Body Count: Moral Poverty...and How To Win America's War against Crime and Drugs, 200–201
Book profits, 18, 92
Boot: An L.A.P.D. Officer's Rookie Year, 204
Booth v. Maryland, 21, 23, 76, 169–170
Bordenkircher v. Hayes, 56, 173
Bork, Robert H., 77
Boyle, Joseph E., 68
Brady bill, 97, 106, 142
Brady v. United States, 43
Branch, Elmer, 48
Braswell v. United States, 79
Brennan, William J., Jr., 85, 149, 150, 153, 155, 174, 175
Brewer v. Williams, 55, 161–162
British Bill of Rights, 10
Buckley v. Fitzsimmons, 96
Bullington v. Missouri, 62
Bureau of Justice Statistics (BJS), 86, 185
Burger, Warren E., 44, 58, 61, 62, 65, 72, 137, 152, 201
The Burger Court: The Counter Revolution That Wasn't, 201
Burnham, David, 202

Burnley, Jane Nady, 114
Burns, Arnold, 78
Burns v. United States, 89–90
Bush, George, 80, 82, 86–87, 93
Butler v. McKellar, 83

Cabana, Don, 202
Calabro, Marian, 202
California Department of Corrections v. Morales, 104
California v. Acevedo, 89
California v. Hodari Z., 87
California Victims' Bill of Rights, 63
Callins v. Collins, 98
Campus security, 113
Capital punishment, 103–104, 202
  aggravating and mitigating evidence, 83
  appeals, 61, 67, 84, 91, 95, 97, 101, 102, 106, 144, 176–177, 179–180
  Beccaria on, 112
  Blackmun's opposition, 98
  cruel and unusual punishment (Eighth Amendment) challenges, 11, 48, 50, 82–83, 166–172
  drug-related murders, 79, 80
  federal crimes, 87
  ineffective counsel, 163
  insane criminals, 73, 169
  judge overriding jury recommendations, 103
  juror exclusion for opposition to death penalty, 48, 70, 72, 164–165, 167
  juvenile offenders, 96, 216
  mandatory death sentences, 76, 170
  mentally retarded murderer, 170–171
  Nixon and, 50
  racial inequities, 11, 75, 85, 207
  utter disregard for human life, 96
  See also Victim impact statements
Cardozo, Benjamin N., 202
Careeer criminals, 100, 173, 179
Carlo, Philip, 203
Carlson v. Green, 59

Carrington, Frank G., 61, 112–114, 193, 203
Carrington Victims' Litigation Project, 114
Carter, Edward R., 45
Case outcomes, victims' right to be informed of, 19
Cause and prejudice standard, 178–179
CD-ROMs, 215
Census Bureau reports, 14, 44–45, 49
Chain gangs, 104–105
The Challenge of Crime in a Free Society, 13, 41
Chambers, Robert, 74, 76, 77
Chevigny, Paul, 203
Child abuse defendants, 75, 76
Child Abuse Prevention and Treatment Act, 56
Christopher case, 22
Chronology. *See* Victims' rights chronology
Citizens Initiative 1974, 51
City Crime Rankings, 195
Civil litigation, 113
Clark, Tom, 148
Clemons v. Mississippi, 84
Clery, Connie, 113
Clinton, Bill, 96, 106, 107, 138–139, 142–143
Closed-circuit television of judiciary proceedings, 144
Code of Hammurabi, 36
Coerced confessions, 87, 160–161, 174
Coerced guilty pleas, 43
Coleman v. Balkcom, 61
Coleman v. Thompson, 90, 178
Commentaries on the Laws of England: A Facsimile of the First Edition of 1765–1769, 201
Commissions, 38, 41, 45, 132
Community notification of sex offender whereabouts, 102, 105, 107, 143, 144
Compensation. *See* Victim compensation
The Complete Book of Victims' Rights, 212

Confessions, 70
coerced, 87, 160–161, 174
The Conspiracy of Silence, 215
Constitutional amendments, 5–12, 208
proposed constitutional amendment, 18, 23–29, 107–109, 115–116, 123, 124, 145–146, 214
resources, 215
state amendments, 18, 19, 25, 124
See also Eighth Amendment rights; Fifth Amendment rights; Fourteenth Amendment; Fourth Amendment rights; Sixth Amendment rights
"Constitutional Considerations: Government Responsibility and the Right Not To Be a Victim," 213
Continuations of court proceedings, 19
Conviction rates, 14–15
County of Riverside, Calif. v. McLaughlin, 88
Court overcrowding, 44, 63, 84, 137
Court reform, 44, 67
Reagan vs. "liberal judges," 74
speedy trial deadlines, 49
Court television, 144
Court waiting areas, 19
Cowan v. Montana, 98
Cox Broadcasting Corporation v. Martin Cohn, 52
Crime and Punishment in American History, 205
Crime Control and Justice in America: Searching for Facts and Answers, 207
Crime in America's Top-Rated Cities: A Statistical Profile, 195
Crime prevention, 91, 143, 216–217
Crime State Rankings 1994: Crime in the 50 United States, 196
Crime statistics:
Bureau of Justice Statistics (BJS), 86, 185
cities receiving federal anticrime money, 53–54

Crime statistics *(cont.)*
  costs of crime, 108
  FBI reports, 43, 48
  LEAA reports, 14, 49
  repeat offenders, 70–71, 81
  resources, 195–196
  Violence Commission report for
    the 1960s, 41
*Crime Victim Compensation
    Programs: A Reference Guide to
    the Programs in the U.S.*, 197
Crime Victim Initiative, 14–15, 51
Crime Victims' Bill of Rights, 60,
  67. *See also* Victims' bills of
  rights
Crime Victims Fund, 18, 70, 84,
  105
Crime Victims' Legal Advocacy
  Institute, Inc., 193
Crime victims' rights. *See* Victims'
  rights
The Criminal and His Victim
  (Hentig), 118–119
Crimes and Punishment (Beccaria),
  111
Criminal Code Reform Act, 50
Criminal Injuries Compensation
  Act, 117
*Criminal Justice? The Legal System
  v. Individual Responsibility*, 201
Criminal Justice Policy
  Foundation, 185
Crisis centers, 16, 49
Cruel and unusual punishment,
  10
  capital punishment (Eighth
    Amendment) challenges, 11,
    48, 50, 82–83, 166–172
  execution of insane criminals,
    73, 169
  force by corrections officers, 71,
    94
  prison conditions, 90
  prohibition of sperm
    preservation, 92
  victim impact statements, 20–
    23, 169–172, 76
Cupp v. Murphy, 149
Custis v. United States, 100, 179
Czillinger, Ken, 190

Dahmer, Jeffrey, 104
Databases, 114
The D.A., 211
Davis, Richard Allen, 107, 108
Davis v. United States, 100
*Death at Midnight: The Confession of
  an Executioner*, 202
Death penalty. *See* Capital
  punishment
*The Death Penalty in America:
  Current Controversies*, 200
*Decision: How the Supreme Court
  Decides Cases*, 210–211
Defendant testimony on own
  behalf, 60, 158
*The Defense is Ready: Life in the
  Trenches of Criminal Law*, 199
Delaware v. Van Arsdall, 72
Demos v. Storrie, 87
Dershowitz, Alan M., 204
A Dictionary of Modern Legal Usage,
  197
Directories, 196–197
DNA evidence, 92, 177–178
Dolliver, James M., 213
Domestic violence, 54, 215
  hotline for, 55
  law mandating arrest for, 56
  National Coalition Against
    Domestic Violence (NCADV),
    57, 58
  shelters, 55, 60
Domestic Violence Awareness
  Week, 59
Domestic Violence Coalition, 124
Double jeopardy, 7, 38, 62
Douglas, William O., 167
Drug dealer assets, 78
Drug offense sentencing
  guidelines, 89
Drug-related crimes, 79, 80
Drug testing, 71, 73, 135
Drug war, 73
Drunk drivers, 85, 115
Duckworth v. Eagan, 83, 165
Due process, 5, 39
  Fifth Amendment rights, 7
  Fourteenth Amendment
    extension to states, 5, 12, 38,
    39, 173

Dunaway v. New York, 57, 154–155
Dunn, William, 204
Durham v. United States, 45–46
Dusky, Lorraine, 204

Edge of the Knife: Police Violence in America, 203
Edwards v. Arizona, 62, 158, 164
Eighth Amendment rights, 10–11, 11, 70, 166–173. *See also* Cruel and unusual punishment
Eikenberry, Ken, 114–116, 123
Elias, Robert, 204
Emergency shelters, 60
Encyclopedia of the American Constitution, 215
Encyclopedia of World Crime, 215
Engle v. Isaac, 62, 176
English law, 201
Epstein, Lee, 197
Escape from prison, 58
Estelle v. Smith, 62, 158
Evans, James, 205
Evidence, 6, 60
    DNA, 92, 177–178
    Supreme Court reforms, 50
    See also Exclusionary rule;
        Fourth Amendment rights
Exclusionary rule, 64, 79, 103, 147–154
    Eikenberry and, 114
    good faith exception, 69, 77, 91, 152–153
    inevitable discovery exception, 68
    reaffirmed, 83
    Reagan's proposed reforms, 73
    Supreme Court cases, 6, 12, 39, 54, 60, 69, 75, 107

Fairbairn, Robert Henderson, 25
Fay v. Noja, 174–175
Federal Bureau of Investigation (FBI) reports, 43, 48
Federal Crime Control Act, 142–143
Federal crime prosecution guidelines, 57–58
Federal death penalty, 87
Federal rule of Evidence 615, 23, 25–26

Feinstein, Dianne, 24, 108, 109, 145
Felker v. Turpin, 180–181
Fifth Amendment rights, 7–8, 38, 40, 59, 60, 62, 79, 60, 62, 63, 68, 70, 87, 155–161. *See also* *Miranda v. Arizona*
First National Day of Unity, 58
Flaste, Richard, 199
Fletcher, George, 205
Florida constitutional amendment, 124
Florida v. Bostick, 90
Florida Victim/Witness Protection Act, 123
Ford, Gerald, 52
Ford v. Wainwright, 169
Fortas, Abe, 42
Foucha v. Louisiana, 94
Fourteenth Amendment, 5, 11–12, 38, 39, 56, 72, 173–174
Fourth Amendment rights, 5–7, 11–12, 38, 39, 56, 57, 69, 72, 154–155, 173–174
Frankfurter, Felix, 147–148
Fraud, 85
Friedman, Lawrence M., 205
The Frozen Republic: How the Constitution is Paralyzing Democracy, 208
Fry, Margery, 39, 116–117
Furman, John Henry, 48, 50
Furman v. Georgia, 11, 167

Gangs: Turning the Corner, 216
Gannett Co. v. DePasquale, 57, 162
Garland case, 1–2
Garlotte v. Fordice, 105
Garner, Bryan A., 197
Garofalo, Raffaele, 119
Garoogian, Andrew, 195
Garoogian, Rhoda, 195
Gaylin, Willard, 2
Gender-based juror disqualification, 99
Genovese, Kitty, 39
Georgia v. McCollum, 95
Gibran, Kahlil, 118
Gideon v. Wainwright, 19
Ginsburg, Douglas H., 77, 78
Ginsburg, Ruth Bader, 96

Goldman, Ron, family of, 205
Goldwater, Barry, 13, 39
Goodseal case, 45
Grady v. Corbin, 85
Graham v. Connor, 82
Grassroots victims' groups, 16
Great American Trials, 197–198
Great Courtroom Lawyers: Fighting the Cases That Made History, 202
Gregg v. Georgia, 11, 54, 167–168
Guilty: The Collapse of Criminal Justice, 210
Gun control, 52–53, 82, 91, 96–97, 106, 142, 143

Habeas corpus cases, 62, 87, 105, 174–181
    death penalty appeals, 67, 91, 95, 97, 101, 102, 106, 144, 176–177, 179–180
    state inmate access to federal court, 90, 94, 178–179
Hagen, Margaret A., 206
Haight, Lois Herrington, 17, 119–121
Hammurabi's code, 36
Harmelin v. Michigan, 91, 172–173
Harris v. Alabama, 103
Haven House, 55
Hearsay, 9
Hemard, Jean, 119
Hentig, Hans von, 39, 117–119, 122
Hep-Cats, Narcs, and Pipe Dreams: A History of America's Romance with Illegal Drugs, 207
Hernandez v. New York, 88–89
Herrera v. Collins, 96
Herrin, Richard, 1
His Name Is Ron, 205
History of Victims' rights. *See* Victims' rights chronology
Hoffer, Marilyn, 205
Hoffer, William, 205
Holbrook v. Flynn, 71, 164
Homeless, 217
Hoover, J. Edgar, 43, 48
Horton, Willie, 80, 93
Hotlines, 16, 55
Howley, Susan, 26

Hudson v. Louisiana, 61
Hudson v. McMillian, 94
Hudson v. Palmer, 69, 155
Hughey v. United States, 84
Hullinger, Charlotte, 121, 190
Hullinger, Robert, 121, 190
Hung Jury: The Diary of the Menendez Juror, 212
Hurtado v. California, 12, 38
Hutchinson, Earl Ofari, 206
Hyde, Henry, 24, 108
Hypnosis, 76

Illinois v. Gates, 151–152
Illinois v. Krull, 75
Illinois v. Perkins, 85
In My Father's Name: A Family, a Town, a Murder, 200
"Including Victims in the Criminal Justice Equation: Community Justice in the Next Century," 214
Independence Institute, 185
Ineffective counsel, 68, 163
Inmate privacy rights, 69
Insanity defense, 50, 64, 65–66, 67–68, 70, 98, 123, 163
    Justice Assistance Act, 141
Insanity Defense Reform Act, 100
The Insider's Guide to Law Firms 1993–94, 196

Jackson, Jesse, 207
Jackson, Lucious, Jr., 48
Jail conditions, 44–45
Jakobetz v. United States, 92, 177–178
James v. Illinois, 83
Jenkins v. Anderson, 60, 158
Jenner, Albert E., Jr., 50
John Marshall: Definer of a Nation, 211
Johnson, Lyndon B., 13, 42
Johnson v. Texas, 96
Jonnes, Jill, 207
Jury, 9, 198–199
    exclusion of death penalty opponents, 48, 70, 72, 164–165, 167
    gender-based exclusions, 99

instructions, 62, 175–176
justifications for peremptory
	challenges, 105
race-based exclusions, 72, 95, 174
right to trial by, 9
Justice Assistance Act, 18, 69, 141–
	142
Justice for Children, 124
Justice for Surviving Victims, 123
Juvenile offenders, 47, 216
	death penalty for, 96
Juvenile victim testimony, 88

Kanka, Megan, 105, 107, 144
Katzenbach Commission, 13, 40
Keeney v. Tamayo-Reyes, 94, 178–
	179
Kennedy, Anthony M., 77, 78,
	98–99, 172
Kentucky v. Rawlings, 60
Kentucky v. Stincer, 76
Keve, Paul W., 207
King, Rodney G., 99
Klaas, Polly, 107, 108
Knapp case, 209
Knappman, Edward W., 197
Knight, Alfred H., 207
Kyl, John, 24, 108, 109, 145

Landlord liability, 113–114
Law Enforcement Assistance
	Administration (LEAA), 13–
	15, 41, 42, 44–45, 49, 55–56, 139
Law on the Net, 205
Lazare, Daniel, 208
*Legal Lynching: Racism, Injustice,
	and the Death Penalty*, 207
Legal representation:
	ineffective counsel, 68, 163
	intentional misconduct, 69
	perjury, 71
	for poor defendants, 81
	right to counsel, 10, 161–166
	See also Miranda v. Arizona
Legal Services Corporation, 80
Levi, Edward H., 51
Levin, Jennifer, 74, 76
Lex talionis, 36
Liability issues, 113–114
Liberal judges, 74

*The Life of the Law: The People and
	Cases that Have Shaped Our
	Society, from King Alfred to
	Rodney King*, 207
Life-support, 81–82
Lightner, Candy, 58
Lockhart v. McCree, 72, 164–165
Lombroso, Cesare, 119

Magee, Doug, 208
Magna Carta, 7
Malloy v. Hogan, 8, 40, 155–156
*Mama's Boy: The True Story of a
	Serial Killer and His Mother*,
	210
Mandatory death sentences, 76,
	170
Mandatory sentencing laws, 59,
	98–99
Manson, Charles, 94
Mapp v. Ohio, 6, 148–149
Marbury v. Madison, 37
"The Marcia Clark Verdict," 214
Marital rape, 54, 56
Marshall, John, 37, 211
Marshall, Thurgood, 89–90, 162,
	163
Maryland v. Garrison, 75, 153
Massachussetts v. Sheppard, 69, 152–
	153
Matsch, Richard P., 25–26
McCarty, Francis, 40
McCleskey v. Kemp, 75
McCleskey v. Zant, 87, 178
McFarland v. Scott, 101, 179–180
McKoy v. North Carolina, 83
McMann v. Richardson, 43
Mcmillan v. Pennsylvania, 73
McNeil v. Wisconsin, 89
McVeigh case, 25–26
Medication, 94
Medina v. California, 95
Meese, Edwin, 15–16, 74–75
Megan's law, 105, 107, 144
Mendelsohn, Beniamin, 39, 122–123
Mentally ill defendants, 94, 95
	execution of, 73, 169
	See also Insanity defense
Mentally retarded murderer,
	170–171

Michigan v. Harvey, 83
Michigan v. Jackson, 72, 164
Michigan V. Jackson, 72
Michigan v. Lucas, 88, 165–166
Miller, Jerome G., 208–209
Minimum sentencing guidelines, 66
Minnick v. Mississippi, 86
Miranda v. Arizona (and subsequent "Miranda rights" applications), 10, 42, 58, 74, 85, 156–158
  ambiguous request for attorney, 100
  McNeil v. Wisconsin restriction, 89
  Justice Department opposition to, 74–75
  public safety exception, 68, 159
Missing children, 69
Missing Children's Act, 64, 140
Mitchell, John N., 42, 46, 47, 48, 138
Moody v. Dagget, 55, 175
Morgan, Daniel David, 72
Morgan, Kathleen O., 196
Morgan v. Illinois, 95
Morris, Norval, 209
Mothers Against Drunk Driving (MADD), 58, 64, 124, 186
Mu'Min v. Virginia, 89, 166
Murder is Not Entertainment (MINE), 190
Murray v. Giarratano, 82

Nader, Ralph, 209
Napoletano, Nick, 210
National Association for the Advancement of Colored People (NAACP) Legal Defense Fund, 11
National Center for Missing and Exploited Children (NCMEC), 69
National Center for State Courts, 186
National Center on Child Abuse and Neglect, 56
National Coalition Against Domestic Violence (NCADV), 57, 58
National Coalition Against Sexual Assault (NCASA), 56

National Commission of Reform of Federal Criminal Laws, 40
National Commission on Law Enforcement and Observance, 38
National Commission on Reform of Federal Criminal Laws, 45, 132
National Commission on the Cause and Prevention of Violence, 41
National Council on Crime and Delinquency (NCCD), 187
National Criminal Justice Reference Service (NCJRS), 187–188
National Institute of Justice (NIJ), 188
National Legal Aid and Defender Association (NLADA), 26
National Organization for Victim Assistance (NOVA), 15, 24, 53, 188–189
National Organization for Women (NOW), 16, 54
National Rape Task Force, 16
National Victim Center (NVC), 70, 124, 189–190
National Victim Constitutional Amendment Network (National VCAN), 24, 124, 128
National Victims' Rights Week, 17, 61, 125
Natural rights, 4
The Nature of the Judicial Process, 202
Negligence, 113
Nejelski, Paul A., 55
New York v. Burger, 76
New York v. Quarles, 68, 159
New Zealand, 39, 117
The Night Stalker: The True Story of America's Most Feared Serial Killer, 203
Nix v. Whiteside, 71
Nix v. Williams, 68
Nixon, Richard, 13, 42, 45, 46, 50, 132–138
No Contest: How the Power Lawyers Are Perverting Justice in America, 209

Not Too Young To Die: Capital Punishment for Juvenile Offenders, 216
Notification of case developments, 27
Notification of sex offender whereabouts, 102, 105, 107, 143, 144
Novak, Greg, 123

O'Connor, Sandra Day, 62, 159, 160, 163, 166, 175–176, 180
Office for Victims of Crime (OVC), 66
Ohio v. Huertas, 86
Oklahoma City bombing trial, 25–26
Omnibus Crime Bill, 85, 86
Omnibus Crime Control Act of 1968, 14
Omnibus Crime Control Act of 1970, 44, 139
Omnibus Crime Control and Safe Streets Act, 41
Omnibus Victim and Witness Protection Act, 18, 125–126
On Crimes and Punishments, 200
O'Neal v. McAninch, 103
Oregon v. Elstad, 70, 160
Organizations, 183–193
   National Organization for Victim Assistance (NOVA), 15, 24, 53, 188–189
   National Organization for Women (NOW), 16, 54
   National Victim Constitutional Amendment Network (National VCAN), 24, 124, 128
   Parents of Murdered Children (POMC), 121–122, 124, 190–191
   Victims' Assistance Legal Organization, Inc. (VALOR), 61, 113, 193
Ornelas v. United States, 107, 153–154
The Oxford History of the Prison: The Practice of Punishment in Western Society, 209

Pagan, Noel, 81–82
Palko v. Connecticut, 12, 38
Parents of Murdered Children (POMC), 121–122, 124, 190–191
Parker v. North Carolina, 43
Parloff, Roger, 209
Parole Block Program, 190, 191
Parole Reorganization Act, 139–140
Parole revocation hearing, 55, 175
Patrick, John J., 198
Payne v. Tennessee, 22–23, 90, 171–172
Penal Philosophy (Tarde), 118
Penalties for Crime against Government Officials, 64
Pennsylvania v. Ritchie, 75
Penry v. Lynaugh, 83, 171
People Against Crime Together, 124
People Against Violent Encounters, 124
Peremptory challenges, 105
Pienciak, Richard T., 210
Pietkiewicz, Victor, 127
Plea bargaining, 23, 26, 56, 173
Postmortem: The O.J. Simpson Case, 199
Powell, Lewis F., Jr., 49, 149, 150
"Preppy" murder case, 74, 76, 77
President's Commission on Law Enforcement and the Administration of Justice, 13, 40
President's Commission on Organized Crime, 135–136
President's Task Force on Victims of Crime, 17, 20, 23, 63, 112, 114, 115, 119, 123, 125, 133–135
Preston, Bob, 24, 123–124
Pretrial detention, 47, 68, 75, 173–174
   Justice Assistance Act, 141
   Sixth Amendment right to a speedy trial, 8–9
   warrantless arrests and, 88
Pretrial hearings, public right to be present at, 57, 76, 162
Print resources, 195–214

Prison conditions, 44–45, 58, 65, 71, 90, 94
Prison construction allocations, 102–103
Privacy rights, 69
Probable cause, 6, 57, 155
Probation, 38
Protection, 19, 64, 84, 140
Psychiatric care, 70, 94, 163
Psychiatric exam, 158
Psychiatric expert testimony, 206
Public defender misconduct, 69
Public housing, 106
Public opinion, 12–13, 67
Publishing profits, 18, 92
Punishment, 209
    Beccaria on, 111–112
    chain gangs, 104–105
    See also Capital punishment;
    Cruel and unusual
    punishment; Sentencing
Purkett v. Elem, 105

Quinn, T. J., 214

Racial inequities, 206, 208–209
    death penalty, 11, 75, 85, 207
    jury exclusions, 72, 95, 174
Racial Justice Act, 85
Ramsey, Martha, 210
Rape, 210
    laws, 17, 52
    National Coalition Against
    Sexual Assault (NCASA), 56
    previous sexual relationships
    and, 88, 165–166
    public identification of victims,
    52
    shield laws, 17
    spousal rape, 54, 56
Rape crisis centers, 16, 49
Rape crisis hotline, 16
Reagan, Ronald, 17–18, 54, 61, 63, 64, 65, 68, 73, 74, 78, 124–126, 140
*Reasonable Doubts: The O. J.
    Simpson Case and the Criminal
    Justice System*, 204
Recidivism, 70–71, 81, 100, 179
Referenda, 102

Reform Act, 64
Rehnquist, William H., 49, 61, 72, 73–74, 77, 81, 84, 151, 154, 166, 172, 174, 180
Reno, Janet, 96
Repeat offenders, 70–71, 81, 100, 173, 179
Resources, 195–217
Restitution, 84
Rhode Island v. Innis, 162
Rhodes v. Chapman, 62
Riggins v. Nevada, 94
"Rights and Needs of Victims of
    Crime: The Judges'
    Perspective," 213
Rock v. Arkansas, 76
Roper, Roberta, 126–128
Rothman, David J., 209
Rothwax, Harold J., 210
Rowland, James, 20, 54

A Safe Place, 217
Saffle v. Parks, 83
Sandoval v. California, 99
Save Our Sons and Daughters, 191–192
Scalia, Antonin, 72, 74, 171
Schad v. Arizona, 90
Schall v. Martin, 68, 173–174
Schwartz, Bernard, 210–211
Scott, Laura, 20
*Search and Destroy: African-
    American Males in the Criminal
    Justice System*, 208–209
Search and seizure. *See*
    Exclusionary rule; Fourth
    Amendment rights
Self-defense laws, 41, 45
Self-incrimination. *See* Fifth
    Amendment rights
Senate Joint Resolution 6, 145–146
Sentencing:
    federal guidelines, 89–90
    Justice Assistance Act, 141
    mandatory, 59, 66, 98–99
    multiple (consecutive)
    sentences, 158
    1987 federal reform, 79
    three-strikes laws, 102, 107
    victims allocation law, 25

See also Capital punishment;
    Victim impact statements
Sex offenders, notification of
    whereabouts of, 102, 105, 107,
    143, 144
Sexual abuse victim testimony, 88
Sexual assault:
    National Coalition Against
        Sexual Assault (NCASA), 56
    rape classified as, 17
    See also Rape
Shannon v. United States, 100
Shelters, 55, 60
Simmons v. South Carolina, 100
Simon, Jules, 119
*Simon and Schuster v. New York
    Crime Victims Board*, 92
Simpson case, 199, 204, 205, 206,
    214
Sinthasomphone, Konerak, 104
Sixth Amendment rights, 8–10, 55,
    68, 70, 71, 72, 78, 83, 88, 89,
    161–166
    proposed changes for victims'
        rights, 18, 115–116, 123
Smith, Jean Edward, 211
Smith, Wesley J., 209
Smith, William French, 117
Social welfare theory, 117
Son of Sam law, 92
*Sourcebook of Criminal Justice
    Statistics*, 196
Souter, David H., 85
South Carolina v. Gathers, 22, 23, 82,
    170
Sovereign immunity, 113
Speck, Richard F., 48
Speedy trial deadlines, 44, 49
Sperm preservation, 92
Spiegelman, John D., 72
Stanford v. Kentucky, 83, 170–171
State constitutions, 18, 19, 25, 124
State inmates, federal court access,
    94, 178–179
Steele, M., 214
Stephanie Roper Committee &
    Foundation, Inc., 192, 127
Stephanie Roper Family
    Assistance Committee, 127
Stevens, John Paul, 63, 67, 172

Stewart, Potter, 149, 162, 167–168
*Still Unequal: The Shameful Truth
    About Women and Justice in
    America*, 204
Stone v. Powell, 54, 149
Strickland v. Washington, 68, 163
Subpoena rights, 9–10
Sullivan, John J., 211
Sullivan v. Louisiana, 96
Sumeria, 35–36
Sumner v. Shuman, 170
Sunny von Bulow Victim Avocacy
    Center, 124
Supreme court cases, 146–181
    Eighth Amendment, 11, 70,
        166–173
    exclusionary rule, 6, 12, 39, 54,
        60, 69, 75, 107, 147–154
    Fifth Amendment, 8, 40, 59, 60,
        62, 63, 68, 70, 87, 155–161
    Fourteenth Amendment, 12, 56,
        72, 173–174
    Fourth Amendment, 57, 69,
        154–155
    resource materials, 197–198,
        210–211, 212
    rules of evidence, 50
    Sixth Amendment, 55, 68, 70, 71,
        72, 78, 83, 88, 89, 161–166
    victim impact statements,
        21–23, 169–170
    See also Constitutional
        amendments; Habeas corpus
        cases; Victims' rights
        chronology; *specific cases,
        justices*
*The Supreme Court Compendium:
    Data and Developments*, 197
*The Supreme Court Justices: A
    Biographical Dictionary*, 198

Tague v. Louisiana, 58
Tarde, Gabriel, 119
Task Force on Family Violence, 66,
    68
Task Force on Victims of Crime,
    17, 20, 23, 63, 112, 114, 115,
    119, 123, 125, 133–135
Taylor, Lawrence, 211
Terrorism, 106

Testimony on own behalf, 60, 158
Thinking About Crime, 213
Third party negligence, 113
Thomas, Clarence, 91, 180
Thornton, Hazel, 212
Three-strikes laws, 102, 107
Tibbs v. Florida, 63, 159
Timmendequas, Jesse, 144
Tisson v. Arizona, 75
Tort liability, 113–114
Tower v. Glover, 69
*Triple Jeopardy: How Determined
    Lawyers Fought To Save One
    Man's Life,* 209
Twining v. New Jersey, 8, 12, 156

*Uniform Crime Reports for the
    United States,* 196
United States v. Bailey, 58
United States v. Felix, 94
United States v. Frady, 62, 175–176
United States v. Havens, 60, 150
United States v. Jakobetz, 92, 177–178
United States v. Leon, 69, 152–153
United States v. McVeigh, 25–26
United States v. Mistretta, 79
United States v. Muñoz-Flores, 84
United States v. Nichols, 25–26
United States v. Payner, 60, 150–151
United States v. Salerno, 75
United States v. Salvucci, 60, 151
Urofsky, Melvin I., 198
U.S. Sentencing Commission, 136
U.S. Parole Commission, 135
Uviller, H. Richard, 212

Velde, Richard W., 45, 47
Vera Institute of Justice, 192–193
Victim and Witness Protection
    Act, 64, 84, 140
Victim classification, 118–119, 122
Victim compensation:
    California program, 40
    Fry and, 116–117
    government funds, 18, 53, 70,
        84, 105, 126, 142
    resource, 197
    third party negligence, 113
Victim Constitutional Amendment
    Network (VCAN), 24, 124

Victim impact statements, 18, 25,
    54–55, 64, 76, 82, 86, 90–91,
    125–126
    constitutional challenge as
        "cruel and unusual
        punishment," 20–23, 169–172
Victim-offender relationships,
    117–119
Victim Rights Clarification Act, 26
Victim/witness programs, 14–15,
    51
Victim/witness protection, 19, 64,
    84, 140
Victimology, 39
    Hentig and, 118–119, 122
    Mendelsohn and, 122–123
The Victims (Carrington), 112, 203
Victims allocution law, 25
Victims' advocates, 15, 19–20
Victims' Assistance Legal
    Organization, Inc. (VALOR),
    61, 113, 193
Victims' assistance programs, 49,
    51
Victims' bills of rights, 25, 26, 60,
    63, 67, 95, 101, 109, 124
Victims of Crime Act of 1984
    (VOCA), 18, 70, 126, 142
Victims' ombudsman, 27
Victims' rights:
    history of, 3–4
    political origins, 13
    proposed constitutional
        amendment, 18, 23–29, 107–
        109, 115–116, 123, 124, 145–
        146, 214
    right to attend judicial
        proceedings, 23, 25–26, 116,
        123, 135
    See also Victim compensation
Victims' rights chronology, 35–109
    ancient times to 19th century,
        35–37
    19th century to 20th century,
        37–38
    1905–1951, 38–39
    1960s, 39–42
    1970s, 42–57
    1980s, 57–83
    1990s, 83–109

"Victims' Rights Constitutional
  Amendment: A Bad Idea
  Whose Time Should Not
  Come," 213–214
Victims' Rights Week, 52
*Victims Still: The Political
  Manipulation of Crime Victims,*
  204
Victor, Joseph L., 211
Victor v. Nebraska, 99
Videotapes and audiotapes, 215–
  217
Violence Against Women Act, 143
Violence Commission, 13, 41
Violent Crime Control and Law
  Enforcement Act, 101–102,
  142–143
*Virtual Justice: The Flawed
  Prosecution of Crime in
  America,* 212
Von Bulow, Sunny, 70, 189

Wainwright v. Witt, 70, 168
Wallace, Scott, 26–27
The Warren Court: A Retrospective,
  211
*We, The Jury: The Jury System and
  the Ideal of Democracy,* 198–199
Weaver, Mark, 82
Weed, Frank J., 1
Weeks v. United States, 6, 147
Weld, William F., 91
Whalen v. United States, 59, 158

*What Murder Leaves Behind: The
  Victim's Family,* 208
Wheat v. United States, 78, 165
*Where I Stopped: Remembering Rape
  at Thirteen,* 210
White, Byron R., 96, 150, 179
White v. Illinois, 88
Whitley v. Albers, 71
*Whores of the Court: The Fraud of
  Psychiatric Testimony and
  the Rape of American Justice,*
  206
Wickersham Commission, 38
Wilins v. Missouri, 83
Wilson, Debra, 212
Wilson, James Q., 213
Wilson v. Seiter, 90
Wisconsin Crime Victims' Bill of
  Rights, 60
*With Justice for Some: Victims'
  Rights in Criminal Trials,* 205
Witherspoon v. Illinois, 48, 167
Witness fees, 19, 38
Witness subpoena, 9–10
Wolf v. Colorado, 6, 12, 39, 147
Wolff v. Rice, 54, 149
Women's movement, 16
*Women in Law: A Bio-
  Bibliographical Sourcebook,* 198

*The Young Oxford Companion to the
  Supreme Court of the United
  States,* 198

Leigh Glenn is a professional journalist who has published internationally. Ms. Glenn has written for the *St. Petersburg Times*, the *St. Petersburg News, Colby Magazine,* and the *Moscow Times.* She currently concentrates her reporting skills on legislation and issues affecting franchised auto dealers in the metropolitan Washington, D.C., area.